CW00542544

REVERSE RI'

Spiritual Knowledge Is True Communion

REVERSE RITUAL

Spiritual Knowledge Is True Communion

Rudolf Steiner
Friedrich Benesch

With an introduction by
Christopher Schaefer

ANTHROPOSOPHIC PRESS

Copyright © 2001 Anthroposophic Press
Introduction Copyright © 2001 Christopher Schaefer

Published by Anthroposophic Press
PO Box 799 Great Barrington, MA 01230
www.anthropress.org

All rights reserved. No part of this book may be reproduced in any form without the written permission of the publisher, except for brief quotations embodied in critical reviews and articles.

Spiritual Communion of Humanity translated by Eva Knausenberger, edited by Marsha Post, from the German *Verhältnis der Sternenwelt zum Menschen und des Menschen zur Sternenwelt: Die geistige Kommunion der Menschheit* (GA 219), with permission from Rudolf Steiner Nachlassverwaltung, Dornach, Switzerland, 1984.

The Reversed, Cosmic Ritual translated by Eva Knausenberger, edited by Marsha Post, from the German *Der kosmische, der umgekehrte Kultus,* with permission from Verlag Die Pforte, Basel, Switzerland, 1958.

Brotherhood and the Struggle for Existence manuscript translation edited by Michael Lipson from the German *Die Welträtsel und die Anthroposophie* (GA 54), with permission from Rudolf Steiner Nachlassverwaltung, Dornach, Switzerland, 1983.

Preparing for the Sixth Epoch manuscript translation edited by Michael Lipson from the German *Das Geheimnis des Todes: Wesen und Bedeutung Mitteleuropas und die europäischen Volksgeister* (GA 259/260) with permission from Rudolf Steiner Nachlassverwaltung, Dornach, Switzerland, 1980.

Human Encounters and Karma translated by Christopher Bamford from the French *Les Rencontres Humaines et le Karma,* with permission from Editions Anthroposophiques Romandes, Geneva, Switzerland, 1983.

Library of Congress Cataloging-in-Publication Data

Steiner, Rudolf, 1861–1925.
    Reverse Ritual: spiritual knowledge is true communion / Rudolf Steiner,
Friedrich Benesch; with an introduction by Christopher Schaefer.
        p. cm.
    Includes bibliographical references.
    ISBN 0-88010-487-2
    1. Anthroposophy. 2. Spiritual Life. I. Benesch, Friedrich. II. Title.

BP595.S894 R48 2001
299'.935—dc21   00-068987

10 9 8 7 6 5 4 3 2 1

Book design by
STUDIO 31
WWW.STUDIO31.COM

Printed in the United States of America

Table of Contents

INTRODUCTION

Christopher Schaefer, Ph.D.

SACRAMENTAL AND SPIRITUAL COMMUNION

In July 1984, I participated in a large conference in Spring Valley, New York, with the theme "The Christ in Our Times and the Transformation of Humanity." I had been asked to give a workshop on "Social Life as Christian Transformation" with Dietrich Asten, a friend and Council member of the Anthroposophical Society in North America. Dietrich gave the fifth lecture of the conference on "Sacramental and Spiritual Communion," raising the question of the different ways in which the human being can be in dialogue, in communion, with the spiritual world. The talk was preceded and ended by a silent Eurythmy presentation called "The Question of Destiny." Shortly after having completed his talk, while leaving the stage, Dietrich died. The lecture was his final act and legacy and my first significant introduction to this complex yet vital set of questions about the nature and differences between the Sacramental Communion of the Christian Churches and the Cosmic Ritual or the Spiritual Communion of Anthroposophy. It is a vital set of questions because it deals directly with our understanding and practice of both inner development and community development, and because it asks us to be in a direct and conscious dialogue with spiritual beings.

Dietrich Asten's lecture, included as an appendix to this volume, is an excellent short introduction to the differences between Sacramental Communion — the cultic act of communion practiced with the mediating role of a priest — and Spiritual Communion or the cosmic ritual, which Steiner described as a cognitive meditative possibility for our time.[1]

What would otherwise be mere abstract knowledge is transformed into a relationship of will and feeling toward the world. The world becomes the Temple, the House of God. When a human being as a knowing being summons up powers of will and feeling, he becomes a sacrificing being. His fundamental relationship to the world changes from knowledge into *cosmic ritual*. The first thing that must come to pass if Anthroposophy is to fulfill its mission in the world is that the human being's relationship to the world must be recognized to be one of cosmic ritual.[2]

Sacramental Communion in the Christian churches is a distinct set of ritualistic acts, moving from the revelation (reading of the gospel), to the offering, to the transubstantiation (the transforming of the bread and wine by the healing power of Christ), to partaking in communion. As a sacrament, it is based on the gift of Christ to humanity at the Last Supper, in which he gave the wine and the bread to his disciples, saying, "This is my body, which is given for you,"and "This cup is the new testament in my blood, which is shed for you." It is a set of acts in which the priest brings the divine presence into physical reality. In this way, a community of believers can experience itself together as a community in Christ.

The other, the cosmic or reverse ritual described by Steiner, is less formed. It requires the human being either alone or with others to awaken to the soul spiritual element in the world or in others, and so to raise ordinary experience to a spiritual level.

Steiner describes these differences in the following manner. "I would put it thus: the community of the cultus seeks to draw the angels of heaven down to the place where the cultus is being celebrated so that they may be present in the congregation (Sacramental Communion), whereas the anthroposophical community seeks to lift human souls into supersensible realms so that they may enter the company of angels (Spiritual Communion)."[3]

Friedrich Benesch, a Christian Community Priest and for many years the guiding spirit of the Priest Training Seminar in Stuttgart, Germany, has researched the questions of Sacramental and Spiritual Communion comprehensively and in depth. His two short books on the subject, *Das Religiöse der Anthroposophie* (The Religious in Anthroposophy) Vol. I (Verlag die Pforte, Basel), and *Ideen zur Kultusfrage* (Ideas on the Question of Ritual), Vol. II (Verlag die Pforte, Basel), are, to my mind, indispensable aids to understanding Steiner's thoughts and intentions about sacramental and Spiritual Communion and the spiritual sources of community life.[4] Their terse and direct style, the clarity of presentation and the extensive use of Steiner citations make these works a very important resource for anyone seeking a deeper understanding of this subject. The abridged translation by Eva Knausenberger makes the substance of Volume I available to English readers.

Benesch's unique contribution in the translated volume is the detailed manner in which he explores the reverse ritual, or Spiritual Communion, as different from the sacrament of communion in form, sequence, and direction. He likens Spiritual Communion to the process of birth, which begins with an excommunication from the spiritual world — a leaving behind of communion with spiritual hierarchies. The next stage is the transformation, the *transubstantiation* of spirit into matter as a soul spirit being connects to an embryo. In this process, the cosmic, celestial human being *offers* its substance to a newly forming earthly being. In the process of birth and early childhood the *revelation* of the "I am" gradually comes to expression in walking, talking, memory and "I"consciousness. He describes Spiritual Communion occurring in the same sequence: the *communion* with nature as the experience of spirit, involving the purification of human perception and the *cleansing* of thought, the *transubstantiation* through an understanding of our body's relationship to the stars and planets, the *offering* in sharing our thoughts with the cosmos and other human beings, and, finally, the *revelation*, our experience of the earth and of life as the manifestation of the Logos.[5] For Benesch, to practice the cosmic ritual, the path of Spiritual Communion, is to experience the religious in Anthroposophy.

In Volume I, Benesch suggests both reversals in intention and sequence as differences between Sacramental and Spiritual Communion. I think the question of a reversal in sequence is open to question, as I believe the "reverse" of the reverse ritual also refers to the difference in gesture, with sacramental communion bringing the spiritual into earthly manifestation and Spiritual Communion raising human consciousness to the supersensible. Indeed, in his second volume, Benesch is much less definite about the sequence. He devotes himself to describing the Revelation, the Offering, the Transubstantiation and Communion as mysteries to be understood and experienced, recognizing that Spiritual Communion is a much less definite process in form and sequence than Sacramental Communion.[6]

THE NATURE OF SPIRITUAL COMMUNION

In reflecting on the nature and practice of Spiritual Communion, I think it is essential to distinguish between three levels of activity. The first is the conscious recognition that, as human beings, we are a direct revelation of the spirit through the process of conception, birth, development, and death. We are a cosmic creation and revelation with our body, soul, and spirit, and the reality of repeated earth lives. Bringing this to consciousness can give us a profound sense of reverence and gratitude for what has been given to us, individually and collectively, by the spiritual world.

A second level of Spiritual Communion is our individual inner activity as thinking, feeling, and willing beings who are able to bring the promptings of the spirit to consciousness, to manifestation, and to deed.

A third level of activity is that of dialogue with the spirit in groups and communities. Benesch's contribution focuses primarily on levels one and two, while the essay by Athys Floride on human encounters and karma gives a moving and very helpful description of Spiritual Communion in relationships and community life.[7] The two essays complement each other and, together with the lectures by Steiner, constitute an invaluable resource for active spiritual work.

In attempting to understand Spiritual Communion as an individual spiritual activity, the question of how this process works with the different soul forces arises. In the introduction to the second volume of Goethe's scientific works, Steiner writes:

> When thinking takes hold of ideas, it fuses together with the ground of existence; that which works outside enters the spirit of man — he becomes one with the world of reality on the highest level of potency. Becoming aware of the idea in the world of reality is the true communion of man.[8]

This cognitive experience of communion — of a spiritual beholding and articulation of the Logos in the world — is one way in which Spiritual Communion can be experienced. It is, I believe, a path described in *The Philosophy of Freedom*, by Steiner, and elaborated by thinkers such as Georg Kühlewind.[9] An essay by Friedemann Schwarzkopf called "Spiritual Communion" has been of particular value to me in understanding this cognitive path to Spiritual Communion.[10] I believe that through active thinking we can all have the experience, that appropriate and living thoughts are the gifts of angelic beings who want us to be aware of their presence and their gift.

The arts are another path to Spiritual Communion through the transformation and purification of feeling. In his essay on Goethe as the Father of a New Aesthetics, Steiner writes that the artist can raise matter into the sphere of the divine: "The beautiful is not the divine in a visible garment but, quite to the contrary, it is visible reality in a divine garment."[11] The artist can so create that matter reveals the spirit it contains, and we can experience this reality as nourishing and enriching.

A path to Spiritual Communion through the will is also possible and is, to my mind, the main content of Steiner's book, *How to Know Higher Worlds*.[12] As Dietrich Asten writes:

> By fulfilling the demands placed on him, the student will contribute to the liberation of the human race. He lays his gifts on the sacrificial altar of humanity. Through such deeds he can become one with the Greater Guardian who is, as we know, no other than Christ. This union with the Greater Guardian of which the book [*How to Know Higher Worlds*] so clearly speaks is in reality a communion of the human being with Christ through human acts of will.[13]

It is the path of "achieved idealism" also described by Steiner in *The Inner Aspect of the Social Question*,[14] in which our deeds respond to the needs of the world out of a feeling of spiritual responsibility.

In his translated essays, Benesch describes Spiritual Communion as a journey from thinking through feeling to willing — from the Relationship to Nature, to the Body, to others so that we may finally be "the seed bed of a Christ-permeated world."[15] In his untranslated second book, he shows how each stage, each Mystery, is contained in the other, with no set sequence of time or soul orientation.

> ... One slowly learns to see—the Cosmic Ritual doesn't have a time structure, it also doesn't have a particular sequence in which one stage proceeds from the other. It has a cosmic order and structure similar to the cosmos itself. Therefore, the human being seeking the experience, the practice of the cosmic ritual, has access to each of the spheres immediately and directly. He or she can begin with the Revelation of Christ or with the Communion through cognition or with the working of stars in the process of transformation or with the spirit-filled thoughts of another in a gesture of offering...[16]

It would follow from this that a starting point in the journey to Spiritual Communion can be made through any of the soul faculties—through thinking, feeling or willing—depending on the orientation and gifts of the individual. Insofar as both Sacramental and Spiritual Communion are ways of being in dialogue with the spiritual world, the level of inner development of the individual, the stage of awareness, will determine what manner of dialogue is possible. Yet, even in the absence of clairvoyant capacities, we can experience the presence of spirit beings as a grace, a blessing that can be felt and remembered. A phrase of Steiner's, that "we should become conscious of the Spiritual Communion of mankind" and that the more lively and alert our consciousness is "the more easily we can find our way to this communion" suggests that the cosmic ritual, that Spiritual Communion takes place in daily life, but that we are seldom conscious of it.[17] A few years ago, I was asked to give a talk on Angels — not a usual topic of presentation for me — at the New York Open Center. I was preparing at home on a beautiful autumn day, and having finished, asked, "Well, what have I left out?" A loud voice in me said, somewhat humorously, "You've left out celebrating with us!" It was quite right, and I rectified the omission. I am quite certain that the angelic world wants us to be aware of their presence and is anxious to actively assist us if we only ask.

Spiritual Communion as Community Building

A significant issue that is part of any sustained reflection about Sacramental and Spiritual Communion is the social community aspect of these two rituals. The sacramental ritual is a community-building ritual by virtue of the fact that it takes place within a congregation and is mediated by a priest. According to Steiner, its power as a community-building activity is due to the fact that it brings members of the congregation into a felt connection with their pre-birth experiences in the spiritual world.[18] The cosmic ritual can be an individual experience through individual cognitive and meditative activity, but it can also be the basis of a new community building impulse. In *Awakening to Community,* "Brotherhood and the Struggle for Existence" and "Preparing for the Sixth Epoch," the latter two included in this volume, Steiner describes work in spiritually-oriented groups as providing an awakening to the soul-spiritual of the other and through common striving allowing spirit beings to be present in new community forms.[19] In meeting, conversation and encounter we can experience each other as soul and spirit beings in communion. This possibility and experience is sensitively described by Athys Floride in his essay *Human Encounters and Karma,* in which he shows how the Revelation occurs in initial meeting, is deepened through experiencing the profound humanity of the other [Offering], then transformed through experiencing the forces of karma [Transubstantiation], finally leading to an experience of [Communion].[20] The process of achieving communion through meeting the other in the cosmic ritual in this manner is shown by Steiner to be the earthly mirror of our meeting in the spiritual world between death and a new life:

> Thus at the first stage after death the human being moves among the spirit-physiognomies of those who are connected with him by destiny: he beholds these physiognomies. Human beings learn to know each other in the spirit-form, they learn to know each other's moral and spiritual qualities. But at this first stage it is a beholding only, a seeing; although it means that the souls come into intimate connection, it is no more than a beholding. Then begins the period that I described as that of the growth of mutual understanding. The one begins to understand the other; he gazes deeply upon him and looks into his inner nature, knowing the while that the sure working of destiny will link the future to the past. Then the great process of transformation begins, where the one is able to work

upon the other out of a profound knowledge and understanding, and the plastic molding of the spirit is taken up and changed to music and to speech. And here we come to something more than understanding; the one human being is able to speak to the other his own warmth-filled, creative work. On Earth we speak with our organs of speech; by means of these we tell each other what we know. Our words live in the physical body as something fleeting and transient; and when we express what we want to say by means of our speech-organs, in that moment we completely shut off that which lives behind the merely material. But now imagine that what a man thus utters, what goes over into the fleeting word, were an expression of himself, were not alone a manifestation of him, but were at the same time his very being. Such is the intercourse of human beings in the middle period of the time between death and a new birth — differentiating each of his own being and revealing themselves one to another. Word meets word; articulate word meets articulate word; inwardly living word meets inwardly living word. The human souls are themselves words; their symphony is the symphony of the spoken Cosmic Word in its very being (communion). There, men live in and with one another; there is no such thing as impenetrability. The word, which is the one human being, merges into the word, which is the other human being. And it is there those links of destiny are formed which work on into the next incarnation and express themselves in the sympathy or antipathy which one human being feels when he encounters another.[21]

This picture of meeting, of a true intimacy between human beings in the spiritual world, is a powerful archetype and a call to us on earth to experience the soul spiritual with and through each other.

Working with groups in different communities is part of my work as an advisor and consultant. I experience the

description of Spiritual Communion by Floride and the archetype of meeting in the spiritual world given by Steiner as having practical consequences for all meetings, if we seek
connection to the spirit. We enter a meeting space as a Board,
Finance Committee, College of Teachers or some other group,
and we sit down. We can then, in quiet, behold/perceive each
other and share a verse, saying, or meditation. This perceiving
and sharing can be seen as a kind of attunement to the presence of the spirit. It is akin to the gospel reading of the communion service, for both we and the verse or saying are the
revelation of the spirit.

   The meeting or the conversation then begins. If we have
come prepared and listen intensely to one another — both the
content and the person — we are making an offering of our
consciousness. This process of conscious listening is difficult,
for it entails silencing our own reactions and responses in
order to be really present for the other and for what is to be
revealed in conversation. With the beholding and sharing of a
verse we are expressing a common intention. Through conscious listening we are beginning to create a chalice, a cup that
can hold spiritual substance and being. The third step, that of
transubstantiation, occurs again and again when we see and
experience the best of each other and are grateful for our col-
leagueship and karmic connection. Anger, annoyance, impa-
tience, and discomfort drive away positive working spirits and
invite other forces into our conversation. To create Spiritual
Communion, we are called upon to see the highest in each
other, an activity movingly described by Steiner in his Faithfulness Verse:

> Create for yourself a new, indomitable perception of
> faithfulness. What is usually called faithfulness passes so
> quickly. Let this be your faithfulness:
> You will experience moments — fleeting moments —
> with the other person.
> The human being will appear to you then as if filled, irra-
> diated, with the archetype of his Spirit.

And then there may be — indeed, will be — other moments. Long periods of time, when human beings are darkened. But you will learn to say to yourself at such times: "The Spirit makes me strong. I remember the archetype. I saw it once. No illusion, no deception shall rob me of it."

Always struggle for the image that you saw. This struggle is faithfulness.

Striving thus for faithfulness, we shall be close to one another, as if endowed with the protective power of angels.

If we are able to meet these three conditions and create the requisite mood of soul, we can be graced by a commonly experienced presence of the spirit. This experience of a star- and presence-filled space is something we have all had at one time or another, in conversation and in meeting. If we can more consciously work on the steps and the mood of sacramental conversation then this experience of Spiritual Communion can become the basis of a new meeting and community culture in all our work, in schools, and in curative homes, hospitals, and businesses. Working in this way, we will be co-creating with the spirit and practicing "preparing for the sixth epoch,"the title of the last lecture by Steiner in the study section of this volume.

What I have described, an elaboration of Athys Floride's essay, is also the content of two well-known essays by Marjorie Spock: "On Goethean Conversation" and "Reflections on Community Building," both of which are available from Anthroposophic Press, and both of which are important resources for understanding the sacrament of conversation. Both the Benesch and Floride essays describe the nature and steps of sacramental and Spiritual Communion from a human and earthly perspective. If we now ask ourselves what the spiritual process is that takes place in Spiritual Communion, then the clearest description I am aware of in Steiner's work is the Teachers Imagination that he gave to the first Waldorf teachers in the Stuttgart School. In the imagination, he describes how behind each teacher stands their angel, lending support and strength; then above the circle of teachers weave the archangels, creating a chalice of courage. Lastly, the time spirit, the being of Michael, bestows a drop of inspiration, of true spiritual insight, to the group of colleagues. I believe this to be a true spiritual imagination of what is happening in the process of Spiritual Communion for any group of spiritually active colleagues genuinely seeking to work with pressing issues of our time. The angels, archangels, and archai can strengthen and inspire us if we consciously turn to them for guidance and help.

In the last ten years, there has been an increasing amount of reflection and work on dialogue groups and sacred conversation, stimulated in large part by the work of David Bohm and, in a different way, by M. Scott Peck.[22] This work was reviewed and elaborated by the Fetzer Institute and the Institute of Noetic Sciences (IONS) in a series of Group Service and Synergy Conferences in 1998 and 1999. The Fetzer summary report by Robert Kenny describes a clear horizontal and vertical dimension to Spiritual Communion, that is, both a concern about the quality of relationships and authenticity between people (horizontal), and a joint commitment to working with spirit (vertical).[23]

Another way of describing this distinction is to refer to the vessel or container built by the group making the presence of positive, inspiring spiritual beings possible. Out of my experience working with many types of groups, I can fully support the conditions that Kenny mentions as essential for Spiritual Communion. These include:

- A mutual commitment to each other and a clear and shared human and spiritual purpose
- Developing an atmosphere of safety, confidentiality, trust, and respect.
- Speaking from the heart and out of experience

- Inclusivity and respect toward different human and spiritual orientations
- A willingness to play
- An ability to deal with differences and with conflict
- Creating a sacred space open to guidance and inspiration
- A joint commitment to inner development and learning
- A meeting that is prepared, held, and guided by a clear process and form of facilitation

When these conditions are met, a true chalice has been created through which group members can experience:

- An enhanced level of trust in self and others
- A sense of being known and seen
- A greater sense of authenticity and creativity
- A sense of spiritual presence and guidance
- Mutual encouragement
- Satisfaction at connecting inner values with life
- An increased desire to serve and contribute to a better world
- A greater sense of individual and community health

These are also the conditions and effects of Spiritual Communion so clearly and simply described by Steiner in the America or Threefold Verse given to Ralph Courtney, an early student of Anthroposophy and one of the founders of the Threefold Community in Spring Valley, NY:

May our feeling penetrate into the center of our heart
and seek in love to unite itself with human beings
sharing the same goals and with spirit beings,
who bearing grace and strengthening us from realms of light
and illuminating our love
are gazing down upon our earnest, heartfelt striving.

This book of essays and lectures is a valuable resource and stimulus for practicing sacramental conversation and bringing the sacred into art, cognition, and deeds of social service. The lectures by Steiner in this volume bring together some of his most important reflections on Sacramental Communion. The lecture of December 30, 1922 also describes his different relationship to the Christian Community, which he helped but remained separate from, and the Anthroposophical Society, which he founded and was to lead following the Christmas Foundation Meeting of January 1-7, 1923. The five lectures by Steiner are followed by the Benesch book and two more related lectures by Steiner, while both Asten and the Floride essays are contained in the appendix.

We have the opportunity in this new century to co-create with spiritual beings directly in all spheres of life. Indeed, without such conscious co-creation and dialogue with spiritual beings, I do not think we will be able to make progress with the host of issues we face as humanity. Steiner, as a great spiritual teacher of the 20th century, has provided a moving and detailed description of a new landscape of possibilities for human and spiritual co-creation in the 21st century. Our task is to grasp these possibilities and to practice a conscious dialogue with the spirit. This book can help us in understanding and fulfilling this task.

Christopher Schaefer
Spring Valley, NY
October 2000

Christopher Schaefer, PhD, is a faculty member at Sunbridge College, an advisor and consultant, and a member of the Social Science Section of the School of Spiritual Science. He is the co-author of *Vision in Action: Working with Soul and Spirit in Small Organizations,* Lindisfarne Press, and of the forthcoming *Partnerships of Hope: Building Waldorf Schools and other Communities of the Spirit.*

1 Dietrich Asten, *Sacramental and Spiritual Communion*, Anthroposophic Press, 1984.

2 Rudolf Steiner, *Man and the World of the Stars, the Spiritual Communion of Mankind*, Anthroposophic Press p. 187-188, 1963 (December 31, 1922).

3 Rudolf Steiner, *Awakening to Community*, Anthroposophic Press, p. 157.

4 Friedrich Benesch, *Das Religiöse der Anthroposophie, der kosmische, der umgekehrte kultus*, Verlag die Pforte, Basel, 1985. *Idden zur Kultusfrage.*, *Das Religiöse der Anthroposophie*, Verlag die Pforte, Basel, 1986.

5 F. Benesch, *Das Religiöse der Anthroposophie*, pp. 13-14.

6 F. Benesch, *Ideen zur Kultusfrage*, p. 27.

7 Athys Floride, *Human Encounters and Karma*, Anthroposophic Press, 1990.

8 Rudolf Steiner, *A Theory of Knowledge Based on Goethe's World Conception*, Anthroposophic Press, 1968.

9 Rudolf Steiner, *Philosophy of Spiritual Activity*, Anthroposophic Press, 1986.

Georg Kühlewind, *The Logos Structure of the World*, Lindisfarne Press, 1993.

10 Friedemann Schwarzkopf, *Spiritual Communion*, Dec. 31, 1992, 20465 Placer Hills Road, Colfax, CA 95113.

11 R. Steiner, *Goethe as the Father of a new Aesthetics*, 1888, in GA. 30.

12 R. Steiner, *How to Know Higher Worlds*, Anthroposophic Press, 1994.

13 Dietrich Asten, *Op. cit.*, pp. 10-11.

14 R. Steiner, *The Inner Aspect of the Social Question*, Rudolf Steiner Press, London, 1974.

15 F. Benesch, *Op.cit.*, (this translation), p.20.

16 F. Benesch, *Ideen zur Kultusfrage*, pp. 28, 29.

17 R. Steiner, *Man and the Stars*, p. 185.

18 R. Steiner, *Awakening to Community*, in particular — *Brotherhood and the Struggle for Existence*, Mercury Press, 1980. *Preparing for the Sixth Epoch*, Anthroposophic Press.

19 Ibid.

20 Athys Floride, *Op. cit.*

21 R. Steiner, Hague, November 14, 1922.

22 M. Scott Peck, *A World Waiting to be Born* Bantam, 1993 and also *The Different Drum: Community-Making and Peace.*

23 Robert Kenny, *Group Service and Synergy: Report to the Fetzer Institute*, 1999.

Part One

CHAPTER I

MIDSUMMER AND MIDWINTER MYSTERIES

Dornach, December 23, 1922

The Mystery on which the Christmas festival is based can give us cause to compare it with other Mysteries that emerged out of other conditions in the course of human evolution. The Christmas Mystery — when it is conceived of as a Mystery — is a *Winter* Mystery. It arose from conceptions of the spiritual world that had primarily to do with the link established between human beings and the scene of their life on Earth at the beginning of winter.

When we consider the Mysteries that were celebrated in certain parts of Asia long before the founding of Christianity, in which many sublime cosmic thoughts were given expression, or when we compare the Christmas Mystery with Mysteries that were celebrated also in pre-Christian times in Middle, Northern, and Western Europe, we are struck by the fact that they were preeminently *Summer* Mysteries, connected with the union between human beings and all that takes place in earthly life during the time of summer. But we understand all this only if we focus first on the part of human evolution that came before the Mystery of Golgotha.

Looking back into the very ancient times we find that the Mysteries were institutions of human beings who still possessed the faculty of instinctive clairvoyance. The human beings belonging to that ancient humanity were still able, in certain states of consciousness between those of full sleep and waking, in states where dreams were expressions of reality, to gaze into the spiritual worlds from whence human beings descend into physical bodies on the Earth. Every human being in those times could speak and think about the spiritual worlds, just as we today can speak about the ordinary knowledge we have learned in school. I have, as you know, often said that what the people of those ancient times beheld of the spiritual-supersensible world presented itself to them in pictures — not the pictures of dreams but somewhat resembling them. Whereas we know quite well that the pictures in our dreams are woven from our reminiscences, that they rise up from the organism and, unlike our thoughts, do not mirror reality, people of those times knew through the very nature of the imaginations of the old clairvoyance that they were the expressions, not of any external, material reality or historical reality, but of a spiritual world hidden behind the physical world. Thus the spiritual world was revealed to human beings at first in pictures.

But it must not be imagined that those human beings of an earlier epoch had no thoughts. They *had* thoughts, but they did not acquire them as we acquire our thoughts today. If we today are to have thoughts, we must exert ourselves inwardly; we must shape and form our thoughts within ourselves. A similar activity was required in ancient times when spiritual realities were received as pictures. One may well be amazed at the power and brilliance of the thoughts of that old humanity, but the thoughts were not thought out by the people; they were received as revelations.

Now just as we have schools and colleges today, so in those times there were Mysteries — institutions in which science, art, and religion were united. No distinction was made between belief and knowledge. Knowledge came in the form of pictures, but belief was based securely on knowledge. Nor was any distinction made between what people fashioned out of various materials into works of art and what they acquired as wisdom. Today the distinction is made by saying that what people acquire in the form of wisdom must be true, but that what they embody in their materials as painters, sculptors, or musicians — that is fantasy!

Goethe was really the last survivor of those who did *not* hold this view. He regarded as truth just as much what he embodied in his materials as an artist as what he took to be science. The philistinism expressed in the distinction between the artistic and the scientific did not, in fact, appear until comparatively late, indeed until after Goethe's time. Goethe was still able, when he saw the works of art in Italy, to utter the great words, "I surmise that in the creation of their works of art the Greeks proceeded by the same laws by which nature itself creates and of which I am on the track." In Weimar, before going to Italy, he and Herder had studied the philosophy of Spinoza together. Goethe had attempted to immerse himself in a divine-spiritual that permeates all the beings in the human being's environment. He tried, however, to track this divine-spiritual in the details, right into the leaf and flower of the plant. And the way in which he built up for himself a picture of the plant-form and the animal-form in his botanical and zoological studies was the same, an activity of the soul, as the procedure he adopted in his artistic creations.

Today it is considered unscientific to speak of one and the same truth in art, in science, and in religion. But as I have said, in those ancient centers of learning and culture, art, science, and religion were one. It was actually the leaders in these Mysteries who began gradually to separate out particular thoughts from those that were revealed to people with their instinctive clairvoyance and to establish a wisdom composed of thoughts. On all sides we see thought-wisdom emerging in the Mysteries from clairvoyant vision. Whereas the majority of people were content with pictorial vision, were satisfied to have the revelation of this spiritual vision presented to them in the form of myths, fairy tales, and legends by those who were capable of doing so, the leaders of the Mysteries developed a thought-wisdom. But they were fully aware that this wisdom was *revealed*, not acquired by the human being.

We need only think ourselves into this quite different attitude of soul. I will put it in the following way: when we conceive a thought today, we ascribe it to our own activity of thinking. We form chains of thoughts in accordance with laws of logic — which are themselves the laws of our own thinking.

The humans of ancient times *received* the thoughts. They paid no heed at all to how the connections between thoughts should be formulated, for they received them as finished revelations. But this meant that the human beings of old did not live in their thoughts the same way we live in ours. We regard our thoughts as the possessions of our soul; we know that we have worked to acquire them. They have, as it were, been born from our own life of soul; they have arisen out of ourselves, and we regard them as our property. Human beings of ancient times could not regard their thoughts as their own property. Thoughts were illuminations that had come to them together with the illuminated pictures. And this gave rise to a very definite feeling and attitude toward the wisdom-filled thoughts. People said to themselves as they contemplated their thoughts: "A divine being from a higher world has descended into me. I partake of the thoughts that in reality other beings are thinking — beings who are higher than the human being and who inspire me, who live in me, who give me these thoughts. I can therefore only regard the thoughts as having been vouchsafed to me by grace from above." Because of this human beings of old felt the need at certain seasons to offer these thoughts in turn to the higher beings through their feelings, as it were. And this happened in the Summer Mysteries.

In the summer the Earth is more given up to its own environment, to the atmosphere surrounding it. It has not contracted because of the cold or enveloped itself in raiment of snow; it is in perpetual intercourse with its atmospheric environment. Hence human beings too are given up to the wide cosmic expanse. In the summer they feel themselves united with the upper gods. And in those ancient times people sought out at the midsummer season, the time when the Sun is at the zenith of its power, certain places they regarded as sacred, in order to establish contact with the upper gods. They availed themselves of their natural connection in summer with the whole etheric environment, in order to make a sacrificial offering out of their deepest feelings to the gods who had revealed their thoughts to them.

The teachers in the mysteries spoke to their pupils somewhat as follows: "

> Every year at midsummer, a solemn offering must be made to the upper gods in gratitude for the thoughts they vouchsafe to human beings. For if this is not done it is all too easy for the Luciferic powers to invade human thinking, and then human beings are permeated by these powers. They can avoid this if every summer they are mindful of how the upper gods have given them these thoughts and if, at the midsummer, they let these thoughts flow back again, as it were, to the gods.

In this way the people of ancient times tried to safeguard themselves from Luciferic influences. The leaders of the Mysteries called together those who were in a sense their pupils and in their presence enacted a solemn rite, which culminated with the thoughts that had been revealed by the upper gods being offered up to them in upward-streaming feelings.

The external rite consisted in solemn words being spoken into rising smoke, which was thus set into waves. This act was merely meant to signify that the offering made by the human being's inmost soul to the upper gods was being inscribed into an outer medium, the outer smoke, through form-creating words. The words of the prayer inscribed into the rising smoke only the feelings that the soul desired to send upward to the gods as an offering for the thoughts they had revealed.

This was the basic mood out of which the celebration of the Midsummer Mysteries proceeded. These midsummer festivals had meaning only as long as human beings received their thoughts through revelation.

But in the centuries immediately preceding the Mystery of Golgotha — beginning as early as early as the eighth and ninth centuries B.C. — the thoughts that were revealed from above grew dark, and more and more the faculty awakened in human beings to acquire their thoughts through their own efforts. This induced in them an entirely different mood.

Whereas formerly they had felt that their thoughts were coming to them as it were from the far spaces of the universe, descending into their inner life, they now began to feel the thoughts as something unfolding within themselves, belonging to them like the blood in their veins. In ancient times, thoughts had been regarded more as something belonging to the human like the *breath* — the breath that is received from the surrounding atmosphere and continually given back again. Just as we regard the air as something surrounding us that we draw into ourself but always give out again, so they felt their thoughts as something they did not draw into themselves but received through revelation and had to be given back again and again to the gods at the time of midsummer.

The festivals themselves were given a dramatic form in keeping with this attitude. The leaders of the Mysteries went to the ceremonies bearing the symbols of wisdom; and as they conducted the sacrificial rites, they divested themselves of the symbols one by one. Then when they went away from the ceremonies, having laid aside the symbols of wisdom, they appeared as fools who had to acquire their wisdom again in the course of the year. It was like a confession on the part of those sages of ancient times. When they had made the solemn offering it was as though they declared to their followers, "We have become fools again."

To share in this way in the course taken by the seasons of the year, entering as midsummer approaches into the possession of wisdom, then passing into a state of being a fool, and then in turn becoming wise again — this was actually felt by people to be the means of escape from the Luciferic powers. Thus, they strove to experience the cosmos. As the cosmos lets winter alternate with summer, so they wanted to let the time of wisdom alternate in themselves with the time of entry into the darkness of ignorance.

Now there were some whose wisdom was needed all year round, and who for this reason could not act or adopt the same procedure as the others. For example, there were teachers in the Mysteries who practiced the art of healing — for that too was part of the Mysteries. Naturally, it would not do for a doctor to become ignorant in August and September (if I may use the present names of the months), so these people were allowed to retain their wisdom; but in return they made the sacrifice of being only servants in the Mysteries. Those who were the leaders in the Mysteries became ignorant for a certain time every year.

Reminiscences of this have remained here and there, for example, in the figure described by Goethe in his poem *Die Geheimnisse* (The Mysteries) as the "Thirteenth," the one who was the leader of the others but was himself in a state of dullness rather than wisdom.

The attitude toward the guiding wisdom of humankind was entirely different from what it became afterward when human beings began to regard their thoughts as produced by themselves. Whereas formerly they felt that wisdom was like the air they breathed, later on they felt that their thoughts were produced within themselves, like the blood. We can therefore say: In ancient times human beings felt their thoughts to be the air of the breath, and in the epoch of the Mystery of Golgotha they began to feel that their thoughts were like the blood within them.

But then people also began to feel that what they experienced as thought was no longer heavenly, no longer something that descended from above, but rather something that arises in human beings themselves, something that is earthly. This feeling that thoughts of the human being are earthly in origin was still significantly present at the time of the Mystery of Golgotha among those who were the late successors of the leaders of the ancient Mysteries. Those who stood at that time at the height of cultural life said to themselves: Human beings can no longer have such thoughts as had the sages of old, who, with their thoughts, lived together with the gods to a certain extent; they must now develop purely human thoughts. But these purely human thoughts are in danger of falling prey to the Ahrimanic powers. The thoughts that were revealed to human beings from above were in danger of succumbing to the

Luciferic powers; the human thoughts, the self-produced thoughts, are in danger of succumbing to the Ahrimanic powers.

Those who were capable of thinking in this way in the epoch of the Mystery of Golgotha — by the fourth century, however, the insight was lost — experienced the Mystery of Golgotha as the real redemption of humanity. They understood that the spiritual power living with the Sun, which previously could be reached only by superhuman forces, now had to be attained by human faculties, for human beings' thoughts were now within their own being. Hence they had to inwardly raise these thoughts of theirs to the divine. Now that they were earthly thinkers, they had to permeate their thoughts inwardly with the divine, and this they could do through uniting themselves in thought and feeling with the Mystery of Golgotha.

This meant that the festival once celebrated in the Mysteries at midsummer became a *winter* festival. In winter, when the Earth envelops itself in its raiment of snow and is no longer in living interchange with the atmosphere around it, human beings too are fettered more strongly to the Earth; they do not share in the life of the wide universe but enter into the life that is rooted beneath the surface of the Earth. However we must understand the meaning of this correctly.

We can continually be made aware of how in the Earth's environment there is not only that which comes directly from the Sun but also that which partakes in the life of the Earth beneath its surface. I have spoken of this before by referring to some very simple facts. Those of you who have lived in the country know how farmers dig pits in the earth during winter and put their potatoes in them. Down there in the earth the potatoes last splendidly through the winter, which would not be the case if they were simply put in cellars. Why is this? Think of an area of the Earth's surface. It absorbs the light and warmth of the Sun that have streamed to it during the summer. The light and warmth sink down, as it were, into the soil of the Earth, so that in winter the summer is still there within the

Earth. During winter it is summer underneath the surface of the Earth. And this summer under the surface of the Earth in wintertime enables the roots of the plants to thrive. The seeds become roots and growth begins. So when we see a plant growing this year it is actually growing by the forces of last year's Sun that penetrated into the Earth.

Therefore when we are looking at the root of a plant, or even at parts of the leaves, we have before us what is the *previous summer* in the plant. Only in the blossom do we have *this* year's summer, for the blossom is conjured forth by the light and warmth of the present year's Sun. Indeed, in the sprouting and unfolding of the plant we still have the previous year, and the present year comes to manifestation only in the blossom. Even the ovary center of the blossom is a product of the winter — in reality, that is, of the previous summer. Only what surrounds the ovary belongs to the present year. Thus do the seasons interpenetrate, just as different times interpenetrate in the case of sleep in the human being, as I explained yesterday. When the Earth dons its winter raiment of snow, beneath that raiment is the continuation of summer. Then human beings do not unite themselves with the wide expanse but turn their life of soul inward, into the interior of the Earth. They turn to the lower gods.

This was the conception held by those who possessed the heritage of the ancient wisdom at the time of the Mystery of Golgotha. And it gave them the realization that they had to seek the power of the Christ, the power of the new wisdom permeating the evolution of the Earth, in what is united with the Earth. Having passed to the stage of self-produced thoughts, they felt the need to unite these thoughts inwardly with the divine, to permeate them inwardly with the Christ. This they could do at the time when they were most closely bound to the Earth — in deep winter; they could do it when the Earth shut itself off from the cosmos. For then they too were shut off from the cosmos and could come nearest to the God who descended from those far spaces and united himself with the Earth.

It is a beautiful thought to connect the Christmas festival with the time when the Earth is shut off from the cosmos, when in the loneliness of Earth human beings seek to unite their self-produced thoughts with the divine-spiritual-supersensible, and when, understanding what this means, they endeavor to protect themselves from the Ahrimanic powers, as in ancient times they protected themselves from the Luciferic powers through the rites of the Midsummer Mysteries.

And just as the human beings of ancient time, under the guidance of the teachers in the Mysteries, became aware through the midsummer festival that their thoughts were fading into a state of twilight, so those of today who rightly understand the Christmas Mystery should feel strengthened when at Christmas they steep themselves in truths such as have now once more been expressed. They should feel how, through developing a true relation to the Mystery of Golgotha, the thoughts they acquire in the darkness of their inner life can be illumined. For it is indeed so that they realize that in the course of the Earth's evolution the being who in pre-Christian ages could only be thought of as united with the Sun, once passed into Earth evolution and together with humankind indwells the Earth as a spiritual being. In contrast to the old midsummer festivals whose aim was for human beings to pass out of themselves into the cosmos, the Christmas festival should be the occasion when they go into themselves and deepen inwardly, to spiritualize inwardly whatever knowledge they acquire about the great world.

Human beings of old did not feel that knowledge was their own possession but that it was a gift, and every year they gave it back again. Today human beings necessarily regard their world of thought, their intellectual knowledge, as their own possession. Therefore, they must take into their heart the spirit being who has united with the Earth; they must link their thoughts with this being so that instead of remaining with their thoughts in egotistic seclusion, they will unite them with that being of Sun and Earth who fulfilled the Mystery of Golgotha.

In a certain respect the ancient Mysteries had what might be called an "aristocratic" character. Indeed the principle of aristocracy really had its origin in those old Mysteries, for it was the priests who enacted the sacrifice on behalf of all the others.

The Christmas festival has a "democratic" character. For what modern people acquire that really makes them human is their inner store of thoughts. And the Christmas Mystery is only truly seen in the right light when one does not make the sacrificial offering for another, but shares with the other a common experience: in the face of the Sun Being who came down to the Earth. And in the early period of Christian evolution, until about the fourth century, it was this equality that was felt to be particularly significant for Christianity. It was not until then that the old forms of the Egyptian Mysteries were resuscitated and made their way via Rome to Western Europe, overlaying the original Christianity and shrouding it in traditions that will have to be abandoned if Christianity is to be rightly understood. For Rome invested Christianity with a character that was through and through the character of the old Mysteries. Christianity itself requires absolutely this finding of the spiritual-supersensible in human beings *not* at a time when they pass out of themselves and are given up to the cosmos, but when they are firmly *within* themselves. And this is most of all the case when they are united with the Earth at the time when the Earth itself is shut off from the cosmic expanse — that is to say, in midwinter.

I have thus tried to show how it came about that in the course of the ages the midsummer festivals in the Mysteries changed into the midwinter Christmas Mystery. But this must be understood in the right sense. By looking back over the evolution of humanity we can deepen our understanding of what is presented to us in the Christmas Mystery. In contrast with ancient times, human beings can rightly feel what they are to become more and more by seeking the secrets within themselves that they once sought outside themselves.

It is from this point of view that my *Outline of Esoteric*

Science is written. If such a book had been written in ancient times (then, of course, it would not have been a book but something different) the starting point of the descriptions would have been in the starry heavens. But in the book as it is, the starting point is the human being: contemplation, first of the inner aspect of the human being, and proceeding from there to the universe. The inner core of the human being is widened to Old Saturn, Old Sun, Old Moon, and, in turn, to the future epochs of the Earth's evolution.

In ancient times, human beings seeking knowledge of the world started from the stars they looked at outwardly, then endeavored to take into their inner being what the stars said to them. They studied the Sun in this way. The Sun revealed a very great deal to the imaginative cognition of those days. To the orthodox modern scientist the Sun is a ball of gas — which of course it cannot be for unbiased thought. When human beings of ancient times contemplated the Sun externally, it was to them the bodily expression of a soul-and-spiritual entity, just as the human body is an expression of a soul-and-spiritual entity. They saw much in the Sun. And when they had read in the cosmos what the Sun had revealed, they could point to their own heart, and say: Now I understand the human heart, for the Sun has told me what the nature of the human heart is. And likewise in the other heavenly bodies and constellations, human beings discovered what they themselves are.

It was not possible to proceed in this way in my book *Outline of Esoteric Science*. Although it is too soon yet for all the relevant details to have been worked out, the procedure is that we think, first, of the human being as a whole, with heart, lungs, and so on, and in understanding the organs individually we come to understand the universe. We study the human heart, and what we read there tells us what the Sun is, tells us something about the nature of the Sun. Thus through the heart we learn to know the nature of the Sun; that is to say, we proceed from within outward. In ancient times it was the other way around: first of all human beings learned to know the

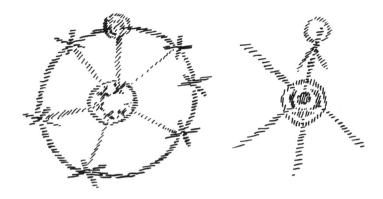

nature of the Sun, and then they understood the human heart. In the modern age we learn what the heart is, what the lung is, and so, starting from the human being, we learn to know the universe.

The ancients could only express their awareness of this relation of the human being to the universe by looking upward to the Sun and the starry heavens at the time of midsummer, when conditions were the most favorable for feeling their union with the cosmos. But if we today would realize with inner intensity how we can come to know the universe, we must gaze into the depths of the inner human being. And the right time for this is in midwinter, at Christmas.

Try to grasp the full meaning of this Christmas thought, for there is a real need today to enliven old habits such as these — for they have become old habits — so that we become sincere again in our experience of the course of the year, for example. All that many people today know about Christmas is that it is a time for giving presents, also, perhaps, a time when in a very external way, thought is turned to the Mystery of Golgotha!

Such externalizing and making superficial are what is really to blame for the great calamity into which human civilization has drifted today. It is there that the real blame must be placed; it lies in clinging to habits, and in being unwilling to face the necessity of *renewal*, for example, of what the Christmas thought, the Christmas feeling should be. We need such renewal through and through.

This impulse of renewal is needed because we can only become human in the true sense by finding the spiritual part of our being in the world. It is a "World Christmas" that we need, a birth of the spiritual life, as I have often said, precisely at this time. Then we shall once again celebrate Christmas as honest human beings; again there will be meaning in the fact that at the time when the Earth is shrouded in her raiment of snow, we try to feel that our world of thought is permeated with the Christ. The world of thought today is like the blood within us, in contrast to the old world of thought, which was like the breath.

We must learn to live more intensely with the course of time than is the custom today. About twenty years ago the idea came up that it would be advantageous to have a fixed Easter — a festival still regulated by the actual course of time. The idea was that Easter should always be on April 1, so that account books would not always be thrown into confusion because of the dates of the festival varying each year. Even the experience of the flow of time was to be drawn into the materialistic trend of evolution. In view of other things that have happened as well, it can be understood if materialistic thought were ultimately to accept this comfortable arrangement. For example, we begin the year with the present New Year's Day, the first of January, in spite of the fact that December (*decem*) is the tenth month and January and February quite obviously belong to the previous year, so that in reality the new year can begin in March at the earliest — as indeed was actually the case in Roman times. But it once pleased a French king (whom even history acknowledges to have been an imbecile) to begin the year in the middle of the winter, on the first of January, and humanity conformed to it.

Strong and resolute thoughts are needed to admit honestly to ourselves that saving human evolution depends upon our allying ourselves with *wisdom*. Many things indicate that human beings have by no means always done so, and have very often allied themselves with ignorance, with nescience. Take hold of the Christmas thought in such a way that we become honest in it to connect with the being who said, "I am the Way, the Truth and the Life." But the way to the Truth and the Life in the spirit has to be deliberately sought, and for this it is necessary for modern humanity to immerse itself in the depths of midnight in order to find the light that kindles itself in the human being.

The old tradition of the first Christmas Mass being read at midnight is not enough. We must again realize in actual experience that what is best and most filled with light in our nature is born out of the darkness prevailing in ourselves. For this is indeed a truth: *The light is born out of the darkness.* And from this darkness *light* must be born — not always further darkness.

Try to permeate the Christmas thought with the strength that will come to your souls when you feel with all intensity that the light of spiritual insight and spiritual vision must pierce the darkness of knowledge of the other kind. Then in the Holy Night Christ will be born in the heart of each one of you, and you will experience together with all humanity a World Christmas.

CHAPTER II

THE MYSTERIES OF THE HUMAN BEING'S NATURE AND THE COURSE OF THE YEAR

Dornach, December 24, 1922

If we would deepen our thoughts in a manner suitable for the present age, this can best be done in the way indicated yesterday, namely, by looking back over the process of human evolution in order to recognize from the spiritual guidance of humanity what tasks human beings have today. It must not be overlooked, of course, that the most important part of the Christmas thought is that in the night just beginning the Light of Christ shone into the evolution of humanity at the point of time when, through this event, through this integration of the Mystery of Golgotha into earthly life, meaning was given to human life on Earth and therewith to the Earth itself.

Yesterday I spoke to you of how an important role was played in the times before the Mystery of Golgotha by the festivals celebrated in the Mysteries at midsummer, when human beings, together with the Earth, open their being to the cosmos and can enter with the soul into union with powers belonging to realms beyond the Earth. We heard how among certain peoples the leaders of the Mysteries, following the path along which at midsummer, at our St. John's Tide, the human soul can be led into the divine-spiritual worlds, offered up the feeling-permeated thought world to the divine-spiritual powers. They did this because they realized that whatever revealed itself to them in the course of the year was exposed to the temptations of the Luciferic powers unless at midsummer, when the Earth spreads wide her wings into the cosmic expanse, these thoughts were felt to be grace bestowed by the divine-spiritual beings.

I went on to show how the evolutionary process brought it about that for a certain section of humankind, the midwinter festival quite naturally replaced the midsummer festival. Even in our present vapid Christmas thoughts something is still left of this midwinter festival. The birth of the Savior in the midwinter night is celebrated either in religious communities or by human beings in the stillness of their own hearts because they feel they must again find the way to the light of the Spirit and are conscious that at this time of the year they are most similar to the Earth and its life when they go into their own selves. For the Earth too, at this time, is shut off from the cosmos; enveloped in its raiment of snow it lives in cosmic space as a being pressed into itself.

However, Christmas thoughts played a part already in the times when people celebrated mainly the midsummer festival, but in the pre-Christian era the meaning of the Christmas thought was not the same as it is today. At that time the sublime Sun Spirit still belonged to the cosmos, had not yet come down to the Earth. The whole condition of the human soul at midwinter, when together with the Earth human beings felt themselves to be in cosmic isolation, was different from what it is today. And we learn to know what this condition was if we turn our attention to certain Mysteries that were celebrated mainly in the south in times long, long before the Mystery of Golgotha. Initiation in those Mysteries, the initiation science of that day, was conferred upon candidates in the old way. And among certain ancient peoples this initiation science consisted in the candidate learning to read the book of the world — I do not mean anything that is conveyed by dead letters written on paper, but what the beings of the universe themselves communicate. Those who have insight into the secrets of the cosmos know that everything growing and thriving on the Earth is through and through an image of what shines down from the stars out of the cosmic expanse.

Those who learn this cosmic reading, as we today learn the far simpler kind of reading by means of dead letters, know that they must see in every plant a sign revealing something of the secrets of the universe, and that when they let their gaze survey the world of plants or animals, this surveying is itself a reading. And it was in such a way that the initiates of certain ancient Mysteries read to their pupils. They did not read to them out of a book but communicated to them what they experienced under the inspiration of the so-called Year God concerning the secrets of the course of the year and their significance for human life. In this way an ancient wisdom read what concerned human life in the beings and happenings of the world. When the sages of old communicated such things to their pupils, they were inspired by divine-spiritual beings such as the Year God.

Who was this Year God who belonged to the rank of the Primal Powers, the Archai, in the Hierarchies? He was a being to whom certain of those versed in initiation science lifted their hearts and in so doing were endowed by him with the power and inner light enabling them to read one thing from the budding plants in spring, another from the ripening of the early fruits in summer, another when the leaves redden in autumn and the fruits ripen, and yet another when the trees glitter under the snowflakes and the Earth with her rocks is covered with a veil of snow. This "reading" lasted for a whole year through spring, summer, autumn, and winter; and in it the secrets of the being of the human itself were unveiled between the teachers and the pupils. And then the cycle began anew.

Some idea of what these ancient initiates taught to their pupils under the inspiration of the Year God may be conveyed in the following way. The attention of the pupils was drawn, first of all, to what is revealed in spring, when the snow is over and the Sun is gaining strength, when the first buds of the plants are appearing out of the revived forces of the Earth. The pupils were made aware of how a plant growing in the meadows and a plant growing in the shade of the trees in a forest speak differently of the secrets of the universe. They were made aware of how in the various plants the warmth and light of the Sun speak differently out of the cosmic expanse in the round or the serrated leaves.

And through what could be revealed in this way under the influence and inspiration of the Year God, through the letters budding forth from the Earth itself, the teachers in the Mysteries unveiled to the pupils, in the manner of that time, the secrets of the physical body of the human being.

The teachers pointed to what in the Earth brings forth the physical, to the force of the Earth shooting into the plant. At every single place on the Earth to which the pupils' attention was directed, there was a different "letter." These letters — which were living plant beings, or living animal forms — were then combined as we today combine single letters into words. In sharing thus in the life of spring, the human being was reading in nature. The initiations bestowed by the Year God consisted in this reading. And when spring came to an end, at about the time of the month of May, the human being had the impression: Now I understand how the human physical body takes shape and is formed out of the womb of the universe.

Then came the summer. The same letters and words of the great cosmic Logos were used, but it was pointed out to the pupils how the letters change their forms now when the Sun's rays, stream differently and its light and warmth, work in a different way — how the first buds, which had spoken of the secrets of the human physical body, open themselves to the Sun in the blossoms. These many-colored blossoms were now letters used by the pupils; each blossom made them feel how the Sun's ray lovingly kisses the plant forces springing up from the Earth. And in the wonderfully delicate and tender process of the cosmic forces weaving over the Earth forces in the blossoming plants, they read how the Earth strives outward into the cosmic expanse. They lived in union with the Earth as it opened itself to the cosmos, to the distant stars, lived with the Earth itself in the infinitudes.

What lay hidden in these infinitudes revealed itself to

human beings as they gazed at the letters that were the blossoming plants. They read from these letters how the human being, as it descended from the spiritual worlds to physical existence on Earth, gathered together etheric substance from every quarter of the heavens to form its own etheric body. The human being was thus able to read the secrets enshrined in this etheric body from everything that later came to pass again between the Earth and the cosmos in the Cosmic Word. The signs of the Cosmic Word are inscribed upon the very surface of the Earth in that it lets the plants bloom and gives particular forms of life to the animals at the time of midsummer.

When autumn approached, the pupils saw how the letters of the Cosmic Word were again changing. At this time the warmth and light of the Sun are withdrawing and the plants are obliged to resort to what the Sun itself has conveyed to the Earth during summer. In return, the plants breathe out the blossoming life they have received during summer but at the same time develop within their wombs the ripening fruits that bring the cycle of plant life to completion, inasmuch as the plant then bears the seed forces within it. In turn, human beings unveiled what the Cosmic Word inscribed on the surface of the Earth itself in the ripening plants; and they solved the riddle of what the forms taken by animal life in the autumn can reveal. They read the deepest secrets of the universe in the flight of birds, in all the changes that take place in the lower animals and in the insect world as autumn approaches: in the way the insect world seeks refuge in the Earth and the changes of form it undergoes, and in the Earth's contracting and withdrawing into itself in the face of the dead silence. They read what they felt to be the Earth's brooding upon itself in the cosmos.

This was brought to expression very clearly in certain festivals that were celebrated in the latter half of September and still have traces left in rural districts in the form of the Michaelmas festival. Through these festivals people reminded themselves that when all the paths in the Earth which led out into the cosmos have failed, they had to unite themselves with something that is not bound up with the happenings of the physical and etheric worlds: they had to turn their souls to the spiritual content of the cosmos. And even in the faded, pale Michaelmas festival, there is still a reminiscence of humanity turning to that spirit of the Hierarchies who will lead in a spiritual way when external guidance by the stars and the Sun has lost its power.

Through everything that people read in this way — a reading that was also contemplation — they permeated themselves with the secrets of the human astral body. Autumn was the season when those who were initiated and inspired by the Year God read the secrets of the human astral nature from the being of nature and contemplated these with him.

It was at this autumn season that the initiates said to their pupils: Hold fast to the being who stands before the countenance of the Sun! Think of this being — indicated by the name Michael — who stands before the countenance of the Sun, for you will need the power when you have passed through the gate of death into the supersensible worlds, when you have to go through again whatever has remained in your astral being from Earth existence. Secrets of the human astral body were thus drawn from what revealed itself as Logos, as the Word, in the ripening but also in the withering plants, and in the insects creeping away into the earth. People already knew that if they wished to seek true humanity for this part of their being, they had to turn their gaze to the spiritual world. It was for this reason that the souls of those who were candidates for initiation were directed to the being we can commemorate under the name of Micha-el.

But then came the season at whose middle is our present Christmas. This was the time when those who were inspired and initiated by the Year God pointed out to their pupils the mysteries that are revealed when water covers the Earth in the artistic forms of snowflakes. The reading, which in autumn had already become reflection and contemplation, now became an inner life; what in earlier seasons of the year had been soul observation, running parallel with the outer physical work, now became inner spiritual work. The reading became mystical deepening. Human beings knew that they could only comprehend the deepest essence of their I-being when they listened to the secrets projected by the Cosmic Word, the Cosmic Logos, into everything that takes place in nature at the time when the Earth is swathed in its mantle of snow and when life around and on the Earth is contracted by cold. It was incumbent upon those who were initiated and inspired by the Year God to learn to understand his writing from the indications that were given in the season of winter. Their observation was sharpened so that it could follow the processes at work in the seeds that had been laid into the Earth and in the life of the insects as they hibernated within the contracting forces of the Earth. The human being's gaze was led from physical light into physical darkness.

In certain Mysteries the pupils were told: Now you must gaze at the Midnight Sun, at the Sun at midnight! You must behold the Sun *through* the Earth. If the eyes of your soul penetrate with the power that can follow the plants and the lower animals into the Earth, then the Earth itself will become transparent to your inmost soul. It is when the Earth's forces are most contracted, as compared with the universe, that human beings can so bring themselves to *see through* the Earth and behold the Sun as the Midnight Sun, for the Earth is then inwardly spiritualized; whereas at midsummer, they behold the Sun with their physical senses when they turn their gaze from the Earth to the cosmos. To behold the Sun at the midnight hour in a deep winter night was something the pupils of the initiates of the Year God should learn. And it was their duty to communicate the secrets revealed to them by the Midnight Sun to those who were faithful followers of the Mysteries but could not themselves become initiates or actual pupils of the Mysteries.

And more and more it came about in those ancient times that when the initiates pointed to the Sun at the midnight hour in the depth of winter, they were obliged, in a certain way, to make known to their pupils that human beings on Earth feel their I deserted and forsaken. For those who possessed the greatest knowledge, the festival of midwinter became more and more a festival of pain and suffering through which human beings were to learn that within earthly existence they cannot find the way to their I; they should learn from what is to be read in the signs written by the Logos upon the Earth in midwinter how they with their I had been forsaken by the cosmos, for it was the *Earth* alone that they sensed, and what the I most yearns for, the force of the Sun, was covered by the Earth. The Sun did indeed appear at the midnight hour, but human beings felt ever less strength to come to the Sun Being. At the same time, however, the making aware that the human I was forsaken in the cosmos was the prophetic indication that the Sun Being would come to the Earth, would permeate the being of the human being in the course of evolution, would appear in order to heal a humanity ailing because of its loneliness in the cosmos.

This already points to the fact of the evolution of humanity through which the winter festival of pain and suffering changed precisely among the peoples of the south into a festival of inner joy through the appearance of Christ upon Earth. And what was revealed as the Sun Being descended from the cosmos into earthly existence was shown by those who still proclaimed the event in symbols, in that they pointed out that the message had gone forth to all human beings on Earth that the ancient festival of suffering was now transformed into a festival of rejoicing. In the inmost depths of the shepherds' hearts, where their dreams were woven, the words resounded: "The Divine reveals itself in the heights of the cosmos, and peace will spring forth on Earth to human beings who are of good will." Such was the proclamation in the simple hearts of shepherds.

And at the other pole, the message of the entry of the Cosmic Spirit into earthly matter could come from the surviving relics of ancient Star Wisdom to those who were the most deeply imbued with magical knowledge.

Today, when we speak of the Christmas Mystery, we must

think of all that is experienced through it against the background of the ancient festival of suffering; we must think of how the power has entered the course of human evolution by which human beings can wrest themselves free from everything that weighs them down, fettering them to the Earth. We must be able to formulate the Christmas thought in such a way that we say to ourselves: The inspirations of the Year God that revealed to the old initiates how the Earth withdraws from the universe in the depths of winter and enters a time of self-contemplation are still true; human beings can still understand how the secret of the human I is connected with this secret of the year. But, surrounded with pictures of Christ Jesus entering into earthly human life, they can learn out of their human insight, out of their discerning feeling, out of the wisdom of their heart, to experience in all its depths the thought of the Holy Night.

But they will only be able to experience it truly if they also really have the will to follow the Christ as he reveals himself through all the ages. The task of the initiates of the ancient initiation science was to unveil the mysteries of human nature out of the course of the year. We must understand what the year reveals, but we must also be able to look into the *inner nature of the human being*. And when we do this, anthroposophical spiritual science shows us how the letters that are written in heart and lungs, in the brain, and in every part of the human organism unveil the secrets of the cosmos, just as those secrets were unveiled to those inspired by the Year God in the letters of the Logos they read in the budding plants, in the animals, and in their manner of life on the Earth. We must learn to look into the inner being of the human being. The inner being of the human being must become a script from which we then read the course of human evolution. Then we must devote ourselves to the meaning and purpose of that evolution, and through inner vision unite ourselves with that which wants to weave and flow through the evolution of humanity as spiritual forces. And because this evolution is forever advancing, we must experience the Mystery of Golgotha and the Mystery of the Holy Night anew in every epoch. We must fully experience what the Spirit who sought out for himself the body that was born in Bethlehem on Christmas night spoke: "Lo, I am with you always, even to the end of the days of Earth." Then we must also have a spiritual ear for the perpetual revelation of the Logos through the being of the human being. Humanity must learn to listen to the inspirations of this God of humanity, who is Christ himself, as human beings learned long ago to listen to the inspirations of the Year God.

Humanity will then not confine itself to contemplation of what is transmitted in the Bible concerning the spiritual sojourn of Christ Jesus on Earth, but will understand that ever since then Christ has united himself with the human being in earthly life, and that he reveals himself perpetually to those who are willing to listen. Humanity in our time will then learn to understand that just as the Christmas festival once followed the Michael festival of autumn, so the Michael revelation, which began at a time in autumn in the last third of the nineteenth century, should be followed by a sacred Christmas festival through which human beings will come to understand the spirit birth needed along their path on Earth, so that the spiritualized Earth may eventually be able to pass into future forms and conditions of existence. We are now living in an age when there should not merely be a yearly Michaelmas festival followed by a yearly Christmas festival, but when we should understand the Michael revelation of the last third of the nineteenth century in the depths of our souls out of our own human nature, and then seek the path leading to the true Christmas festival, namely, to the permeation with the very Spirit we strive to know.

Then we shall understand the words in the Gospel, "*I have yet many things to say unto you, but you cannot bear them now.*" Humanity is so constituted that it is capable of bearing more and more of what Christ has to say. Humanity is not intended to listen only to those who want to hinder progress, who point to what was once written down in dry letters concerning the Mystery of Golgotha and do not want the power of that Mystery to reveal itself in a living manner to human beings through the ages. Today is also not the time to listen to those who would like to remain at a standstill in the springtime of the world, which reveals outer physical nature in its brightest glory but cannot reveal the spiritual. Today is the time when the path must be found from the Michael festival to the midwinter festival, which should, however, contain a *Sunrise of the Spirit*. We will never find this path if, in the evolution of humankind and of Earth, we surrender to the illusion that there is light in external life, in external civilization, in external culture today; we must realize that in those spheres there is darkness. But in this darkness we must seek the light that Christ willed to bring into the world through Jesus.

If we then follow, with the same devotion with which the shepherds and the Magi from the East sought the way to the manger in the Christmas night, if with the same devotion we follow the trail that can be read in the being of the human being in letters that are still blurred but that will become clearer and clearer, then it will be granted to us to celebrate anew the Christ Mystery of the Holy Night — but only if we have the will to seek the light *in the darkness*.

Today we often call by the name of "science" not what clarifies the world (*clarify* comes from the clarity of light), but what sheds darkness and obscurity instead of bringing light. These darknesses must comprehend the light!

If we try with depth of feeling in mind and soul and with strongest power of will to find the light of the Spirit in the darkness, then that light will shine as did the Star that announced the birth of Jesus to the shepherds and the Magi in the great Christmas night.

We must learn to place the Christmas thought into the historic evolution of humanity. We do not have to wait for a new Messiah, for a new Christ. Much has been revealed to humanity through nature, which in the course of the last few centuries has been leading us deep into the darkness of matter. We must wait for what can now be revealed to humanity through a living understanding of the ever-living Christ Jesus.

Thus, we must not fix the Christmas thought into a conventional yearly festival, but make it fluid so that it might light the way for us as did the Star at Bethlehem.

It was of this Light, this radiant Star, that I wished to speak to you on this Christmas Eve. I would like to have done something to ensure that you unite the will that is inspired, weakly though genuinely, by anthroposophical spiritual science with that other will to follow the Star that most certainly shines forth in very truth to humankind all through the Holy Night.

To permeate oneself with this Light in deep and intimate stillness is the deepest and truest Christmas consecration for our time. Everything else should, in reality, be no more than an outward sign for this true Christmas feeling, which we can carry over from this Christmas evening to Christmas morning tomorrow. Then this Holy Night can be for us not merely a symbol but a symbol that can become a living force. And we shall also be mindful of how deeply we ought to unite with the spiritual striving that, in all true human beings, leads on into the future and, at the same time, is the true Christmas striving, the striving toward that Spirit who willed to incarnate in the body born in Bethlehem in the world-historic Christmas Night.

THE COSMIC RITUAL ARISES FROM OUR LIVING TOGETHER WITH THE COURSE OF COSMIC EXISTENCE

Dornach, December 29, 1922

The object of the lectures I gave here immediately before Christmas was to indicate the human being's connection with the whole cosmos and especially with the forces that pervade the cosmos. Today I shall again be dealing with the subject matter of those lectures but in a way that will constitute an entirely independent study.

The life of human beings, as far as it consists of experiences of outer nature as well as of the inner life of soul and spirit, lies between two poles; and many of the thoughts that necessarily come to human beings about their connection with the world are influenced by the realization that these two polar opposites exist.

On one side, our life of thinking and feeling is confronted by what is called "natural necessity." We feel ourselves dependent upon firmly working laws, which we find everywhere in the world outside us and which also penetrate through us, inasmuch as our physical organisms and also our etheric organisms are part and parcel of this outer world. On the other hand, we have the feeling — this feeling must arise in every healthy human nature — that human dignity would not be fully attained if freedom were not an integral element in our life between birth and death. These are the polar opposites: *necessity* and *freedom*.

You are aware that in the age of natural science — the subject I am dealing with in another course of lectures here[1] — there is a strong tendency to extend the sway of necessity that is everywhere in evidence in external nature to whatever originates in human beings themselves; many representative scientists have come to regard freedom as an impossibility, an illusion that exists only in the human soul, because when human beings are faced with having to make a decision, reasons for and reasons against it work upon them. These reasons themselves are, however, under the sway of necessity; hence — so say these scientists — it is really not we who make the decision but whatever reasons are the more numerous and the weightier. They triumph over the other less numerous and less weighty reasons, which also affect us. We are therefore carried along helplessly by the victors in the struggle between impulses that work upon us of necessity. Many representatives of this way of thinking have said that we believe ourselves to be free only because the polar-opposite reasons for and against any decision we may be called upon to make are so complicated in their totality that we do not notice how we are being tossed hither and thither. One category of reasons finally triumphs; one scale in a delicately poised balance is weighed down, and we are carried along in accordance with it.

Against this argument is not only the ethical consideration that human dignity would not be maintained in a world where the human was merely a plaything of conflicting yes-and-no impulses, but also the fact that the feeling of freedom in the human will is so strong that unbiased people have no sort of doubt that if they can be misled about its existence, they can equally well be misled by the most elementary sense perceptions. If the elementary experience of freedom in the sphere of feeling could prove to be deceptive, so too could the experience of red, for instance, or of C or C-sharp, and so on. Many representatives of modern natural scientific thought place such a high value upon *theory* that they allow the theory of a natural necessity that is absolute and has no exceptions, and is supposed to embrace human actions and human will, to tempt them into disregarding altogether an experience such as the sense of freedom!

But this problem of necessity and freedom, with all the phenomena associated with it in the life of soul — and these phenomena are very varied and numerous — is a problem linked with much more profound aspects of universal existence than natural science or the everyday experience of the human soul. For at a time when the human being's outlook was quite different from what it is today, this disquieting, perplexing problem was already a concern of the human soul.

You will have gathered from the other course of lectures now being given here that the natural scientific thinking of the modern age is by no means very old. When we go back to earlier times we find views of the world that were as one-sidedly *spiritual* as they have become one-sidedly naturalistic today. The farther back we go, the less of what is called "physical necessity" we find in human thinking. Even in early Greek thought there was nothing of what we today call physical necessity, for the Greek idea of necessity had an essentially different meaning. But if we go still farther back we find, instead of necessity, the working of forces, and these, in their whole compass, were ascribed to a divine-spiritual *Providence*. Expressing myself in a rather trivial manner, I would say that to a modern scientific thinker, the nature forces do everything, whereas the thinker of ancient times conceived of everything being done by spiritual forces working with intentions and aims just as human beings themselves do, only with far more comprehensive intentions than the human being's could ever be. Yet even with this view of the world, entirely spiritual as it was, human beings turned their attention to the way in which their will was determined by divine-spiritual forces; and just as today, when their thinking is in line with natural science, they feel themselves subject to the forces and laws of nature, so in those ancient times they felt themselves subject to divine-spiritual forces or laws. And for many who in those days were determinists in this sense, human freedom, although it is a direct experience of the soul, was no more valid than it is for our modern naturalists. These modern naturalists believe that physical necessity works through the actions of human beings; human beings of ancient times thought that divine-spiritual forces, in accordance with their intentions, work through human actions.

It is only necessary to recognize that the problem of freedom and necessity exists in these two completely opposite worlds of thought to realize that quite certainly no examination of the surface aspect of conditions and happenings can lead to any solution of this problem which penetrates so deeply into all life and into all evolution.

To grasp the meaning of this question that so stirs us, we must look more deeply into the process of world evolution — world evolution as the course of nature, on the one side, and as the unfolding of spirit, on the other — and this is only possible through the anthroposophical point of view.

The course of nature is usually studied in an extremely restricted way. Isolated happenings and processes of a highly specialized kind are studied in the laboratories, brought within the range of telescopes, or subjected to experiment, which means that observation of the course of nature and of world evolution is confined within very narrow limits. And those who study the domain of soul and spirit imitate the scientists and naturalists. They shy away from taking into account the whole human being in connection with the life of the soul. Instead, they specialize in order to bring some particular thought or sentient experience into small relationships, hoping in this way eventually to build up a psychology, just as efforts are made to build up a body of knowledge of the physical world out of single observations and experiments conducted in laboratories, clinics, and so forth.

Yet, in reality, these studies never lead to any comprehensive understanding of either the physical world or the world of soul and spirit. As little as it is the intention here to disparage the justification of these specialized investigations — for they *are* justified from points of view often referred to in my lectures — just as strongly it must be emphasized that unless the world itself, unless nature itself, reveals to us somewhere or other what results from the interworking of the details, we will never be able to build up from our single observations and experiments a picture of the structure of the world that is illumined by the actual world happenings. Liver cells and minute activities of the liver, brain cells and minute cerebral processes can be investigated, and greater and greater specialization may take place in these domains; but these investigations, because they lead to particularization and not to the whole, will give no help toward forming a view of the human organism in its totality, unless from the very beginning we have a comprehensive, intuitive idea of this totality to help us form the separate investigations into a unified whole. In like manner, as long as chemistry, astrochemistry, physics, astrophysics, and biology restrict themselves to the investigation of isolated details, they will never be able to give a picture of how the different forces and laws in our world environment work together to form a whole, unless we develop the faculty of perceiving outside in nature something similar to what can be seen as the totality of the human organism, in which all the separate processes of liver, kidneys, heart, brain, and so forth, are included. In other words, we must be able to point to something in the universe in which all the forces we behold in our environment *work together to form a self-contained whole.*

Now it may be that only much later certain processes in the human liver and human brain will be detected with enough accuracy to be accepted by biology. But in any case, as long as human beings have been able to look at other human beings, they could and can always say that the processes of liver, stomach, heart, etc., work together within the boundary of the skin to form a whole. Without being obliged to look at each and all of the separate details, we have before us the sum total of the chemical, physical, and biological processes belonging to the nature of the human being.

Is it possible also to have before us as a complete whole the sum total of the forces and laws of nature that are at work around us? In a certain way it is possible. But, in order not to be misunderstood, I must emphasize the fact that such totalities are always relative. For instance, we can group together the processes of the outer ear and then have a relative whole. But we can also group together the processes in that part of the organ of hearing that continues on to the brain and then we have another relative whole; taking the two groups together, we have another, greater whole, which in turn belongs to the head, and this again to the whole organism. And it will be just the same when we try to comprehend in one complete picture the laws and forces that come primarily into consideration for the human being.

Now, a first complete whole of this kind is the course of the day. Paradoxical as this seems at first hearing, in this cycle of day and night a number of natural laws around us are gathered together into one whole. During the course of a day and night, processes are going on in our environment and penetrating through us which, if separated out, prove to fall into the most varied physical and chemical processes. We can say that the cycle of the day is a *time organism*, a time organism embracing a number of natural processes that can be studied individually.

And a greater "totality" is the course of the year. If we review all the changes affecting the Earth and humankind during the course of the year in the sphere surrounding us — in the atmosphere, for example — we shall find that all the processes taking place in the plants and also in the minerals from one spring to the next form a *time-organic* whole; otherwise they appear to different scientific investigations to be scattered as separate phenomena. They form a whole, just as the processes taking place in the liver, kidneys, spleen, and so forth, form a whole in the human organism. The course of the year is actually a summing up — the expression is not quite exact but words of some kind have to be used — of what we investigate singly in natural science.

Speaking in what sounds a rather trivial way, but you will realize that the meaning is very profound, we might say that if we are to avoid having the very abstract relationship to surrounding nature that we have to the descriptions of chemical and physical experiments or to what is often taught today in botany and zoology, the time organisms of the course of the day and the course of the year in the cosmos must be placed before us. There they find their own kind as it were. And this we want to contemplate a little.

Let us begin by thinking of the *cycle of the year*. Reviewing it as we did in the lecture before Christmas, we find a whole series of processes in the sprouting, growing plants, which first produce leaves and later on blossoms. An incalculable number of natural processes reveal themselves from the life in the root, on into the life in the green leaves, and on into that of the colored petals. And we have an altogether different kind of process before us when we see in autumn the fading, withering, and dying of outer nature. We have actually collected the world happenings around us into an organic unity. In summer we see what sprouts on the Earth, including the animal world, especially the lower animals. Think of all the activity in the insect world during the summer, how this activity seems to rise up from the Earth and is given over to the cosmos, especially to the forces coming from the Sun. We see how the Earth opens out all its organs to the cosmos and how its life and activities rise toward the cosmic expanse. From autumn through winter, we see how everything that from the time of spring onward sprouts and reaches out toward the cosmic expanse, falls back again into the earthly realm, how the Earth, as it were, gradually increases its hold upon all growing life, brings it to the stage of apparent death, or at least to a state of sleep. We see how the Earth closes all its organs against the influences of the cosmos. Here we have two contrasting processes in the course of the year, embracing countless details but nevertheless representing a complete whole.

If, with the eyes of the soul, we survey this yearly cycle, which can be regarded as a complete whole because from a certain point it simply repeats itself, recurring in approximately the same way, we find in it nothing other than physical necessity. And in our own earthly lives we human beings follow this physical necessity. If we were to follow it entirely, we would be completely under its domination. Now, it is certainly true that those forces of nature that come especially into consideration for us as Earth-dwellers are present in the course of the year. We will consider other closed cycles in the coming days, but the Earth does not change so quickly that the minute changes taking place from year to year make themselves noticeable during our life, however old we may live to be. So by living each year through spring, summer, autumn, and winter, we partake with our own physical bodies in physical necessity.

It is important to contemplate in this way, for it is only actual experience that gives knowledge; no theory ever does so. Every theory starts from some special domain and then proceeds to generalize. Real knowledge can be acquired only when we start from life and from experience. We must not therefore consider the laws of gravity *by themselves*, or the laws of plant life, or the laws of animal instinct, or the laws of mental coercion, because if we do we think only of their details, generalize them, and then arrive at entirely false generalizations. We must have in mind where the nature forces are revealed in their cooperation and mutual interaction. That is in the *cyclic course of the year.*

Now even superficial study shows that humans are relatively free in their relation to the course of the year. Anthroposophy shows this even more clearly. In anthroposophy we turn our attention to the two alternating conditions in which every human being lives during the twenty-four hours of the day, the sleeping state and the waking state. We know that during the waking state the physical, etheric, and astral bodies and the ego organism form a relative unity within the human being. In the sleeping state the physical and etheric bodies remain behind in the bed, closely interwoven, and the ego and the astral body are outside the physical and etheric bodies.

If with the means provided by anthroposophical research, of which you will have read in our literature, we study the physical and etheric bodies of the human being during sleep and during waking life, the following comes to light. When the ego and the astral body are outside the physical and etheric organism during sleep, a kind of life begins in the physical and etheric organism that is to be found only in external nature in the mineral and plant kingdoms. And the reason the physical and etheric organism of the human does not gradually pass over into a sum total of plant or mineral processes is due only to the fact that it is organized in a way that corresponds to the Ego and astral body which are within it for certain periods. If we returned too late with our ego and astral body, our physical and etheric bodies would pass over into a mineral and vegetative form of life. The tendency to become vegetative and mineralized commences immediately after we fall asleep, and this tendency has the upper hand during sleeping life.

If we look, with the methods of anthroposophical research, at human beings while they are asleep, we see in them — of course with the inevitable variations — a faithful copy of what the Earth is throughout spring and summer. Mineral and vegetative life sprouts forth, of course in quite a different way from what happens in the green plants growing out of the earth. Nevertheless, with one variation, what goes on during sleep in the human physical and etheric organism is a faithful image of the period of spring and summer on the Earth. Human beings of the present epoch are organized for this external nature. We can survey it with our physical eyes. We behold its sprouting, budding life. As soon as human beings attain to *Inspiration* and *Imagination*, a view of summer is revealed to them through the sleep period of the physical human being. Sleeping means that spring and summer arrive for the physical and etheric bodies. A budding, sprouting life begins.

And when we wake, when the ego and astral body return, all this budding life in the physical and etheric bodies withdraws, and for the eye of the seer life in the physical and etheric organism begins to be very similar to the life of the Earth during autumn and winter. When we follow the human being through one complete period of sleeping and waking life, we have before us, in miniature, an actual microcosmic reflection of spring, summer, autumn, and winter. If we follow the human physical and etheric organism through a period of twenty-four hours, contemplating it in the light of spiritual science, we pass microcosmically through the course of a year. Accordingly, if we consider only that part of human beings that remains behind in the bed when they are asleep or moves around when they are awake during the day, we can say that the course of the year is fulfilled microcosmically in them.

But now let us consider on the other side that which releases itself in sleep: the ego and the astral body of the human being. If again we use the methods of spiritual investigation, namely Inspiration and Intuition, we find that the ego and the astral body are given over while we are asleep to spiritual powers within which they will only be able to live consciously in the normal condition in a later epoch of the Earth's existence. From the time of going to sleep until the time of waking, the ego and the astral body are withdrawn from the world just as the Earth is withdrawn from the cosmos during winter. During sleep, the ego and the astral body are actually in their winter period, so that in the being of the human being during sleep there is an intermingling of conditions that are present at the same time only on *opposite* hemispheres of the Earth's surface; during sleep, the human physical and etheric bodies have their summer and the Ego and astral body have their winter.

During waking life, the conditions are reversed. The physical and etheric organisms are then in their winter period, and the ego and astral body are given over to what can stream from the cosmos to the human being in the waking state. So the ego and astral body have their summer period, when they come down into the physical and etheric. Once more we have the two seasons side by side, but now winter in the physical-etheric organism and summer in the ego and astral organism.

The Earth must also have summer and winter at the same time, but they cannot be intermingled. In the human being, microcosmic summer and winter intermingle all the time. When we are asleep, our physical summer mingles with spiritual winter, and when we are awake, our physical winter mingles with spiritual summer. In external nature, summer and winter are separated in the course of the year. In the human being, summer and winter mingle all the time from two different directions. In external nature in a given area on Earth, winter and summer follow one another in time. They must be sketched one after the other, thusly:

In the human being, winter and summer are simultaneous, only they interchange, so that at one time there is spirit summer together with body winter (waking life), and at another, spirit winter together with body summer (sleeping life). These streams must be drawn beside each other in a peculiar way for the human being:

The laws and forces in external nature around us cannot neutralize each other in any one region of the Earth, because they work in sequence, one after the other in time; but in the human being they *do* neutralize or offset each other. The course of nature is such that, just as through two opposing forces a state of rest can be brought about, so can an untold number of natural laws neutralize and offset each other. This happens in human beings with respect to all laws of external nature, inasmuch as we sleep and wake the way we do. The two conditions appear as natural necessity only when they succeed each other in time; they are coincident and consequently neutralized in us, and *it is this that makes the human being a free being.*

For that reason, freedom can never be understood until it is realized how the summer and winter forces of our spiritual life can neutralize the summer and winter forces of our outer physical and etheric nature.

External nature presents pictures to us that we must *not* see in ourselves, either in the waking or in the sleeping state. On no account is this to happen. On the contrary, we must say that these pictures of the course and order of nature lose their validity within the constitution of the human being, and we must turn our gaze to something else. For when the course of nature no longer disturbs us within human nature, it becomes possible for the first time to gaze at the soul-spiritual-moral being of the human being. And then we begin to have an ethical and moral relationship to the human being, just as we have a natural relationship to nature.

When we look at our own being with the aid of knowledge acquired in this way, we find, shoved into one another, conditions that in the external world are spread across the stream of time. And there are many other things of which the same could be said. If we contemplate our inner being and understand it rightly in the sense I have indicated today, we bring it into a relationship with the course of time that is different from the one we are accustomed to today.

The purely external mode of scientific observation does not reach the stage where the investigator can say that in the being of the human being you must sense sounding together what can only be heard as separate tones in the course of time. If you develop spiritual hearing, the tones of summer and winter can be heard sounding simultaneously in the human being, and they are the same tones that we hear in the outer world when we enter the flow of time itself. Time really becomes space. The whole surrounding universe resounds toward us, also in relation to time, pulled apart in the widths of space, that which resounds from our own being as from a center, gathered as it were in a single point.

This is the moment when scientific study and contemplation becomes artistic study and contemplation. It is when art and science no longer stand in stark opposition as they do in our naturalistic age, but are interrelated in the way sensed by Goethe when he said, "Art reveals a kind of secret of nature without which we can never fully understand it." From a certain point onward it is imperative that we understand the artistic form and structure of the world. And once we have taken the path from the purely scientific conception of the world to artistic understanding, then we take also the third step, which leads to religious deepening.

When we have found the physical and the soul and the spiritual cosmic forces working together in the inner center of our being, we can also behold them in the cosmos. Human willing rises to artistic creating and finally achieves a relationship to the world that is not merely a passive knowing but a positive, active surrender. Human beings no longer look into the world abstractly, with the forces of their heads; more and more they look into it with their *whole* being. Living together with the course of the cosmos becomes a happening different in character from their connection with the facts and events of everyday life. It becomes a ritual, and the cosmic ritual comes into being in which human beings can have their place at every moment of their lives. Every earthly ritual is a symbolic image of this cosmic ritual. This cosmic ritual is higher in comparison with every earthly ritual.

If what has been said today has been thoroughly grasped, it will be possible to study the relationship of the anthroposophical world conception to any particular religious ritual. And this will be done during the next few days: we shall consider the relationship between anthroposophy and the various forms of ritual.

[1]Origins of Natural Science, course of 9 lectures given at Dornach from December 24, 1922, to January 6, 1923.

CHAPTER IV

THE RELATION OF THE MOVEMENT FOR RELIGIOUS RENEWAL TO THE ANTHROPOSOPHICAL MOVEMENT

Dornach, December 30, 1922

I have often said in this place that in more ancient times in the evolution of humanity, science, art, and religion formed a harmonious unity. Anyone who is able in one way or another to gain knowledge of the nature of the ancient Mysteries knows that within these Mysteries knowledge was sought as a revelation of the spiritual in its picture form, in the way that was possible in those times. That way can no longer be ours, although in this age we must again advance to a knowledge of the spiritual nature of the world. A pictorial knowledge of the spiritual underlies all of the ancient conceptions of the world. This knowledge came to direct expression not merely by being communicated in words, but through methods that have gradually become those of our arts: bodily picture-like presentation in the plastic and graphic arts, and presentation through tone and word in the musical and spoken arts. But from this second stage came a third stage, that of the religious, ritualistic revelation of the nature of the world, through which the whole human being felt uplifted to the divine-spiritual ground of the world, not merely in thought nor merely in feeling as happens through art, but in such a way that thoughts, feelings, and also the inmost impulses of the will surrendered themselves to this divine-spiritual. And the means by which the outer acts of will of the human were to be permeated by the spirit were the offerings, the ritual acts. Human beings felt the living unity in science (as it was then conceived), art, and religion.

The ideal of the spiritual life of the present day must proceed to once more gain knowledge that can bring to realiza-

43

tion what Goethe already divined: a *knowledge* that raises itself to *art*, not symbolical or allegorical art, but true art, which means creating and forming in tones and in words — an art that also deepens into direct *religious experience*. Only when we grasp anthroposophical spiritual science in such a way that we see this impulse within it do we actually understand its true being. Obviously humanity will have to take many steps in its spiritual development in order to actualize such an ideal. But it is precisely the patient devotion to taking these steps that the anthroposophical movement must actuate.

Now I should like, in these lectures yet to be given, to speak from a particular viewpoint about this impulse of the anthroposophical movement that I have just characterized. Perhaps at the close of what I have to say, you will understand what is really the deeper cause of my words. Let me say beforehand that already for a long time now the anthroposophical movement has not coincided with the Anthroposophical Society, but the Anthroposophical Society, if it would fulfill its being, must really carry the whole impulse of the anthroposophical movement. The anthroposophical movement has taken hold of wider circles than merely the Anthroposophical Society. Hence it has come about that in more recent years the anthroposophical movement's way of working had necessarily to be different from what it was when the movement was essentially contained within the Anthroposophical Society. But the Anthroposophical Society can only fulfill its real nature when it feels itself to be the kernel of the anthroposophical movement.

Now in order not to speak merely theoretically but to make what I have just said really intelligible, I must tell you a little about something that has recently taken place in connection with a movement that is distinct from the anthroposophical movement, because if I did not do this misunderstanding might easily arise.

I will therefore narrate briefly the manner in which a certain movement having a religious, ritualistic character has arisen, a movement that indeed has much to do with the anthroposophical movement, but should not be confused with it: it is the religious movement that calls itself "The Movement for Religious Renewal,"[1] for the renewal of Christianity. The position of this movement with respect to the anthroposophical movement will become clear if we take our start from the forms in which this Movement for Religious Renewal has developed.

Some time ago a few enthusiastic young theological students came to me. They were about to conclude their theological studies and enter practical pastoral work. They said to me, in effect: At the present time, when students receive, with a really devoted Christian heart, the theology offered at the universities, they feel at last as if they had no firm ground under their feet for the practical work of a minister that is before them. The theology and religion of our time have gradually assumed forms that do not really enable them to instill in their pastoral work that which must proceed as a living power from the Mystery of Golgotha, from the consciousness that through the Mystery of Golgotha the Christ Being who formerly lived in spiritual worlds has since united himself with human life on Earth and now works on further in that life. I became aware that in the souls of those who came to me there was the feeling that if Christianity is to be kept alive, a renewal of the entire theological and religious impulse would be necessary. This would be necessary if Christianity is to be maintained so that it can be the really vital force for our whole spiritual life. And it is clear that the religious impulse assumes its true significance and meaning only when it takes hold of the being of the human being so deeply that it pervades everything that the person brings forth out of his or her thinking, feeling, and will.

In order to help those who came to me with what they were striving for and could find only where anthroposophical spiritual science is making its way into the world today, I pointed out first that one cannot work out of some individual enthusiasm, but that it is a question of gathering together, as it were, the same striving in wider circles, even though that striving may be more or less unconscious. I said to these people that theirs was obviously not an isolated striving, that they were perhaps feeling more intensely than others, but that they were feeling in their hearts only what countless human beings of the present day are also feeling. And I remarked that if it is a question of religious renewal, one must start from the broad base of that large number of persons out of whose hearts springs the impulse to strive for that renewal.

After some time the people in question came to me again. They had fully accepted what I had said to them and now they were able to tell me that they had been joined by a considerable number of other young theological students who were in the same position, that is to say, who were dissatisfied with the present theological and religious aims at the universities and yet were about to take on the practical duties of ministers of the church; and there seemed every prospect that the circle would grow.

I said that it was quite obvious first of all that it is not only a question of having a band of preachers and ministers, but that such a movement for religious renewal should draw in not only those who can teach and perform the duties of pastors, but above all those — and they are very numerous — who possess more or less dimly in their hearts a strong religious impulse, a specifically Christian impulse, which, in view of the way in which theological religion has developed, cannot be satisfied. I pointed out that there are thus circles of people in the population who are not within the anthroposophical movement and who, from the whole tenor of their minds and hearts, do not immediately find their way to the anthroposophical movement.

I remarked further, that for the anthroposophical movement it is ultimately a case of seeing clearly and distinctly that we are living in an age when, simply through the world's evolution, a number of spiritual truths, truths regarding the actual spiritual content of the world, can be found by human beings when they become spiritual researchers. And if human beings do not become spiritual researchers but strive for the truth in the way it must disclose itself to them when they are conscious of their human worth and dignity, then they can understand through their ordinary, sound human reasoning — provided it is *really* sound — the truths discovered by spiritual researchers.

I went on to say that the anthroposophical movement is based on the fact that those who find their way into it know that what is of main importance is that the spiritual truths now accessible to humanity should take hold of human hearts and minds as *knowledge.* The essential thing is that *knowledge* should enter, first and foremost, the spiritual life. It is of course not the case that those in the anthroposophical movement need be versed in the various sciences. One may be in the anthroposophical movement without possessing any impulse or any inclination toward natural science, for the truths of anthroposophy are perfectly comprehensible to the human intellect if it is healthy and unclouded by prejudice. If already at the present time a sufficiently large number of persons through the disposition of their hearts and minds were to find their way to the anthroposophical movement, then all that is necessary for religious aims and religious ideals would also gradually develop together with anthroposophical knowledge out of the anthroposophical movement.

But there are a great number of people who have the above-mentioned urge toward a renewal of religion, a renewal of Christian religion, and who, simply through being in certain circles of the cultural life, cannot find their way into the anthroposophical movement. What is necessary for these people at the present time is that a path suited to them should be found, leading to the spiritual life appropriate to human beings of the present day.

I pointed out that it was a matter of forming communities; what is to be reached in anthroposophy can be attained first of all in the single individual, but out of the knowledge gained in an individual way there must flow by an absolute inner necessity the ethical and religious social activity that is requisite for the future of humanity.

It is therefore a question of giving something to those people who are at first unable to set out directly along the path to the anthroposophical movement. The spiritual path appropriate for human evolution at its present stage must be sought by forming communities in which heart, soul, and spirit work together.

So what I had to say to the seekers at that time out of the needs of our human evolution may be summed up approximately in these words: It is necessary for the evolution of modern humanity that the anthroposophical movement should grow more and more, in accordance with the conditions that underlie it, and should not be interfered with in this growth out of its underlying conditions — which are that the spiritual truths desiring to come to us from the spiritual world should first of all enter the heart directly, so that we may be strengthened by them. We will then find the way, which will be on the one hand an artistic way, and on the other a religious-ethical-social way. The anthroposophical movement has gone along this path since its inception, and for the anthroposophical movement *no other path* is necessary, if only this path be rightly understood. The need for another path arises for those who cannot directly take this one, but who, through community building and cooperative endeavor within the community, must follow a different path, one that only *later* will join the anthroposophical path.

In this way the prospect was opened for two movements to travel side by side. There is the anthroposophical movement, which attains its true aims when it adheres, in accordance with its meaning and strength, to what it originally contained and is not led astray by any special fields of work that are bound to open up as time goes on. Even the field of scientific works for example, must not encroach upon the impulse of the general anthroposophical movement. We must clearly understand that it is the anthroposophical impulse that determines the anthroposophical movement, and that, although various fields of scientific work have recently been started within the anthroposophical movement, it is absolutely necessary that the power and energy of the general anthroposophical impulse should not be weakened. In particular, the anthroposophical impulse must not be drawn into the forms of thinking and ideation prevailing in various fields of science — which ought actually to be vitalized by it — and be colored by those forms to such an extent that anthroposophy becomes, let us say, chemical as chemistry is today, physical as physics is today, or biological as biology is today. That absolutely must not happen. It would strike at the very heart of the anthroposophical movement. What is essential is that the anthroposophical movement shall preserve its spiritual purity, but also its spiritual energy. To this end it must embody the essential nature of the anthroposophical spirituality, must live and move in it and bring forth out of the spiritual revelations of the present day everything that seeks to penetrate also into the life of science.

Side by side with this — so I said at that time — there could be such a movement for religious renewal, which of course has no significance for those who find the way into anthroposophy, but does have significance for those who, to begin with, cannot find this way. And as there are great numbers of such people, a movement like this is not only justified, but also necessary.

Taking for granted therefore that the anthroposophical movement *will remain what it was and what it ought to be*, I gave something, quite independent of the anthroposophical movement, to a number of persons who, *from their own impulse, not mine*, wished to work for the Movement for Religious Renewal; I gave what I was in a position to give with respect to what a future theology needs; and I also gave the contents of the ceremonial and ritual required by such a new community abuilding.

What I have been able to give to these people out of the conditions pertaining to spiritual knowledge at the present time, I have given as a human being to other human beings. What I have given them *has nothing to do with the anthroposophical movement*. I have given it to them as a private indi-

vidual and in a way that emphasizes with the necessary firm-
ness that the anthroposophical movement may not have anything to do with this Movement for Religious Renewal, and
that, above all, I am not the founder of this movement and
rely upon this being made quite clear to the world. To individuals who wished to found this Movement for Religious
Renewal I have given the necessary counsel suited for the practice of an authentic and spiritually powerful ritual, filled with
spiritual substantiality, to be celebrated in a right way with
the forces from the spiritual world. When I gave this advice, I
never performed a ritualistic act myself; I only showed, step by
step, to those who wished to enact the ceremonies, how they
have to be performed. That was necessary. And today it is also
necessary that *this should be correctly understood* within the
Anthroposophical Society.

The Movement for Religious Renewal therefore was
founded independently of me, independently of the Anthroposophical Society. I only gave advice. The one who started it,
the one who performed the very first ceremony in this movement, performed it under my guidance, but I had no part
whatever in the founding of this movement. It is a movement
that originated out of itself but received counsel from me,
because when advice is justifiably asked in any particular
sphere of work, it is a human duty to give it if one can.

Thus it must be understood, in the strictest sense of the
word, that alongside the anthroposophical movement another movement has started, founded out of itself and *not* out of
the anthroposophical movement, for the reason that outside
the Anthroposophical Society there are numbers of people
who cannot find their way into the anthroposophical movement itself, but who will be able to come to it later on. Therefore strict distinctions must be made between the
anthroposophical movement, the Anthroposophical Society,
and the Movement for Religious Renewal. And it is important
that anthroposophy should not be looked upon as the founder
of this Movement for Religious Renewal.

This has nothing to do with the fact that the advice that

makes this religious movement into a real spiritual community in a form suited to the present stage of human evolution was given in all love and also in all devotion to the spiritual powers who are able to place such a movement in the world today. So this movement has originated in the right way only when it considers what is within the anthroposophical movement as a forerunner and as something that *gives it a sure ground* when it leans upon the anthroposophical movement and seeks help and counsel from those who are within the anthroposophical movement, and so on. Taking into account the fact that the opponents of the anthroposophical movement today consider every method of attack justifiable, we have to make points such as these quite clear, and I must here declare that everyone who is honest and sincere about the anthroposophical movement would be obliged to deny any statement to the effect that the Movement for Religious Renewal was founded at Dornach in the Goetheanum and by the Goetheanum. For that is not the case; the facts are as I have just presented them.

Thus, in view of the way I myself have helped the Movement for Religious Renewal to find its feet, I have necessarily had to picture to myself that this movement models itself on the anthroposophical movement and regards the anthroposophical movement as its forerunner, that it will look for adherents outside the Anthroposophical Society, and that it would consider it a grave mistake to carry into the Anthroposophical Society the endeavor that is indeed necessary outside that Society. For the Anthroposophical Society is not understood by those who belong to it and do not understand that they can be counselors and helpers of this religious movement, but cannot directly immerse themselves in it. If they were to do so, they would be working on two things: firstly, on the ruin and destruction of the Anthroposophical Society; secondly, on making fruitless the Movement for Religious Renewal. All the movements that arise within humanity in a justifiable way must indeed work together as in one organic whole, but this working together must take place *in the right way*. In the human organism it is quite impossible for the blood system to become nervous system, or for the nervous system to become blood system. The several systems in the human organism have to work distinctly and separately from one another; it is precisely then that they will work together in the right way. It is therefore necessary that the Anthroposophical Society with its content remain anthroposophy, unweakened in any way by the newer movement; and that one who understands what the anthroposophical movement is should be able to see — not in any presumptuous, arrogant sense, but as one who reckons with the tasks of the age — that those who have found their way into the Anthroposophical Society *do not need a religious renewal*. For what would the Anthroposophical Society be if it first needed religious renewal!

But religious renewal is needed in the world, and because it is needed, because it is a profound necessity, a hand was extended to aid in founding it. Matters will therefore proceed in the right way if the Anthroposophical Society remains as it is, if those who wish to understand it grasp its essential nature and do not think that it is necessary for them to belong to another movement that has taken its content from anthroposophy, although it is true in a real sense that anthroposophy has not founded this Movement for Religious Renewal but that it has founded itself.

Therefore anyone who does not clearly distinguish these things and keep them apart is actually, by becoming lax about the essential impulse of the anthroposophical movement, working for the destruction of that movement and for the removal of the foundation and backbone of the Movement for Religious Renewal. If those who stand on the ground of the Movement for Religious Renewal think they must extend this movement to the anthroposophical movement, they remove the ground from under their own feet. For everything of the nature of worship and ritual is finally bound to dissolve away when the "backbone" of knowledge is removed.

For the progress of both movements it is essential that they be held clearly apart. Therefore in the beginning, since everything depends on our developing the strength to carry out what we have set our will to do, it is absolutely necessary in these early days that the Movement for Religious Renewal should work in all directions in circles *outside* the anthroposophical movement; also, in the acquisition of material means (in order that the matter be clearly understood I must also speak about these things) it should not encroach on sources which in any event only flow with great difficulty for the anthroposophical movement, nor, because it does not at once succeed in finding adherents among non-anthroposophists, should it, for example, make proselytes within the ranks of anthroposophists. Were it to do so, it would be doing something that would inevitably lead to the destruction of both movements. It is really not a matter today of going forward with a certain fanaticism, but of being conscious that we can do what is necessary for the human being only when we work out of the necessity of the thing itself.

What I am now stating as consequences were also equally the *preliminary conditions* for lending my assistance in the founding of the Movement for Religious Renewal, for only under these conditions could I assist it. If these preliminary conditions had not been there, the Movement for Religious Renewal would never have originated through my advice.

Therefore I ask you to understand that it is necessary for the Movement for Religious Renewal to know that it must adhere to its starting point, and that it has promised to look for its adherents outside the sphere of the anthroposophical movement, for it is there they can be found in the natural way, and it is there they must be sought.

What I have said to you has not been said because of any anxiety that something might be dug away from the anthroposophical movement, and it has certainly not been said out of any personal motive, but solely out of the necessity of the case itself. And it is also important to understand *in what way alone* it is possible to work rightly in each of these spheres of activity. It is indeed necessary that with important matters we state quite clearly how the case stands, for at the present time there is far too great a tendency to blur things and not to see them clearly. But clarity is essential today in every sphere.

If therefore someone were to exclaim, "The very one who himself put this Movement for Religious Renewal into the world now speaks like this!" ... Well, my dear friends, the whole point is that if I had at any time spoken differently about these things, I would not have lent a hand toward founding this Movement for Religious Renewal. It must remain with its starting point. What I am now saying, I am of course saying merely so that these things may be correctly understood in the Anthroposophical Society and so that it shall not be said (as is reported to have happened already) that the anthroposophical movement did not succeed, so now they have founded the Movement for Religious Renewal as the right thing.

I am quite sure that the very excellent and outstanding individuals who have founded the Movement for Religious Renewal will oppose any such legend most vigorously, and will also sternly refuse to make proselytes within the anthroposophical movement. But, as has been said, the matter must be rightly understood within the anthroposophical movement itself.

I know that there are always some who find it unpleasant to hear explanations like these, which are necessary from time to time, not in order to complain in one direction or another, nor for the sake of criticism, but solely in order to present something once and for all in its true light. I know there are always some who dislike it when clarity is substituted for nebulous obscurity. But this is absolutely essential for the welfare and growth of the anthroposophical movement as well as of the Movement for Religious Renewal. *The Movement for Religious Renewal cannot flourish if it in any way damages the anthroposophical movement.*

This must be thoroughly understood, especially by anthroposophists, so that whenever it is necessary to stand up for what is right in the matter, they may really be able to do so. When, therefore, there is any question about attitudes of anthroposophists toward Religious Renewal, they must be clear that their attitude can only be that of advisers, that they give what they can give in the way of spiritual possessions, and that when it is a case of participating in the ceremonies, they do this in order to help those ceremonies on their way. Those who understand themselves to be anthroposophists can be spiritual helpers only of the Movement for Religious Renewal. But this Movement for Religious Renewal must be sustained in every way by persons who, because of the particular configuration and disposition of their spiritual life, cannot yet find their way into the Anthroposophical Society itself.

I hope that none of you will now go to someone who is doing active work in the Movement for Religious Renewal and say that this or that has been said against it in Dornach. Nothing has been said against it. In love and in devotion to the spiritual world, the Movement for Religious Renewal has been given counsel in a justified manner from out of the spiritual world, in order that it could found itself. But anthroposophists must know that it has founded itself out of itself, that it has formed the *fact* of its ritual (but not, it is true, the content of its ritual) out of its own force and its own initiative, and that the essential core of the anthroposophical movement has nothing to do with the Movement for Religious Renewal.

Certainly no wish could be stronger than mine that the Movement for Religious Renewal shall grow and flourish more and more, but always in adherence to the original conditions. Anthroposophical groups must not be changed into communities for religious renewal, either in a material or in a spiritual sense.

I was obliged to say this today, for, as you know, counsel and advice had to be given for a ritual, a ritual whose growth in our present time I earnestly desire. In order that no misunderstanding should arise in regard to *this* ritual when I speak tomorrow of the conditions of the life of ritual in the spiritual world, I felt it necessary to insert these words today as an episode in our course of lectures.

ADDENDUM

In connection with his lecture on December 30, 1922, Rudolf Steiner gave an account that was published in 1924 in the news-letter "What Is Happening in the Anthroposophical Society?"

Following are some remarks concerning the course on the Apocalypse that was given at the Goetheanum in September.

Inserted in the courses held here in September was one that was held exclusively for the priests of the Christian Community. The members of the Vorstand were the only other people present.

The priests had already expressed the wish for a course on the Apocalypse quite a while earlier.

In 1908 I gave a lecture to the members of the Theosophical Society in Nuremberg, which is in print under the title *Theosophie an der Hand der Apokalypse* [Theosophy in Light of the Apocalypse].

What I said at the time could not be identical with what I had to say this time. At the time our dear friends and members were eagerly awaiting to hear some cognitive facts about the evolution of the human being on Earth and of the Earth within the star system, as it can be known through spiritual scientific research. With such a topic one can connect to the Apocalypse, because its content poses a riddle for anyone who reads the Bible. It is the very last chapter of the Bible and contains prophetic statements about the evolution of humankind and the Earth. In that in the Nuremberg cycle I was able to show that in the image-rich language used by the writer of the Apocalypse we find many statements about the evolution of humankind and the Earth within the solar system, it was possible to put the relationship of the esoteric truths of Christianity to anthroposophy in the right light. I was able, in a certain sense, to present the listeners with the insight that one can hear truths that profoundly touch the eternal depths of human souls, from two sides: one, from the side of esoteric Christian clairvoyant perception, and, two, from the side of spiritual-scientific cognition. And one hears the same thing if one knows how to listen.

This time my task was different. Though I will not report to you the exact content, because in its essence it was meant only for the circle of the priests, I feel called to tell you what anthroposophists ought to know of events within the Anthroposophical Society. The spiritual substance streaming through the priesthood has been the gift from the spiritual world. It was given two years ago at the site of the now burned-down first Goetheanum, and I was its mediating agent. This gift was such that the Christian Community was made to stand in full independence in relation to the Anthroposophical Society. Nothing but such a complete *independence* could be aimed for at the foundation of the Christian Community, since as a movement for religious renewal it did *not* grow out of anthroposophy. The founders of the movement sought a new religious path, not out of anthroposophy but out of Christianity. They had the desire, in grasping the living content of Christianity, supersensible content, to find the connection of the human soul with its eternal world of being. They firmly believed that it should be possible. And yet they felt that the avenues open to them through their previous theological training were not sufficient. And so it happened that these students came to me with their honest desire for a spiritually worthy priesthood. They had become acquainted with anthroposophy, and they were sure that anthroposophy could be the mediator in what they sought. But they did not seek the path of anthroposophy; they sought a specifically religious path.

I pointed out to them that both the ritual and the teaching content could be mediated through anthroposophy, but that the anthroposophical movement itself sees its task of caring for the life of the spirit from other sides.

Through the efforts of these students, *Dr. Rittelmeyer* stepped up to a spirit-oriented Christian priesthood. He was both a Christian priest *and* an anthroposophist in the truest sense of the word. He had, albeit without the ritual and yet in a wider spirit-endowed sense, lived the Christian renewal in the creative work of his person. The practical question was, of course, how Dr. Rittelmeyer was going to accept the gift of the Christian renewal from the Anthroposophical Society. What stand was he going to take to what is wanted? Because as far as the anthroposophical movement was concerned, Rittelmeyer was a person who had united Christianity and anthroposophy in the outer harmony of his bearing and working, and also in his inner harmony of heart.

And Rittelmeyer said "Yes" with full heartfelt conviction. And thus the solid starting point was established for an independent movement for Christian renewal. What was ready to happen could come about and be inaugurated here in the Goetheanum two years ago.

Ever since then the community of priests has energetically gone forward on its path. A creative activity, rich in blessing and healing has since unfolded.

Two years later to the day of the founding, this course took place, because the priests felt a need to enter into a more intimate relationship to the Apocalypse.

It was my belief that I could aid them in attaining this closer relationship. On my paths within the world of the spirit I was able to retrace the trail of the Apocalypse.

And so I intended through this course to make possible a representation that would transmit this "priest book," in the truest sense, to the priests as a spiritual guide. The act of consecration stands in the center of the creative work of the priesthood; from here it radiates what the spirit world would penetrate into the human world in ritual fashion. The Apocalypse can stand in the center of the priest's soul, and from there can stream into all priestly thinking and into the priestly feeling, what the offering human soul is supposed to receive from the spirit world through grace.

This then is how I conceived the task of the course for the priests, when I was asked to give it. And in this sense it has been given.

[1] This movement was the beginning of *The Christian Community,* as it has since been called.

CHAPTER V

SPIRITUAL KNOWLEDGE IS A TRUE COMMUNION: THE BEGINNING OF A COSMIC RITUAL SUITABLE FOR THE PRESENT AGE

Dornach, New Year's Eve, 1922–3

(The fire that destroyed the first Goetheanum was discovered one hour after this lecture ended.)

The day before yesterday I spoke of how the cycle of the year can also be found in the human being. I pointed out that the forces of nature around us take place in a time organism during the cycle of a year, so that we can see the interaction and cooperation of occurrences that otherwise appear like isolated processes and facts in nature.

Now the essential difference between this nature cycle and its image in the human being is that events that take place *successively* in a particular region of the Earth take place *concurrently* in the human being. It is true that, taken as a whole, the human being resembles the Earth globe taken as a whole, inasmuch as when it is winter in one hemisphere it is summer in the other, and so forth. In the case of the Earth, however, the corresponding winter and summer are separated from one another so that if we take the winter influences as they work in one region and the simultaneous summer influences working in another region, the two flow away from one another, and neither is disturbed or weakened in its operation by the other. But now consider how it is with human beings. When we are asleep, our physical and etheric bodies are in a kind of summer condition, in a budding and sprouting life. Spiritual sight shows us this budding and sprouting summer condition of the human physical and etheric bodies during sleep, when the Ego and astral body are separated from them. We can say that while we are asleep there is a kind of successive spring and summer condition in the physical and etheric organism we have left behind. At the same time the Ego and the astral body, which still cooperate in supporting the human organism as a whole, are in a sort of winter condition. Thus here again there are simultaneous summer and winter conditions, but in the human they are not turned away from one another; on the contrary, they work into one another. And it is the same in our waking life. As long as we are awake, our physical and etheric bodies are in a kind of autumn and winter condition. On the other hand the Ego and the astral body, stirred by external impressions and by the thoughts the human being thinks about these impressions, are in full summer or full spring conditions. So that once more we find inner spring, inner summer, and inner winter working together in the human being, not turning away from one another, but shining through each other.

This is what actually takes place, as disclosed by the researches of spiritual science. If we wished to compare the entire Earth with the human being in respect to winter and summer, we would have to turn the opposing hemispheres around. With the human being it is as though by turning the Earth we superimpose the summer of one hemisphere on the winter of the other. Were this possible, we would actually have what may be described as summer conditions canceling winter conditions, and winter conditions canceling summer conditions, producing a kind of equilibrium. Now this is an important fact, not yet realized by external science, which consequently is bound to misunderstand the essential nature of the human being. For in the human being, summer and winter (if I may allow myself the expression, for it really corresponds to what actually takes place) cancel one another.

It is true that human beings bear surrounding nature in themselves, but its activities cancel one another and a condition sets in that actually brings the activities of nature to a state of rest. Just as in a balance that has weights in both pans, the pointer will come to rest at a certain spot and at that spot is affected neither by the weight to the right nor by the weight to the left, but is in equilibrium with respect to the forces that otherwise affect the beam, so too there is in the human a counterpoise resulting from opposing natural forces.

Anyone who studies what I said very briefly about the human being as a threefold being in the appendix of my book *Riddles of the Soul* — studies it really carefully, as people are not yet accustomed to do — will in fact find the following. The human being is made up of an organism of nerves and senses, a rhythmic organism, and an organism of limbs and metabolism. These three organisms work into one another. We may say that the organism of nerves and senses has its principal activity in the head. But the whole human being is, to a certain extent, functionally head. And the same may be said of the other systems, that of the nerves and senses and that of the trunk, limbs, and metabolic activities.

Now, when we take into account the threefold being, we could present the human being schematically in somewhat the following way. We have the nerve-sense organization, the rhythmic organization, and the limb-metabolic organization.

If we take the two outer organisms, the nerve-sense organization and the metabolic-limb system, we find an actual opposition between them, which is very plainly visible to a spiritual scientific anatomy and physiology. When, for example, we are walking, there is  *movement* in our limb organism that is even movement in space. To this movement there corresponds in a certain portion of our nerves and senses organism, our head organism, a kind of *rest*, proportional to the amount of activity or movement in our limb organism. Please try to understand this correctly. I said: a *proportional* amount of rest. Rest is generally thought of as an absolute. A person who is seated is seated, and we do not differentiate the degree of intensity with which he or she sits! This is permissible in a certain connection in ordinary life, where these things do not differ very strongly from one another.

But with our organism of nerves and senses it is different. If we run fast, if our limb organism moves fast, then in our nerve-sense organism there is a tendency to rest, a stronger desire to be at rest than if we were sauntering along slowly. And everything that happens in our limb organism and in our metabolic organism, when, for example, the digestive fluids are being kept active by intestinal movements, corresponds to a tendency to rest in our nerve-sense organism. This comes to expression externally.

The head, the principal seat of the nerve-sense organism, is a lazybones in relation to the limb organism. It behaves much like people who sit in a cab and let themselves be drawn along by the horse. The people remain at rest; and so does our head sit quietly on the rest of our organism. The head is not even interested if, for instance, I wave my arms. When I wave my left arm, a tendency to rest is set up in the right half of my head, and when I wave my right arm, a tendency to rest in the left half. And through this tendency to rest it is possible to accompany our movements with thoughts and ideas. It is quite a mistaken notion of materialistic philosophy that ideas originate from movements in the nerves. On the contrary, if they are ideas about some motion in space, they depend on the tendencies to rest in the nervous system. The nervous system quiets down, and because it becomes quiet and abates its vital activities, thoughts find their way into this state of rest and become real. Those who can observe human beings with the vision of spiritual science and see what happens when they think and when ideas occur to them, can never be materialists, for they know that in the very same measure that thoughts quicken and become active as soul and spirit substance, the nerves grow quiet, lose their vitality and energy, and even become lame in that same measure. The nervous system must, through ceasing its material activities, make room for the soul-spiritual of thought. It is just in such things that we see why we have materialism. Materialism dates from the time when science no longer understood matter. For material science is characterized by a total inability to conceive the nature of material occurrences, to which it therefore attributes all kinds of things that are not there.

So you see, there are opposite conditions in us, tending toward equilibrium. Just as at midsummer natural forces and activities are present that are directly opposed to those of the depth of winter, so do we find opposing forces in the human organism, which however hold each other in balance. Yet we shall only think correctly about these opposing forces that balance one another when we organize the human being in the following way. When we divide the middle system of the human being, the rhythmic system, into two halves, we differentiate essentially (it is not totally exact) a rhythm of the breath and a rhythm of the blood circulation. Then we speak of an upper middle rhythmic system and a lower middle rhythmic system. Between the upper and lower halves is that part of the human which, because it is influenced and permeated from above and below by opposite natural forces, strives most energetically to maintain equilibrium.

If I would therefore insert the opposed natural forces working in the human into my schematic drawing, I must elaborate the drawing in the following way (red). In the upper part of this lemniscate, I have circumscribed the natural forces that are arranged in opposition to those I have circumscribed in the lower half.

So the human being is divided, as it were, into two halves, an upper and a lower. The upper half embraces the nerve-sense system, which extends, of course, over the whole body. The

drawing is schematic. Sometimes we must seek here the "above" in the big toe, because the nerve-sense organs are there too. Thus the drawing is schematic, but it will be easy for you to think of its being applied to reality. Therefore, I have to picture how the nerve-sense system with the breathing system belonging to it on one hand works in the opposite direction to the metabolic-limb system and the blood circulatory system on the other hand. They cancel one another.

The organ in the human in which the adjustment takes place, in which there is a continual striving from beneath upward and from above downward to maintain equilibrium, is the human heart, which is far from being a pump for pumping blood through the body, as modern physiology would have it. It is, on the contrary, the organ that keeps the upper and lower systems in equilibrium. Therefore even in our outer physical organisms we find an expression of the spiritual events taking place within us when we observe how summer and winter conditions are incessantly offsetting one another within us.

On Earth, winter can prevail in a given region precisely because summer does not occur at the same time. Otherwise the summer would balance the winter, that is to say, there would be neither winter nor summer but only equilibrium. This is the real state of things in the human. Human beings are a part of nature, but since the natural forces oppose each other in their organism they cancel one another, and it is as though humans were no longer a part of nature. For that very reason, human beings are *free beings*. Physical necessity cannot be applied to human beings, for in them there is not one physical necessity, but two natural forces, working against one another and canceling each other out. And in this realm where natural forces cancel one another are to be found the soul and spirit of the human being, which are unaffected by the working of nature and must be known through their own lawfulness of soul and spirit.

From this you can see that we must go to an encompassing method of observation if we want to understand the human being, and that a mere application of the external laws of nature, which are orientated in one direction only, is of no use at all.

But now that we have set before us the true nature of the human being, let us see what results follow. We only learn to know the being of human beings when we regard them as bearing within a piece of nature in such a way that the counteracting natural forces cancel one another. If we examine this piece of nature in the human with the eyes of spiritual science, we find that the physical and etheric bodies are penetrated during sleep by mineral and vegetable modes of activity, which are seen to be in the summer condition. Now, in that we are able to observe this budding, sprouting life in the right way, we learn to understand its real significance.

When does this budding and sprouting take place? When the ego and the astral body are not present, when they are away during sleep. And whence comes this budding and sprouting? That is precisely what spiritual vision shows us.

Let us picture the human being asleep. The schematic in bright, green, yellow, red. The physical and etheric bodies lie in the bed. Spiritual vision sees them as soil, as mineral matter, out of which plant life is sprouting. It is a different form of plant life, of course, from the one we see around us, but recognizable as such by spiritual sight. Above gleam the ego and

astral body like a flame, unable to approach the physical and etheric. The sleeping human therefore is a sort of budding, sprouting plot of ground, with a gleaming ego and astral body belonging to it, but detached.

And how is it when we are awake? I must describe this state as follows: The mineral and vegetable portions are seen to be withering and collapsing, while the ego and astral body gleam down into them and burn them up. This is the waking human, with the soil and mineral elements crumbling and the plant element wilting within. The mineral element crumbles during the waking hours. There is a sort of plantlike activity that, although quite different in appearance, gives a general impression of autumn foliage, of drooping, withering leaves that are dying and shrinking; and all through this fading substance, big and little flames are gleaming and glowing. These big and little flames are the astral body and the ego, which are now living in the physical and etheric bodies. And then the question arises: What happens to these gleaming and glowing flames during sleep, when they are separated from the physical and etheric bodies?

When this problem is attacked by spiritual scientific research, we find the answer, which you could yourselves draw from a comparison of various descriptions I have given from time to time. What is this inner power, the power that drives away the flame and gleam of the ego and astral body, and then stimulates the budding and sprouting vegetative life of the summer-like, sleeping physical body, that also causes even its mineral element to evolve a kind of life, so that in the course of its infinitesimal subdividing, it looks like a mass of melting atoms, a continuous mobile mass, everywhere active, fluid-mineral and yet air-like, at all points permeated by sprouting life? It is the reverberating wave of our life before birth. When we are awake during earthly life we bring this to a standstill. So long as the flame and gleam of the ego and astral body are united with the physical and etheric bodies, we annul those stimuli that spring from life before birth and that are present during sleep; we bring them to quiescence. And now we learn first from an inspection of ourselves, how to look at external nature in the right way so that we can say: All natural laws and energies affecting external vegetable and mineral nature are the same as what is mineral and vegetable life in ourselves during sleep, sprouting life and summer. And this means that just as our sleeping physical and etheric bodies point to our past, to a spiritual life in which we lived before birth, so does all external nature that is vegetable or mineral point to the past. If we are to correctly comprehend the natural laws and forces of our external environment, exclusive of the animal element and the physical human, we must recognize that they point to the Earth's past, to the dying away of the Earth. And the thoughts we entertain about external nature are really directed to the dying element of Earth existence.

If this dying Earth existence is to be enlivened again so that it can have impulses for the future, this can come about only as it does in the human being, that is to say, by the insertion of soul and spirit into mineral and vegetable. The soul element enters with animals, and spirit enters then with the human being.

Looked at in this way, the whole world is actually divided into two parts. When we look out into external nature, insofar as this is mineral and plant — and that is the main thing in external nature — we can compare it only with our sleeping physical and etheric organism. When we consider external physical activities, we must say that all other physical actions depend upon these physical activities in mineral and vegetable matter. Consider the process of nourishment. It begins with the taking in of mineral and vegetable matter. The animal takes it a step further in preparing it as food for the human. But all external nature depends, as far as its physical and etheric activities are concerned, on such substantiality as we find in our sleeping physical and etheric organism. Now in the human being, during our waking moments while our physical and etheric organism is in its winter sleep, the ego and astral organism that we bear within us is in a condition of summer, being stimulated by the outer senses and the thoughts that form themselves. This ego and astral organism balances in waking hours the winter condition of the physical and etheric bodies.

And when we come to apply the methods of spiritual science to the cycle of the year, we find in it too a *spiritual summer* condition belonging to its winter and a *spiritual winter* condition belonging to its summer. These conditions do not, however, balance one another as they do in the human. On the contrary, they express themselves in opposite hemispheres, so that on the Earth physical winter is strengthened by the soul-spiritual winter condition, and physical summer by the spiritual summer condition. These occurrences, however, point to the fact that all surrounding nature bears within it its past and its present, even as human beings carry their past and present in themselves.

We actually have the *present* in our physical body only in connection with the activities and lawfulness that penetrate it when we are awake. For our physical and etheric bodies during sleep, we have the inworking of a past, a past moreover that was spent in the spiritual world. We find the same thing in the vegetable and mineral worlds that lie before us and work upon us. They too are a result of past existence. And they become present only through the Earth being cloaked with the soul-spiritual even as the human being is permeated by the soul-spiritual. And the present already contains the germ of the future. But if it is true — and the description I have given you is true — that our physical and etheric organism is an expression of the past precisely when it is independent of the activities of the soul and spirit, then in order to find what works over into the future we must look to our Ego and astral body; and for the Earth too we must seek the future in what is spiritual.

Human beings have evolved to a point where, by help of forces that of course are quite elemental, they have added the Ego and astral body to the physical and etheric bodies. The mineral and vegetable earthly world has not yet accomplished this. The Earth's ego and astral body surround the Earth with soul and spirit but do not permeate her mineral and vegetable activities. The mineral nature of the Earth, as we observe it, shows itself as being unable to let soul and spirit enter, able only to let them surround it and shine around it. The vegetable nature shows itself also unable to admit soul, but in a certain way the upper parts of the plant may be said to be touched with the soul and spirit. Spiritual scientific research shows us the following concerning the plant. If I have the root below, the stem in the middle and the blossom above, then I have to see that in the blossom the upward-striving plant comes into contact with the astral. The astral does not penetrate the plant; it merely touches it. And this touching is the origin of the blossom. The astral surrounding the Earth touches the uppermost portion of the plant, and the flower comes into being. I have often spoken of this in an analogy (which must of course be received with proper delicacy), saying that the flowering of the plant is the kiss exchanged between the sunlight and the plant. It is an astral influence that is, however, no more than a "touching."

So when we look into surrounding nature, we do not see in the mineral and vegetable kingdoms exactly what we see in the human. In ourselves as human being we behold a mineral nature, a plant nature, an astral nature, and an Ego nature, all belonging to one another. (We will leave the animals out for the time being and speak of them on some future occasion.) But we have to find in the mineral and vegetable worlds themselves that on which physical activity essentially depends. These worlds show themselves, in external nature, altogether lacking in astral thought, as well as in experience of the ego, the self-conscious sense of spirit. The latter are not to be found in the world outside, neither in the mineral nor in the plant. For mineral and plant are fundamentally results of the past.

If we observe the Earth's crust and its vegetation aright, we will look upon all the life of the Earth and say: You crystals, you mountains, you budding and sprouting plants, I see in you monuments of a living, creative past that is now dying. But in the human beings themselves — if we are able to have the right perspective on this dying element that brings its energy from pre-earthly existence into and exhausts itself and dies away in the physical and etheric bodies — we see the physical and etheric organism permeated by that of the astral and ego, which shines into the future and is able to unfold freely, as life of thought and ideation in a situation of balanced nature forces. It may be said that we see in human beings *past and future side by side.* In nature on the other hand, insofar as it is mineral or vegetable, we see only the past. The element that already functions as future during the human being's present is the element that confers *freedom* upon him or her. This freedom is not found in external nature. If external nature were doomed to remain just what its mineral and vegetable kingdoms make it, it would be doomed to die, in the same way that the mere physical and etheric organisms of the human being perishes. The physical and etheric organisms die, but human beings do not, because the astral and ego bear within them, not death, but a *becoming.*

If therefore external nature is not to perish, it must be given what human beings have through their astral body and ego. This means that as human beings, through their astral body and ego, have self-conscious ideas, they must, in order to ensure a future to the otherwise dying Earth, insert into the Earth the supersensible and invisible that they have within themselves. Just as human beings must expect their reincarnation in another Earth life from what is supersensible and invisible in them and cannot expect it from their dying physical and etheric bodies, so can no future arise for the Earth from the mineral and vegetable globe that surrounds us. Only when we place into the Earth what it does not have itself can a future Earth arise. What is not there of itself on the Earth is principally the *active thoughts of human beings* who live and weave in their independent nature organisms, which always hold a balance and are on this account free. If we bring these independent thoughts to a real existence, we confer a future on the Earth. But we must first have them. Thoughts that we make in our ordinary knowledge of nature, thoughts about what is dying away, are mere reflections and not realities. But thoughts we receive from spiritual research are quickened in Imagination, Inspiration, and Intuition. If we take them up, they become forms having independent existence in the life of the Earth.

Concerning these creative thoughts I once said in my book *The Science of Knowing* that such thinking represents the spiritual form of communion for humanity. For as long as human beings give themselves up to their mirror thoughts about external nature, they do nothing but repeat the past. They live in corpses of the divine. When they enliven their thoughts themselves, then, communing and receiving communion through their own being, they unite themselves with the Divine Spirit that permeates the world and assures its future.

Spiritual knowledge is thus a real communion, the beginning of a cosmic ritual that is suitable for human beings today, who then can grow because they begin to realize how they permeate their physical and etheric organism with their astral and ego organism, and how as they quicken the spirit in themselves, they lay it also into the dead and dying matter that surrounds them.

Then human beings will experience that when they look upon their own organism in its *solid* condition, they will feel that it links them to the starry universe, insofar as it is a being at rest. Insofar as the starry universe is a being at rest, maintaining, for example, in the signs of the Zodiac a position at rest in relation to the Earth, human beings are connected in their physical organism with those constellations in space. But by allowing soul and spirit to flow into this "form structure" in space, they themselves change the world.

Human beings are also penetrated in like manner by their stream of *fluid*. The etheric organism lives in the fluids and juices of the body. It is the etheric organism that causes the blood to circulate and that brings the other fluids and juices in us into movement. Through this etheric organism we are connected with the *deeds* of the stars, with the *movement* of the planets. Just as the resting pictures in the heavens of the fixed stars act upon, or stand in relation to, the solid structure of the human organism, so do the planetary movements of the system to which we belong stand in relation to the fluids in us.

But the world as it presents itself to our immediate vision is a dead world. Human beings transform it through their own spirit when they share their spirit with the world by quickening their thoughts to Imagination, Inspiration, and Intuition, thus fulfilling the spiritual communion of humanity. We must first become *conscious* of this. This consciousness must become more and more lively and alert. Then more and more we find the way to this spiritual communion. I should like to give you today some words that may serve as a foundation for this consciousness, words that, when allowed to act rightly upon the soul — and this means they must be made to live over and over again in the soul until the soul experiences their moving, living meaning to the full — will then bring something into existence in the human soul that transforms what is dead in the world we are connected with into the living, and quickens the past to life in order that from its death may arise the life of the future. This can happen only when we become aware of our connection with the cosmos in the following manner. The first formulation I write in this way:

In Earth-activity draws near to me —
(I imagine the earthly matter that I take into myself with that which fashions the solid structure of my organism.)

In Earth-activity draws near to me,
Given to me in substance-image,
The Heavenly Being of the Stars.

For it is a fact that when we look at some structure of the
Earth that we take into ourselves as food, we find in it an
image of the constellations of the fixed stars. We take it into
ourselves. With the substance of the Earth that is contained in
Earth activity, we take into ourselves the being of the stars, the
being of the heavens. But we must be conscious that we, as
human beings, in our will, in our love-permeated will, transform what has become matter back into spirit again. In this
manner we perform a real act of *transubstantiation* when we
become aware of our own part in the world so that the spiritual thought-life is quickened within us.

In Earth-activity draws near to me,
Given to me in substance-image,
The Heavenly Being of the Stars.
In Willing I see them transformed with Love!

And when we think of what we take into ourselves that
permeates the fluid part of our organism, the circulation of
the blood and juices, then that, insofar as it originates on
Earth, is an image not of the heavens or of the stars, but of the
deeds of the stars, that is to say, the movements of the planets.
And I can become conscious of how I spiritualize that, if I
stand rightly in the world, through the following formula:

In watery life stream into me,
Forming me through with power of substance-force,
The Heavenly Deeds of the Stars —

That is to say, the deeds of the planetary movements. And
now:

In Feeling I see them transformed with Wisdom!

While I can see how in *will* the being and weaving of the stars change lovingly into the spiritual content of the future; I can also see how in *feeling* a wise change takes place when I receive into myself, in what permeates my fluid organism, an image of heavenly deeds. In this way, we can experience ourselves in willing and in feeling. Surrendering ourselves to the all-wielding power of the universe, of cosmic existence, that is all around us, we can experience what is carried out through us as transubstantiation in the great temple of the cosmos in that we stand within it as one who is celebrating a sacrifice in a purely spiritual way.

What would otherwise be mere abstract knowledge achieves a relationship of will and feeling to the world. The world becomes a temple; it becomes the House of God. When knowing human beings summon up powers of *will* and *feeling*, they become sacrificing beings. The fundamental relationship of the human being to the world rises from knowledge to *cosmic ritual*. The first beginning of what must come to pass if anthroposophy is to fulfill its mission in the world is that the human being's whole relationship to the world must be recognized to be one of cosmic ritual.

I have wished to say this to you, as it were, as a beginning. Next Friday I will speak further about the nature of this ritual in its relation to the knowledge of nature. I especially wanted to say this to you today. I appointed this lecture for this particular day with a special end in view. For today, when the being of time that is given in the cycle of the year is brought before our souls, when such a year, at least for outward perception and experience, comes to an end, we should become conscious of how our relationship to time should take shape, of how we should seek the future out of the *past* and how we know how to work actively for the future, in order to create the spiritual.

One of the poems recited this afternoon began with these words: "Every year finds new graves!" That is profoundly true. But it is equally true that every year finds new cradles. As this year touches the past, so does it also touch the future. And today it lies with the human being above all to grasp this future, to think about the fact that the budding and sprouting life in the external world contains death within it, and that we must seek for *life* with our *own* power of action. Every New Year is a symbol of this truth. If we see, justifiably, on the one hand the graves, let us behold on the other hand the renewing life waiting to receive the seed of the future into itself.

It is our great task this day to observe how the mood of New Year's Eve is in the world around us — all is passing and dying away — but how in the hearts of those who are conscious of their true human nature, of their divine humanity, there must be the mood of New Year, the mood of the beginning of a new era, of the uprising of new life. Let us not merely turn with a superficial festiveness from a symbolical New Year's Eve to a symbolical New Year's Day; but let us so turn our thoughts that they may indeed grow powerful and creative, as evolution requires them to be. Let us turn our thoughts away from the dying phenomena that confront us everywhere in modern civilization like old graves, away from New Year's Eve to New Year's Day, to the Cosmic New Year. But that will come only when human beings decide to bring it to pass.

> In Earth-activity draws near to me,
> Given to me in substance-image,
> The Heavenly Being of the Stars:
> In WILLING I see them transformed with love!

> In watery life stream into me,
> Forming me through with power of substance-force,
> The Heavenly Deeds of the Stars:
> In FEELING I see them transformed with Wisdom.

> Geistige Kommunion.

> Es nahet mir im Erdenwirken,
> In Stoffes Abbild mir gegeben,

Der Sterne Himmelswesen:
Ich seh' im Wollen sie sich liebend wandeln.

Es dringen in mich im Wasserleben,
In Stoffes Kraftgewalt mich bildend,
Der Sterne Himmelstaten:
Ich seh' im Fühlen sie sich weise wandeln.

PART TWO

THE REVERSED, COSMIC RITUAL

Meeting in the Spirit:
The Cosmic Ritual

Reflections on the
Religious in Anthroposophy

FRIEDRICH BENESCH

CHAPTER I

THE MYSTERY OF REVERSAL AND THE CHRISTIAN SACRAMENTAL RITUAL

Rudolf Steiner's spiritual scientific research into human life and conditions of existence in the spiritual worlds between death and a new birth goes essentially in four directions.

1. First there is the transformation of the individual being of the human in laying aside the earthly sheaths and being clothed with cosmic spiritual sheaths on the path of transformation, purification, and the turning inside out of consciousness, from an earthly to a cosmic consciousness: the change from Earth human to celestial human.

2. The second is the living together, growing together, and working together with the Hierarchies in passing through their spheres on the path from the Third Hierarchy over to the Second and the First, and on to lingering in the bosom of the Godhead in the "midnight hour" of the eternal Cosmic Day.

3. The third is a manifest togetherness, on the deepest level, with all those with whom karmic ties exist and the resulting reworking of the past into future karma in cooperation with the Hierarchies, right to the condition of the celestial human being.

4. The fourth is the preparation and pre-forming of the next life on Earth, including enveloping with the members of being of this following incarnation, again during the journey through the spheres of the Hierarchies, to which belongs the final phase of cloaking with the stream of heredity through conception, embryonic development, and early childhood.

Only in the course of the presentations in anthroposophy of this comprehensive earthly-cosmic journey of the human being from different viewpoints do these transformations of the cooperation of the Hierarchies with the deepest being of the human appear as a ritualistic-karmic event, a ritual. These presentations run through the whole of anthroposophy, from the first edition of *Theosophy* (1904) through the detailed descriptions in *Karmic Relationships* (Vols. 1–6, 1924).

Four questions arise in light of these revelations concerning the cosmic journey of the human being as comprehensive karmic-cosmic ritual:

1. What is a ritual as such, in its essential nature? What is the primal phenomenon, the fundamental events of the ritualistic processes?

2. What form does the ritual event have from its own nature? What are the parts of every ritual and the events that make up its celebration?

3. What sequence do the parts of the ritual follow?

4. What are the form and meaning of what takes place as ritual in world events, not only in the life before birth and after death, but also of ritual that can occur between birth and death on Earth?

All processes, deeds, and suffering that can be meant by the word *ritual* presuppose two or more spiritual beings who celebrate the ritual together. An active and passive fundamental relationship of beings to and with each other is established, celebrated, and nurtured as ritual.

The second presupposition is that the process of the ritual event has the form of mutual devotion from being to being in the most comprehensive and deepest sense. Such devotion has its source in a quite specific fundamental relationship, a fundamental attitude that can be characterized in the most comprehensive sense as "devoutness." It is a character, an attitude, a way of acting, and, lastly, a condition of the beings themselves who are performing the ritual.

At first, it appears as if the cultic process consists of a giving or offering by the one side and a receiving of what is offered by the other side of the participating beings. But in a real ritual that is not so. The giving and receiving are always happening simultaneously on both sides. The giving reveals the giver, and, in the receiving, the one who receives is always united with the one who gives — a communion. The nature of giving is always an offering, a delivering up or giving away;

and receiving is always a transformation, both of the one who receives and of the one who gives, becoming thereby a mystical fact, a Mystery.

Hence every real ritual is structured into these four archetypal processes: Revelation, Offering, Transubstantiation, and Communion. We can understand these as parts of a whole, as sequential stages, and as simultaneous spheres in each of which the other three spheres must be present and active. Ritual in itself is also a Mystery.

From this perspective, ritual is possible for human beings not only in the spiritual world between death and birth, but also on Earth between birth and death.

All forms of ritual on Earth have come out of the Mystery centers. Initiates prepared and formed the content of the ritual differently according to the development of humanity at the particular time, as well as with respect to the differences in humanity in the various cultures spread over the Earth. They did so by renewing ever again what had already been formed earlier and also by founding new forms appropriate to the changed conditions that had arisen.

Only the Last Supper performed by the Christ Being contains the direct act of the divine-human Christ Being himself, through the mediating substances of bread and wine, for the Earth and humanity. This ritual proceeds directly out of the Mystery of Golgotha.

In that Rudolf Steiner refounded the Mysteries in the form of anthroposophy, he could, on the one hand, give the help needed for the renewal of the sacramental ritual. On the other hand, he was able to lay the foundation, out of the totality of anthroposophy, for a new ritual, which he himself called the "reverse ritual," the ritual of knowledge, the cosmic ritual, the cosmic communion. In this ritual, the spiritual communion of humanity is celebrated as a new development of the ritual.

Thus, we find two quite distinct forms of ritual for the human living on the Earth: one is the sacramental ritual, the Sacrament; the other is what Rudolf Steiner called the reverse ritual. The first is a complete renewal of already existing ritual forms with the help of anthroposophy. The second is a new creation within anthroposophy itself. Anthroposophy provides the possibility to work toward an understanding of both ritual forms. Both forms contain the four parts, revelation, offering, transformation, and communion, and in both all four take place and unfold their respective spheres. What makes them different from each other, and even opposites, is what Rudolf Steiner called the "reversal" of the one as compared with the other.

The first question that arises in an effort to gain knowledge of the reverse ritual concerns the mystery of *reversal* itself. It can refer both to the starting point and direction of the ritual process as a whole, or it can refer to the sequence of its four parts. So, the reversal can be connected with the starting point, as well as with the sequence of the ritual events.

The mystery of reversal can become apparent when we compare the ritual of birth in the spiritual world with the sacramental ritual. In the sense of spiritual science, the great life-mystery of birth does not begin with the birth from the womb. In reality, that is the end of processes of a sweeping nature that comprises the descent of human beings out of the spiritual world into the earthly world that occurs in the second half of the period between death and a new birth. Processes that take place in the depths of human beings bring about first their release from being surrounded by and interwoven and permeated with spiritual beings. Thus human beings sever themselves from a condition of all-embracing communion and turn away from the spirit world and toward the earthly world.

The turning away from the spiritual beings becomes a kind of existential excommunion. The turning to the earthly world is, first, a transformation of the content of consciousness. In this, the cosmic consciousness gradually turns inside out into an internalized and centralized consciousness that inclines to the Earth. This means that we turn away from the peripheral forces of the cosmos to the centralized forces of earthly existence. This transformation takes place in the form of a rhythmical breathing out into the cosmic circumference and breathing in into the developing inner being of the human before birth. This is described in the first lecture of the cycle *Man and the World of the Stars* (GA 219, the last lectures of which present the reverse ritual; see notes I,4). This brings about a kind of transformation, a transubstantiation, a becoming related to physical matter, also in the form of transformations of spiritual substance into the germ of earthly substance formation. This is a transubstantiation.

This second stage of birth in pre-birth existence then moves into a third stage. The spirit germ of the physical body participates in this stage, taking hold of the centralized forces that work with it from Earth in the stream of earthly heredity to the moment of conception. Seen physically, through the fertilization of the physical ovum a condition of chaos arises in which the descending peripheral forces, which are in the process of transformation, are enveloped and laid claim to by the centralized earthly forces. This third stage of birth is an offering, a sacrifice, of the celestial human to the Earth human.

During the time of embryonic development, birth, and the first months of life, the subjective, personal inner core of the child forms. At this time in the ritual of birth, the fourth stage passes over into revelation. The inwardness of the human soul comes into being. After birth this inwardness develops more and more into the activities that lead to standing upright, walking, speaking, and lastly to thought-deed, to thinking. The final step is that this inwardness expresses then itself, in that it is able to say "I."

What we are looking at here is in truth a cosmic ritual, the mystery of birth: excommunion; transubstantiation from spirit to matter; offering of the higher, heavenly substance to the embrace of the earthly; and revelation in the word out of the now earthly individual inner being through the "I" expressing itself. These are the four fundamental stages of birth, leading from communion through transformation and offering to revelation, which are carried out in cooperation among the fellow human souls that are incarnating, the Hierarchies, the hereditary stream of the ancestors, and the individual incarnating human being. These essential stages of the birth mystery are changed into variations during our life in the form of the more hidden births in the seven-year rhythms of the earthly biography. Their effect weakens after the middle of life.

With the first breath that we draw, the other mystery begins to work, which is the other pole of life between birth and death. This is the mystery of dying, of death. The differentiations of all the death processes work in and permeate our entire life. Beginning with our first breath, they increase particularly after our thirty-fifth year and culminate in death at the end of our earthly life.

The earthly human being comes out of the sphere of birth and lives on in the sphere of death. This sphere brings about, on the one hand, the possibility of earthly consciousness, the I-consciousness, as well as the achieving and experiencing of earthly freedom. On the other hand, it works in the direction of a permanent danger for the earthly human. For the Earth is dying physically and etherically, and finally, so too is the bodily human being after birth, in the ever further waning of the forces of birth. When, however, the soul and spirit of the human get pulled into this dying and are taken hold of and shackled by it, the human being is threatened with the loss of his or her divine-spiritual being as the result of Earth existence. It is a soul-spiritual dying, a burying of the eternal in the temporal.

The Christian sacramental ritual is placed, to begin with, in this sphere of death. It follows the path of birth in the sphere of death in reverse order, beginning where the ritual of birth ends. It begins with the capacity to speak. With this, the human being hears and speaks the human word in the presence of other human beings. Through the first step of the Christian sacramental ritual, the divine Word, the divine revelation, the Gospel, is united with this human word. And so, the first stage of the ritual consists in the Word of God, the Gospel, the mystery of new birth out of death, the Mystery of Golgotha, being proclaimed, heard, experienced, and realized.

This provides the beginning step of the reversal of the ritual of birth, and it continues in the human being led by the Gospel into the sphere of Christ's working in the death realms of the Earth. In the sacramental incense offering, the human being is adapted to the peripheral, to the cosmic-divine, again. This is the mirror image of the next to last stage of the ritual of birth, a reverse offering through which the Godhead frees us from the Earth's embrace.

Through this the possibility unfolds in the third stage of the sacrament for the transformation of the earthly substances of bread and wine into the substance of the divine world itself. This is the reversal of the transformation that happens to the heavenly human on the pre-birth path to the earthly.

In the sacrament the transubstantiation then leads to the communion of the being of the human with the body and the blood of the being of the resurrected Christ. There are manifold disclosures in anthroposophy concerning the nature and meaning of the sacramental ritual. (Some are given in notes I,7–22.)

A third ritual, from anthroposophy, comes to the aid of this earthly Christian sacramental ritual. Rudolf Steiner called it the "cosmic ritual," the "reverse ritual," the "world ritual," or also the "spiritual communion of humanity." (It is presented essentially in GA 219.)

The Christian sacramental ritual arises out of the union of the human being and the Earth with the victory over death through the Mystery of Golgotha. The cosmic-spiritual reverse ritual arises out of anthroposophy, out of the striving to imbue and permeate the world with the Christ Being, in human beings working in harmony with the order of the universe. (See notes II, 2–3.)

This ritual belongs both to the inner spiritual striving of the individual anthroposophist and to the cultivation of anthroposophy together in the branches of the Anthroposophical Society.

If we compare the ritual of the pre-birth descent with the Christian sacramental ritual, we see that already here there is a reversal. The ritual in the sphere of birth occurs from excommunication to the expression of the I. The sacramental ritual, as a permeating of the sphere of death in earthly-material existence with the Christ Being, goes from the Word of God over to the offering and transubstantiation to communion with the Resurrected One through his body and blood. That is, the sacramental ritual goes from the I over the astral and etheric to the physical in the altar communion in bread and wine. The question now is whether what Rudolf Steiner called the reversed, cosmic ritual also consists of the elements of the *I* and the *we* and takes place in the four original processes that are being spoken of in the Christian sacramental ritual.

The ritual of birth has its beginning within the sphere of communion. The human being is united in communion with spiritual beings and emerges out of this communion on the path that leads to the revelation of the "I." This process of birth becomes a ritual for gods and human beings in that the human being unfolds the impulse toward incarnation, and the spiritual beings participate in all the transitions.

Through their birth into the physical body human beings are united with the sense-material world. They live in communion with the earthly world. This communion is a deed of being. It begins to become a ritual, a cultic communion, in all that human beings develop as cognition process, as communion in the consciousness, in addition to this existential communion. With that, the starting point for the reverse ritual is not in the revelation of the divine world to the human being as in the sacrament, but is, as with the birth process, in the communion. And the way in which communion, transformation (transubstantiation), offering, and revelation develop out of this existential communion of the earthly human — so that a reversal of the sacramental ritual can be realized — can become the key for an anthroposophical understanding of this reverse ritual itself.

CHAPTER II

THE REVERSED RITUAL
IN THE SPHERE OF COMMUNION

It is not immediately noticeable in the study and practice of the philosophical writings of Rudolf Steiner given approximately forty years before the lectures on the reverse ritual that already in the philosophic and even more in the Goethean approach, human cognition should have something to do with ritual. One can, however, to a certain extent look back from the end to the beginning, forty years before, and get the impression that in Rudolf Steiner's picking up the thread and carrying on the theory of knowledge presented in the introductions to Goethe's scientific writings, something like a beginning is there for the reverse ritual. This is especially true in the lecture of December 31, 1922, as then precisely this realm of human cognition is pointed out in a double sense as "communion."

There he speaks, to begin with, of how human beings can give something to nature that nature itself does not have: "the active thoughts of human beings." But this is, however, actually the last stage of the cosmic ritual. The first stage consists in the fact that the human being must have these active thoughts, these "independent thoughts." Human beings acquire those in that they can make them their own from spiritual scientific research as thoughts enlivened through Imagination, Inspiration, and Intuition, for then those thoughts become entities "having independent existence in the life of the Earth." The path to such thoughts is presented in Rudolf Steiner's philosophical writings and continues in a wealth of instructions and indications concerning the path of esoteric schooling.

In both the introductions to Goethe's natural scientific writings and in *The Science of Knowing* (GA 2), the working toward these independent thought forms appears to be "the beginning" of the reverse ritual of the human being. Out of the fundamental analysis of modern consciousness in relationship to itself at its four boundaries (the sense boundary of the twelve senses, the soul and memory boundary of our inner being, the boundary of Ego consciousness and the thought boundary of thinking — in all of which the content of our consciousness can initially appear) leads the path to grasping pure or purified experience of the senses, pure experience of the soul, pure experience of the I, and pure thinking.

This purifying of consciousness at its boundaries leads to experiencing pure thinking itself and, indeed, through the transition from intellectual thoughts as corpse and shadow of pre-birth to the re-enlivening of this thinking out of itself because will and love can stream into it. This thinking can be awakened to its own spiritual activity and, through that, be made body-free. The dead, shadow-like intellectual concept is awakened to individual existence. The human being places his or her will and love at its service, and the thought begins, in the sense of Hegel's dialectic, to reveal itself according to its own nature, but then leads far beyond Hegel into the spiritual world.

The thought takes on a life, in the sense of Fichte's morality and Schiller's aesthetics. Lastly, in the sense of Goethean exact fantasy, this living force of thinking fills itself with the force of metamorphosis and brings thereby the thought, with the help of this exact fantasy, to the creative, creating idea in the sense of Goethe and Plato.

Through further enlivening the thinking, that is, developing and penetrating it with the spirit, it can be transformed, in the sense of Rudolf Steiner, to Imagination and lead thereby to an experiencing of the spiritual world.

In this direction toward living, mobile, pure, body-free thinking the human being will come, through various kinds of exercises, to a first communion with the cosmic thoughts of the Hierarchies.

If we take into these thoughts and exercises the results of spiritual scientific research concerning the spiritual world, that is, "thoughts we receive from spiritual research," we will proceed in the direction of Imagination, Inspiration, and Intuition, and right to a real experiencing of such thoughts, especially in the sense of the Goethean metamorphosis efforts, which then finally can lead to the being itself. The idea becomes *entelechy* in the sense of Aristotle or *monad* in the sense of Leibniz. Intuition is the final result, the final stage of this communion. It becomes the revelation of individualities, of persons, in the sense of Schelling and also Novalis.

If we go on to connect these living, mobile, spirit-filled thoughts to the pure experiences, especially of the sense world but also of the inner soul world and the I, then the thoughts can be found as the true reality in the appearances. The ideas become not just the "translator of the gestures of the appearances"; the human being comes to discover the idea in the reality to be the true reality. This communion is thus the first act of the reversed, cosmic ritual. It begins with communion.

From what has just been sketched, it becomes clear that the starting point of this ritual as communion is quite individual. It is the individual I of the anthroposophically striving human being that accomplishes changes at the boundary of thinking and experience, changes that lead to the classic formulation by Rudolf Steiner in the introductions to Goethe's scientific writings: "The perception of the idea in the reality is the true communion of the human being."

What is meant here by communion? In the lecture of December 31, 1922 (GA 219), Rudolf Steiner reminds us of what he said in the introductions to Goethe's scientific writings, namely of the classical formulation just given. It is thus a union with the world of the individual human soul and spirit of the human being striving individually and supported anthroposophically by his or her own schooling and efforts. This stage of the cosmic ritual clearly has an I character.

The words *the perception of the idea in the reality* relate apparently at first to the sense-perceptible reality. It takes place in that partial reality we can perceive with our senses. It is valid to grasp this spiritual communion in connection with the cosmos, with nature, and, finally, with cultural manifestations and the history of humanity. This spiritual communion arises because the human being, with individuality and personal knowing consciousness, fulfills certain basic acts through which he or she unites in self-knowing with the world in order to find the divine behind it.

For instance, we go out into the mountains and observe those regions consisting not of calcite and slate, but of granite and gneiss. We can attempt to unite ourselves with this natural phenomenon through perceptions and observations, and also through empathy and devotion. Then perhaps we can reach the point where the idea of the granite mystery, the granite being, the idea of the being of primal rock, gradually dawns on us, at first in a Goethean manner. Thus we can, in loving observation, perceive what a granite mountain range looks like; how the stone or mineral of these mountains is built up as a solid out of a formerly living being. And then we see how the crystal character of this stone appears to us. We can gradually come to feel how this crystalline rock not only allows the outer light to shine through it, but also is especially permeable to the inner nature of light. This allows the working of etheric and astral forces that come from the cosmos to Earth to stream into this organ of the Earth. The Earth is then permeated by the cosmic forces of the stars, the planets and the fixed stars. When we have gained a certain feeling for this, we can learn to experience through a certain exact-fantasy picture how, for the outer view, the Earth is precisely not just a mass of matter. But much more we experience how this granite matter is permeable to the cosmic influences, the cosmic streams of the extraterrestrial cosmos. We then come to experience how these powerful "mountain-peak giants," as Goethe called them, are a kind of organ for the cooperation of the Earth with the cosmos, so that the Earth is no longer an independent structure, but rather something that is connected with the whole cosmos. The communion experience that arises in this way brings about a special Father feeling in which we can often, when in the course of life we may stand before such nature pictures, get the direct impression: The divine Father-worlds in the Hierarchies were active here in order to build up these wonderful mountains as organs of the Earth. We are reminded of the essay that Goethe wrote about granite in which he expresses a Father experience in his direct, poetic, portentous way. We experience a communion with the Being of the Father God in the world of the granite mountains.

Rudolf Steiner pointed out repeatedly the importance of beginning and practicing this path, from Goethe to anthroposophy, with the outer sense world at first. For in this realm the spiritual communion leads most surely to the development of that selflessness that is existentially necessary for cognition on all higher stages. The results of cognition can ever again be tested and controlled anew on the sense world, and that is the certainty that can lead to "true communion," to exact union with the divine-spiritual in the sense world.

There are also other possibilities to unite oneself with the Earth. We can seek out places where deep ravines are dug into the great masses of sedimentary stone, which exist as canyons on almost every continent. The greatest of these is the Grand Canyon in the western part of North America. There we can look into, and feel into and think into, these layers formed out of land and sea. These layers have the phenomenal ability, because they have gone through weathering processes, to be fertile and to make possible the growth of our earthly creatures and plant world. We have completely different experiences when we look into that than when we look into the granite mountains. We see how the earth is ripped open right to the foundations. In the Grand Canyon, for instance, we can see the totality of the geological layers from the Archaic to, and including, the end of the Mesozoic time. We can actually experience the motherhood of the Earth. We have a sense of a divine Mother Being. Here nature has become something that receives, shelters, nourishes, and carries us. Again we are reminded of Goethe's "Hymn to the Night" in which just this motherly side of nature is presented and expressed in many directions in poetic form.

A further possibility for a communicative meeting with

the Earth being is as follows: We can look at what expresses itself in the Earth organism with certain minerals that have an ore nature and contain the metals: gold ore, copper ore, lead ore, etc. If we try to look into these ore beings, again through exact observation, and follow to where the ores originate, and if we can then determine how they are collected in enormous deposits around the whole Earth or how they permeate the Earth organism in the form of veins, then we can come to something quite different. We can experience how the Earth is permeated by metal elements, which, when one concentrates on them, have a completely different character than the crystals of the mountains or the sedimentary masses of the canyons in the Earth. One gains comprehension of a metal and ore being that the planetary forces have woven into the depths of the Earth. We can come to know that the most manifold forces are present in these metals, and that these forces have conjured something otherworldly into the being of the Earth. We achieve again a communion with a totally different being of nature, with a quite different being of the Earth organism, with its subterranean depths, which Goethe depicted in the form of "Mountanus" in *Wilhelm Meister*.

We can turn to the plant world and attempt to follow in Goethe's footsteps. One sees then how the plant being sprouts and, alternating, undergoes the metamorphosis of its leaf formation, the intensifications and transformations of its whole evolution from germ to the fruit on to seed. And one can learn to experience, to a certain extent, the archetypal plant in the whole occurrence, in order then, with this archetypal plant, to sprout, grow, bloom, and ripen with each individual plant. We experience communion with the plant being. And in living nature one can recognize again the earlier deeds of the gods, which are carried into, placed as mystery into, the whole powerful life world, the plant world of our Earth. Uninterruptedly year after year, they (the earlier deeds of the gods) enliven the being of Earth in the powerful forests and the broad prairies, down to the tiniest plant, lichen, and moss on some stone. One comes in this way to a completely different communion experience. We are reminded of how, for instance, the artist Albert Steffen expressed experiences in a poem about trees in "Wegzehrung":

> Embrace the trees with loving
> And ever grateful mood,
> For in their boughs and branches
> Streams God's own life and blood.
>
> Once Christ, to halt their dying,
> Hung from a cross of wood
> That they might bloom and flourish
> And bear eternal fruit.

It can be a matter of a further communion, a kind of communion with the being of the Son throughout the activity of the plant world. In its streaming life force it becomes an organ of perception, a mediator for the death-conquering life streams of the Christ sphere in the being of the Earth.

Anthroposophy gives us the possibility to come to a communion experience, especially everywhere that it is united with Goetheanism and where this Goetheanism is carried further in the right way. Such a thing can, for instance, also happen, in that we insert such an experience from the plant world into the results of spiritual research; we find indications given by Dr. Steiner in *The Michael Mystery* (GA 26) about why the Earth is a germ or seed in the universe. It is a seed, because an infinite amount of seeds arise in the plant world that never fully form but die as seeds and radiate their seed force into the universe as far as the fixed stars. There they build the elements for the formation of a future cosmos. The being of the plant becomes not only an organ of the Earth, it is not only permeated by the presently working forces of the Son Being, but, much more, it becomes a seed force that bears the germ of a future Earth existence, for the Jupiter stage. One experiences a kind of future communion being. (What is the Earth in reality in the macrocosm? More about that is also in GA 26.)

One thing becomes clear in all these attempts and efforts: This all works when one not only sees with the eye, thinks and conceives with the head, and works further with the imaginations of the fantasy, but when one also tries to bring one's own heart forces into all these processes of "perception of the idea in the reality." This means to set into movement the deepest, most inward I forces of the human being, one's own human nature, in order to immerse oneself with these in the wonders of nature. It is a matter, as it were, of looking through the eyes with the heart, to sense with the heart the fragrance of the world — for instance, what the green forest emits. For without the participation of the heart, the examination of everything remains still somehow outwardly intellectual and superficial. It remains theory. It is not sensed or felt. It does not become totally human experience. We attain to communion first through the movement of the heart to the experiences of thinking, of imagining, and of perceiving. All of this is the first step in the reverse ritual, a ritual that proceeds from the human being. The individual human being participates in this; he or she must attempt to develop all of this. We also see immediately that we can learn in this way to commune with nature step by step. This means to live with, grow with, create with, and also die with this nature — with the spiritual consciousness, with the soul and with the heart, but also with one's own will. That is what the human being can carry into nature and what nature does not have on its own.

Further, something similar is possible when we observe the light in the course of the year. This involves the subtle qualities of what we can perceive directly or indirectly with our eyes. This is not only the glory and fullness of the world of color, for above all it is the fine, subtle metamorphoses that brightness and darkness, light and darkness, go through in the course of the year. The February light looks different from that of summer and different again from that of autumn, the earnest Michaelic Indian Summer we have right now. When we try to accompany these observations with the whole soul, the whole consciousness, we receive a fine sense for what resonates, weaves, and creates in this outer, perceptible light as the inner side, as the finer etheric-astral qualities. We gradually learn to sense the spiritual light in the daylight. Today human beings can actually commune with the course of the year when they bring their Self to meet this active, creative nature in the right way. What actually happens is that the human being becomes devout or reverent on all of these paths.

One must repeatedly think about the fact that precisely Goethe was the human being who not only was, of course, observant and inquisitive in looking at nature, who also not only reproduced it artistically and thereby came to his great nature experiences, but that he was also reverent or devout toward nature. This primally healthy — naïve, one almost wants to say — nature reverence of this human being can gradually be duplicated. The anthroposophical communion, the obtaining of a first step of the reverse ritual as spiritual communion, can allow the human being to become reverent or devout. And this occurs precisely through the fact that the human being begins to penetrate nature with the heart and imbue it with something that he or she has within that nature does not have: heart-warmed, will-enlivened human thoughts.

With such moods, feelings, and attitudes we are reminded of something that we find in the lecture cycle *Metamorphosis of the Soul: Paths of Soul Experience* (GA 58), where Rudolf Steiner speaks on the mission of devotion precisely in relation to the development of the consciousness soul. The love for the divine in the feeling, and the devotion and surrender to the divine in the willing of the human being are what first let this spiritual communing really become a ritual, which is what really matters in the end. (See note III, 2.)

With that it may not be overlooked that it is always a question of two elements: the thought element and the perception element, as feeling element and experience element. And it may not be overlooked that a third element is always there which initially separates the first two. It takes hold of each separately, transforms it, and then finally brings about a merger of the two. Or it makes available the stage or scene of action in the form of the human consciousness and self-consciousness in which they want to unite, according to their own nature, their own connectedness, and their own lawfulness, in the reality of "communion." A full understanding for the esoteric mystery of communion in "perception of the idea in the reality" first becomes possible when both elements of the cognition process — experience, perception, and sense impressions on the one hand and thought, concept, and ideas on the other — go through a transformation, in the sense of a ritual element, before they come into contact with each other.

One can very easily think in an intellectual interpretation, for instance of the theory of knowledge as developed in the first part of *Intuitive Thinking as a Spiritual Path* (GA 4), that cognition means combining a concept with the appropriate perception. Indeed, that produces cognition, but no reality. In order to understand and to experience what "communion" is in cognition, there needs to be a transformation of the idea and of the experience of reality as perception.

Rudolf Steiner describes repeatedly how and through what thoughts, ideas, ideals, and concepts become capable of communion. We only have to point to the lecture cycle *The World of the Senses and the World of the Spirit* (GA 134). The first lecture shows the manner of soul attitude through which perception and thinking are actually so transformed that they become capable of reality. Awe, reverence, conformity, and harmony with the lawfulness of the world, and surrender in the course of the world are the forces for the transformation of thinking. Those are, however, religious forces. Through them thinking first becomes ritualistic.

The equivalent is valid for every kind of perception, experience, and feeling. Among the first references in connection with this, only those in *The Mission of Michael* (GA 194) are selected. It is a question of attention to all the physical-material that appears to the senses, of the "becoming spirit of the flesh" in cognition so that sense perceptions do not remain mere physical perceptions. Rather, through awakening the consciousness for the fading-away part of the sense perceptions, an interweaving of human and world takes place in the realm of will in the human being. The human being then receives the soul element in nature along with the sense perceiving. Thus we gain a Christ relationship with the outer nature (GA 194, lecture of 11/30/19). Freedom from desires and selflessness are the soul prerequisites.

What does all this mean actually?

The thinking that was purified and transformed by the four soul forces given above as the requisite ones in the lecture cycle of GA 134 already has a ritualistic character through those same forces. Human beings do not think; rather they allow the cosmic thought to think in them.

What holds thus for the cosmic thought holds also for the thoughts of other human beings. When another human being expresses his or her thoughts, we can commune, with the help of the four soul forces and soul moods named above, on the thought-sense of these thoughts. This means, in a thinking with them, to really experience with them, to feel with them, and indeed to will with them, and, through this, to perceive the I of the other person expressing these thoughts (interplay of thought-sense and I-sense). We commune with the thinking, speaking I of the fellow human being. A marvelous example of this is the way Rudolf Steiner lets the thinkers of the millennia have their say in his *The Riddles of Philosophy* (GA 18). One experiences a communion with the thoughts and the I of the philosophers, and beyond to the spirit being "Philosophia" and her life rhythms in the four-times-eight-hundred years of the history of philosophy. There is awe-filled reverence, affirmation of the laws of the world, and devotion to the thought deeds of humanity. So then, just as with the thinking of the world and the thinking of our fellow human beings, the perception of the world or of our fellow human beings, as pure experience, take on a ritualistic communion character. For in every kind of perception, will forces flow and weave the rippling cosmic will (GA 134, lecture of 11/28/11) together with the streaming human will (*The Foundations of Human Experience*, GA 293, lecture 8).

It is also true with the following. The pure perception and the impression that develops from it receive a ritualistic character already when the heart forces of devout surrender and the love-filled will flow into the senses. Only when such thinking immerses such perception — when such perception is lifted up into such thinking — does "the perception of the idea in the reality" come into being as the "true communion" of the "reverse ritual."

The whole of the reverse ritual needs the clarification of a concept that has a quite different content in anthroposophy than is usually assigned to it. The reverse ritual in its totality is called the ritual of knowledge. What, however, does knowledge mean here?

In the lecture cycle *From Jesus to Christ* (GA 131), Rudolf Steiner speaks immediately in the first lecture of knowledge as all the spiritual and soul life and experience of the human being, insofar as the human being is, or becomes, conscious of it. In this realm of knowledge he distinguishes five areas: the life of the senses; the life of imagination, thinking, and memory; the aesthetic life; the moral life; and conscience. He says: "In short, what we are first conscious of, the world we live in — whether maya or reality — all that we are conscious of can be encompassed in the term *knowledge-life* in the spiritual" (lecture of 10/5/11; see note II, 5).

To this realm of knowledge-life Rudolf Steiner adds the realm of the unconscious soul life of the human, and finally also the third realm of the unknown behind the perceptible, conscious element of the whole world — but not incapable of being known. It is the mystery of nature.

The whole realm of knowledge-life is religiously assigned to the Spirit, the Spirit God; the realm of the unconscious soul life is assigned to the Son God, and the realm of the foundation of nature in the world and the human being to the Father God. (See note II, 5.)

One thus sees that all conscious human life and experience is knowledge-life and is the realm of the Spirit God.

THE RELIGIOUS-RITUALISTIC ELEMENT IN THE SPHERE OF KNOWLEDGE: HUMAN COGNITION AS OBJECTIVE WORLD PROCESS

When we survey the elements of communion as the first stage of the reverse ritual on the basis of the question of the religious, we find four such elements that pass over into a fifth.

1. The purification of sense perceptions right to the point of an elemental-naïve basic content as guilty-guiltless will process: And what lives subjectively in this side of the cognition process? It is awe. That is, however, already "religious."

2. The purification of thinking right to its spiritual content as pure concept, as pure idea, pure ideal: The thoughts have to be torn away from the intellectualizing caused by Ahriman if they are to serve real cognition. Hegel has already accomplished this (see the lecture "The Eternal in Hegel's Logic" in GA 199; see also note III, 2). But how and when can the soul become devout in relation to the thought life? When it can revere the truth in every form. It is the subjective human demeanor and attitude of reverence and devotion (GA 134; also *How to Know Higher Worlds*, GA 10; see note III, 3), as well as the effort to concentrate the thought life so far that thinking can become the bearer of the imaginations as supersensible pictures. Reverence and veneration are "religious."

3. The manner in which the pure thinking must be set into motion to find its corresponding perception and, vice versa, the way the pure perception must open and allow itself to be permeated by the appropriate thought: This process must be wrested from the Luciferic self-centered striving. Otherwise, illusion, error, dreaming, and fantasy will result. This process can take place only when devoutness changes into

conscious conformity with the lawful necessities that hold sway in cognition and those that work in the world. This refers not only to the laws of nature, but also to moral laws, to the laws of karma and the inherent laws that lead to freedom processes. Only then do the gods, the Hierarchies, hold sway in the power of cognition. And in such a bringing together and permeating of perception with concept, of concept with perception, the concept, the idea, and the ideal open to the lawful creating and working power in every perceived detail. An identifying of the human being who is becoming devout with the thoughts and deeds of the gods leads the I to fit freely into all the world order. The feeling arises of being in wisdom-filled harmony with the laws of the world (GA 134; see note III, 3). Thereby the pure thinking, the correct thinking, becomes permeated with the reality of the world. And then does every human being first become religious and accomplish the ritualistic step from awe in relation to the sense perceptions and veneration in relation to the truth found in thinking to the reality shining forth of the inner identity of perception content and thought content.

4. If, however, this identification is willfully executed — this means hastily and directly brought about by the cognizing human being — then all kinds of prejudices arise in the area of cognition as well as in the form of moral prejudices of every kind. The Luciferic "original sin of humanity" takes place in the form of an *ektroma* (GA 134). The cognizing is not yet ritual. Certainly, the primal foundation of the world lies within thinking, but human beings wanting to know may not do what they Luciferically, arbitrarily want to do. The religious attitude in this process of cognition is, after all, devoutness as patience. That means, however, the thoughtfulness to want to become patiently mature in order to grasp certain truths at all (GA 134; see note III, 3). The transition from thinking to Imagination and from there to Inspiration, as the entrance of the objective world reality into the subjective reality of consciousness, can succeed only in this realm of maturing wisdom that must be patiently awaited and nurtured. Thus the cogniz-

ing consciousness must practice the religious form of patient devoutness. It is only out of the wisdom-filled feeling of being in harmony with the inherent lawfulness of the world that the patient maturing of the cognizing human being can become fully mature judgment. This mature judgment is identical with the inner peace which must hold sway and wait in all striving for knowledge of the higher worlds (*How to Know Higher Worlds*, GA 10; see note III, 3).

5. Such a transforming judgment fitting into such a self-revealing reality through such a transforming immersing of the one in the other and, finally, the cognizing human being putting him- or herself into wisdom-filled harmony with this self-objectifying world process — this creates the last prerequisite for complete human knowledge as religious occurrence. That is the true communion of the cognizing human being with the world and the world with the human being. The foundational processes of cognition in the three preceding elements are permeated with the religious: perception with awe, thinking with reverence, and judgment with harmony with world necessities. This last process allows the cognizing human being to mature in patience and peace and, finally, allows cognition to become ritual through the last stage, which is necessary for the subjective soul attitude. The feeling emerges in all cognition of the perpetually arising temporariness of every such act of cognition, and with it the impulse to an ever new and continued deepening of what has already been accomplished in the cognition process with what has not yet been attained. This also leads to supersensible knowledge, from Imagination and Inspiration to Intuition, through further transformation of the subject seeking knowledge by the appropriate training. However, something of this works also already in the cognition processes that take place within the ordinary consciousness in perception, thinking, and judging.

Through judging, ideas arise as individualized concepts. Judging does not lead into an abstract generality, but always into a totally concrete, particular reality. The judgment is capable of continual deepening. It moves in the direction of a growing truth and a perpetually concretizing reality. That means, however, moving toward accomplishing the whole process of cognition, when the soul conveys its wisdom-filled harmony with the world lawfulness into a soul-spiritual scene of action, in which the world can actually know itself in the human being. Through that, the cognition process becomes fully selfless, and the known reality gains a quite new character. In terms of the sense perceptions, the reality can want to go into the knowledge itself and purify the human perceptive will. In terms of thinking, the world can think itself in the knowledge. The reality can thereby also think with the human being as cognizing being. And finally, in terms of judgment, the world reality builds the judgment on the stage of human consciousness and reveals itself in the judgment. Thereby, cognizing humans, as judges, are included in the world revelation and reveal themselves in their highest being as knowers.

The processes described conceptually here point to the esoteric processes in cognition. With that the question arises about what is necessary as the subjective-religious attitude of the human being in the whole communion process of knowledge. On the path by way of awe, reverence, and wisdom-filled harmony, the soul attitude of devotion and surrender to and with the course of the world arises in the depths: that is, the selflessness in the cognizing human being. In the cycle *The World of the Senses and the World of the Spirit* (GA 134) it is said this way: "Devotion does not work in order to penetrate into these or those truths by force. Rather, it works on itself, on the self-development, and waits quietly, until at a certain stage of maturity, the truth streams in through the revelations proceeding out of the things and permeates us totally." The mood of devotion is to work with patience, which wants to bring us further and further in wise self-development.

The religious stage of devoutness, as devotion or surrender in the course of the world, leads first into the ever further developing knowledge of true reality. The content of the senses only now becomes consciously experienced as what unconsciously constitutes the being of sense perceptions. The sense qualities become a statement that the human being answers, not with an arbitrary judgment but with religiosity.

> In short, we discover that the whole sense world reveals itself to be something that we must call nothing other than will. Insofar as we confront the sense world, all is flowing, wielding will. We are always connected with the world through a will that we sense in everything, that we feel in everything. Thereby we come nearer to reality (GA 134).

From this it becomes clear that from the side of the devout human being, sense perception is gazed revelation, precisely "sense revelation." On the contrary, from the side of the world, from the things, it is overflowing will in the human being — "human beings swim as it were with the things in a common sea of wielding will" (GA 134). Only then is that communion, and indeed communion of the sense world itself through the physical human sense organs, with the unconscious flowing human will in the senses as the one side of this communion.

Why, however, does the world at first become conscious to already awe-filled, devout human beings only as outer sense revelations and only becomes conscious as wielding will to the human beings who have gone through reverence and wisdom-filled harmony and surrender? Because human beings, with their perceiving will, allow only the result of the will of the world, that is, the outer side, to come to them. At first we push away the spirit out of sense revelations through the bodily, physical nature of our sense organization:

> ... we do not then depart from reality when we form concepts of the world and work out of the soul, but rather in that we are born into the physical body, in that we look at the world through the eyes, hear things through the ears, etc. What the senses show us is not the whole of it, is only half of the reality.... Precisely because we are orga-

nized in a certain way, the world is, in a certain connection, semblance or maya, as the Orientals call it. And through our building of ideas about the world, we enclose in the thoughts what we have suppressed because of having gone into the physical body ("The Facts of Evolution of the Human and Humanity," lecture of 9/4/17 in *The Karma of Materialism,* GA 176).

When, through the condition of devotion and surrender, we come to experience the sense perceptions as wielding will, we gain at first just the part of reality that meets us as the world of the senses, with whose outer side we connect ourselves in perceiving. However, what we suppress in perceiving —will— only becomes available to us when we let awe, reverence, harmony, and surrender penetrate sense perception ever anew.

> When we feel this ruling, wielding will in the things confronting us, then our development drives us to a higher stage on its own. Because we have passed through the preliminary stages of feeling in harmony with the world wisdom, reverence and awe to the point of surrender, and devotion, then, through the influence of these conditions within the surrender eventually reached, we learn the possibility of growing together with things with our ether body.... Then we come to the point that when we grow together with the things with our ether body, the things of the world give us the impression that we cannot let them remain as they are in our ideas and concepts, but they change for us in that we enter into a relationship with them (GA 134).

The change in the things lies in the fact that, through experiencing with the things in the etheric, devotion leads us to experience a becoming or fading away in all things; it is a life-mood or death-mood; it is a becoming into the future, a dying away out of the past.

This is something that is a difficult, difficult trial for human beings when they have progressed a little.... in esotericism one calls what one looks upon the world of becoming and fading away. Thus, with the sense world, we look into the world of becoming and passing away, and what is behind it is the ruling, wielding wisdom (GA 134).

In this religious realm of devotion as devoutness permeated by awe, reverence, and patient harmony, cognition enters ever deeper into the human being's grasping of the world. Thereby, discrimination between good and evil becomes possible. The law of nature becomes Providence, becomes moral world order.

"The good is something in the universe that is creative; it means the world of becoming everywhere. And of the evil, the human being feels everywhere that it is outpouring decay" (GA 134). In the wielding wisdom, the cosmic thoughts live in becoming and fading away, in births and deaths, in their deepest being as transformation of the world itself. They live in the rippling, wielding cosmic will as ruling wisdom, and they are precisely what is shoved back in pure sense perception. But then, on the other hand, they are the ideas in pure thinking that create through births and deaths and that can live over into the ether body of the human being from the ether body of the world.

The human soul striving for spiritual knowledge follows, subjectively, in the communion stage of the cosmic ritual, the same path that the Christian sacramental ritual takes. In awe, the mood of a purification of the sense revelation lives. In reverence, we offer ourselves to the experiencing of the pure thought; we offer our consciousness to the life of the idea. In the patient holding back of judgment and in harmony with world necessity on its way to becoming wisdom, the consciousness changes from self-consciousness to cosmic consciousness, and with it the cognizing human being changes. In devotion, human beings eventually let themselves be accepted and included in the objective course of the world. They commune; they achieve communion. Now the soul with its stages of ritualistic devoutness in cognition is yet, on the other hand, only one side, the subjective side, of the cognition process. The objective side is the world that is to be known and that is to reveal itself. And this world also undergoes a ritualistic path in the cognition/knowledge that is a ritual, a communion. This ritualistic path, however, is the reversed way. Human beings are amazed precisely at how the world already communes in the sense perceptions, in the form of wielding world-will, with their own perception-will. That means, however, that the world gives itself, even if only partially, into the senses. Cosmic will melts into human will in perception through the senses in every single concrete experience. That is to say, the world communes in cognition toward the human being — into the human being.

In thoughts, the world transforms itself into human thinking. The cosmic thought meets the human will that is thinking with reverence. The world itself, however, changes itself in the cognizing human being to idea, to a being that is becoming creative. This means that the world, as cosmic thought, transubstantiates in the human being to idea. For the judgment process, the world fulfills an offering. It offers itself to the human being, in order to be able to know itself in the human's wisdom-filled harmony, in that it discloses itself. And finally: In the communion of human beings in the form of their surrender to the course of the world, the world first comes to its revelation in the human; it is a revelation that would not be possible without the human being. And this revelation of the world is devotion in the human being, is communion. It is a matter for the reverse ritual in its first stage, which on the whole is communion, not only of a religious relationship of the subject to the object of cognition, but also of the object to the cognizing subject. Just here is where the mystery of spiritual knowledge lies hidden. Here is knowledge first really ritual. The world "wafts devoutness; He becomes devout" (on the Pink window of the first Goetheanum). Whoever seeks, not models, but examples of how religious knowing proceeds, may look to Goethe and to Novalis. The cognizing human begins with revelation and ends with communion. The world giving itself to be known begins with communion and ends in the human being as revelation. The sequence of the stages of the Christian sacramental ritual works in the same order as the subjective side, the cognizing human being, and in the reverse order from the objective side, the world disclosing itself to cognition. Knowledge becomes ritual; science becomes spiritual science. The mystery of reversal is revealed. This is what Goethe called the "open mystery" and what Novalis called the "magical idealism."

For the I in the physical body's sensing, the world becomes wielding will. For the astral body, it becomes the wielding wisdom of becoming and fading away in the life forces of the ether body. At the same time, the starting point of the four stages of cognition is placed in the freedom of the individuality. For that reason, every individual starts at a different place with the cognition process. Goethe is the phenomenologist. He begins with the sense of awe. Hegel is a thinker. He begins with reverence toward the thought. Fichte is an ethicist. He begins with the judgment, with the harmony with himself; he starts with harmony with the judgment-building I. Novalis, shaken by his destiny, starts with devotion and surrender, with revelation. He is an "apocalyptic."

However, all of them are devout. Their paths of knowledge are of a ritualistic nature. Anthroposophy makes these idealists, as forerunners of the cosmic, reverse ritual, understandable in their deepest efforts for knowledge. Their deepest knowing and thinking becomes devotion, or piety, that wants to immerse itself ultimately in the divine. And since then, they think perpetually into humanity from their after-death existence the question: How and when will the consciousness soul become devout and, thereby, the knowledge truly Goetheanistic, truly apocalyptic?

The peculiar fact that the development of true human self-knowledge, the reality of cosmic knowledge as ritualistic-religious occurrences, and the ritual stages are interwoven with each other in an inner intense manner goes back ultimately to the fact that such knowledge is not mere "knowledge." It is a transubstantiation and communion occurrence in the form of an objective cosmic process that takes place with the human being. In this objective cosmic process, the continuation of the evolution of world development is performed. The world passes over, in the cognizing human being, from its past into its future form. The human being, active and devout, conveys this transition to it. On the other hand, human beings who truly know the reality grasp, in the knowing, their actual world destiny. They fashion their reunion with the gods, whom they have to thank for their origin, but also for their goals and those of the gods themselves. Human beings permeate themselves with the future impulses and future goals of the spiritual world.

In religious-ritualistic cognizing, the human being communes with the world. However, the world also communes with the human being. In such knowledge, human beings move from the revelation of their being, purified in awe and opening itself, on to reverence, which they bring as offering, through their transformation in the laws and necessities of the world, and on to the communion of the patient devotion and offering of their whole being.

The world goes from its communion for the awe as sense appearances, over to its transformation for the reverence from cosmic thought to idea, through its offering into the human being in harmony with the cosmic thought, and on to the revelation of its being for the human being's devotion. The mystery of the opposite sequence in the interrelation of the human being and the world first makes knowledge into communion and communion into reverse ritual.

In most considerations of the theory of knowledge, only the subjective side of knowledge is deliberated on, only what takes place in, through, and for the human being. A real understanding of knowing, as ritual, shows that from the side of the known world also, the whole is not a passive process. In this process, the object is also subject and the cognizing subject is the object of knowledge. For knowledge is not only the experience of reality but also a creating of reality by beings, by human beings and cosmic beings in cooperation.

The view of the closed form of the sacramental ritual can be confusing for an understanding of the open form of the reverse ritual. The image in the sign of the closed form makes the divine-spiritual occurrence, as cosmic reality in the sacrament, an earthly reality. It is earthly ritual.

The reverse ritual cannot be grasped as form; it must be grasped as function, as process, as occurrence in the spiritual. Its form is produced ever anew according to its content at the moment in the respective sphere in which it takes place and for the specific human being performing it. This makes it so difficult to understand.

Knowledge, as ritual, is a whole-human knowledge. Its content is spirit, idea, and being. Its method is art. Its will relationship is religion. The perception of the idea in the reality is a "true communion" then only when it is precisely also religion.

For this reason, human knowledge also has no limits. What appears to be such are, in truth, thresholds that can be crossed through offering and transformation. Seed forces already work in the realm of sense knowledge, and they can be led over into knowledge of the supersensible and subsensible worlds through offering and transformations. This happens, however, already in the study of the results of esoteric research, the supersensible facts of spiritual science. And it is just this understanding for the supersensible in the ordinary consciousness that contains the seed forces that can be led over into supersensible knowledge through offering and transformation, through study and practice of the appropriate methods of self-development. Imagination, Inspiration, and Intuition are ultimately the further unfolding of this knowledge process. The last stage is communion of the being of the human with the spirit being and of the spirit being with the being of the human. In it the human being knows, in that he or she is known. But also here, and precisely here, knowledge is ritual; it is religion.

From this, it is clear that just the occupation with what is esoterically researched and the results of research of the spiritual worlds reported by spiritual researchers needs a religious embedding and permeation if such a study of "spiritual science" is to become real knowledge for the student, if it is to become participation in a reality.

One can study spiritual science with or without religion. Religious attitude determines whether the content of anthroposophy becomes intellectual knowledge or whether it brings about in the student of the spirit that which lifts him or her into the spiritual world. Intellectualism can pull spiritual science down to itself. It can also be refashioned into an idealism that can work itself upward to a spiritual view. The spiritual world is alive in this and works with the ordinary consciousness because it is taken seriously.

Besides the religious elements of awe, reverence, wisdom-filled harmony with the lawfulness of the world, and surrender and devotion to the course of the world, two still more fundamental religious forces play a role in helping the study of anthroposophy to become a cosmic ritual, to become a communion.

One is the earnestness — one can also say "the holy earnestness" — with which anthroposophy can be nurtured. The other element is the devotion toward what perpetually lets the "unknown" become a "known" through such study. The forces of the consciousness soul give the capability for such study. Devotion has the mission of training the thinking in the right manner (see notes III,1–12.). That means, however, to train or educate the consciousness soul. Knowledge without devotion is "loutish."

CHAPTER IV

THE REVERSE RITUAL IN THE SPHERE OF TRANSUBSTANTIATION

Communion experiences, as they were sketched fundamentally and practically in the preceding chapters, bring us, of themselves, to the question, What would be then the following stages, the following actus fundamentalis of the reverse ritual, of the cosmic communion?

The communion experiences lead gradually to a refinement, indeed to a spiritualization of the outer sense perceptions and to an enlivening of thinking. And they lead, in feeling and willing, in loving devotion to the realities of the world on the whole, to a finer spiritualization and sensibilization of the human communing in this manner. Through this becoming sensitive it can be observed that such efforts have a certain retroaction, especially on one's own physical and etheric organizations. The communion in pure thinking, the selfless, loving pure experience and thus the perception of the idea in the reality and the letting of the heart forces stream into the nature beings, works back upon the human organization. The sense perception itself and all that the sense organs carry physically and physiologically, as the sum of the physical, bodily nature, undergo fine changes. Human beings can feel in a sensitive manner the union of their bodily sheaths, their physical and etheric bodies, with the forces and beings of the cosmic world.

In the lecture cycle *The Effects of Esoteric Development* (GA 145), such transformation of the members of the being of the human are presented. Compare the presentations in the lecture of March 22 on the sensitization of the senses, of the physical body, and that of March 23 on the ether body. The descriptions given in this lecture cycle are like a preparation. They lead human beings to notice how forces can arise in their own members, in their sheaths. These forces originate out of spheres from which the human sheaths themselves were ultimately produced. That is the world of the stars (see notes IV,1–3).

With this we come to an understanding of the second stage of the reverse ritual, of the cosmic ritual. It is the transformation, the transubstantiation, which takes place in the physical and etheric of the human being. A beginning experience proceeding from the sense realm leads to this stage. Through the communion experience, human beings come to the ability to perceive finer changes in their physical and etheric condition (also on the path over the senses directed toward the body: sense of taste, sense of life, sense of motion, and sense of balance). Not only are human beings refreshed through nature in their physical constitution to the point of their breath and pulse beat, but, much more, we can notice that something in the physical, bodily nature changes materially. We notice that something there changes and that what is happening there is something that pervades the human physical body from the fixed stars which built up this physical body. The twelvefold nature of the fixed stars (constellations) in the heavens, the twelvefold nature of the human physical body, and the twelvefold nature of the sense organs have the same cosmic origin in the realm of the First Hierarchy in the world of the stars.

Such perception can lead to an experience like what Rudolf Steiner allocated to the individual human being in the lecture of December 31, 1922, on the spiritual, the cosmic communion. The way to the transformation stages of the reverse ritual is described there. I will allow myself to cite from this lecture:

> Concerning these creative thoughts I once said in my book *The Science of Knowing* that such thinking represents the spiritual form of communion for humanity. For as long as human beings give themselves up to their mirror thoughts about external nature, they do nothing but

repeat the past. They live in corpses of the divine. When they enliven their thoughts themselves, then, communing and receiving communion through their own being, they unite themselves with the Divine Spirit that permeates the world and assures its future.

Spiritual knowledge is thus a real communion, the beginning of a cosmic ritual that is suitable for human beings today, who then can grow because they begin to realize how they permeate their physical and etheric organism with their astral and Ego organism, and how, as they quicken the spirit in themselves, they lay it also into the dead and dying matter that surrounds them.

Then human beings will experience that when they look upon their own organism in its *solid* condition, they will feel that it links them to the starry universe, insofar as it is a being at rest. Insofar as the starry universe is a being at rest, maintaining, for example, in the signs of the Zodiac a position at rest in relation to the Earth, human beings are connected in their physical organism with those constellations in space. But by allowing soul and spirit to flow into this 'form structure' in space, they themselves change the world.

Human beings are also penetrated in like manner by their stream of *fluid*. The etheric organism lives in the fluids and juices of the body. It is the etheric organism that causes the blood to circulate and that brings into movement the other fluids and juices in us. Through this etheric organism we are connected with the *deeds* of the stars, with the *movement* of the planets. Just as the resting pictures in the heavens of the fixed stars act upon, or stand in relation to, the solid structure of the human organism, so do the planetary movements of the system to which we belong stand in relation to the fluids in us.

But as the world presents itself to our immediate vision, it is a dead world. Human beings transform it through their own spirit, when they share their spirit with the world, by quickening their thoughts to Imagination,

Inspiration, and Intuition, thus fulfilling the spiritual communion of humanity. We must first become *conscious* of this. This consciousness must become more and more lively and alert. Then more and more we find the way to this spiritual communion. I should like to give you today some words that may serve as a foundation for this consciousness, words that, when allowed to act rightly upon the soul — and this means they must be made to live over and over again in the soul until the soul experiences to the full their moving, living meaning — will then bring something into existence in the human soul that transforms what is dead in the world we are connected with into the living, and quickens the past to life in order that from its death may arise the life of the future. This can happen only when we become aware of our connection with the cosmos in the following manner.

The first formulation I write in this way:

In Earth-activity draws near to me —

(I imagine the earthly matter that I take into myself with that which fashions the solid structure of my organism.)

In Earth-activity draws near to me,
Given to me in substance-image,
The Heavenly Being of the Stars.

For it is a fact that when we look at some structure of the Earth that we take into ourselves as food, we find in it an image of the constellations of the fixed stars. We take it into ourselves. With the substance of the Earth that is contained in Earth activity, we take into ourselves the being of the stars, the being of the heavens. But we must be conscious that we, as human beings, in our will, in our love-permeated will, transform what has become matter back into spirit again. In this manner we perform a real act of *transubstantiation* when we become aware of our own part in the world so that the spiritual thought life is quickened within us.

> In Earth-activity draws near to me,
> Given to me in substance-image,
> The Heavenly Being of the Stars.
> In Willing I see them transformed with Love!

And when we think of what we take into ourselves that permeates the fluid part of our organism, the circulation of the blood and juices, then that, insofar as it originates on Earth, is an image not of the heavens or of the stars, but of the *deeds* of the stars, that is to say, the movements of the planets. And I can become conscious how I spiritualize that, if I stand rightly in the world, through the following formula:

> In watery life stream into me,
> Forming me through with power of substance-force,
> The Heavenly Deeds of the Stars —

That is to say, the deeds of the planetary movements. And now:

> In Feeling I see them transformed with Wisdom!

While I can see how in *will* the being and weaving of the stars change lovingly into the spiritual content of the future, I can also see how in *feeling* a wise change takes place when I receive into myself, in what permeates my fluid organism, an image of heavenly deeds. In this way, we can experience ourselves in willing and in feeling. Surrendering ourselves to the all-wielding power of the universe, of cosmic existence, that is all around us, we can experience what is carried out through us as transubstantiation in the great temple of the cosmos in that we stand within it as one who is celebrating a sacrifice in a purely spiritual way.

What would otherwise be mere abstract knowledge achieves a relationship of will and feeling to the world. The world becomes a Temple; it becomes the House of God. When knowing human beings summon up powers of *will* and *feeling*, they become sacrificing beings. The fundamental relationship of the human being to the world rises from knowledge to *cosmic ritual*. The first beginning of what must come to pass if anthroposophy is to fulfill its mission in the world is that the human being's whole relationship to the world must be recognized to be one of cosmic ritual.

I have wished to say this to you, as it were, as a beginning. (Lecture of 12/31/22, GA 219)

We are talking about a transformation, a transubstantiation, in the physical and etheric and, at the same time, in the willing and feeling of the human being. It is the second stage of the reverse ritual. It proceeds from communion to transubstantiation.

How does the revelation and the description of the cosmic ritual now continue according to Rudolf Steiner? In the preceding presentations the word *offering* appeared repeatedly. The lectures of December 29, 30, and 31, 1922, fell on Friday, Saturday, and Sunday. In the night from Sunday, December 31, 1922, to Monday, January 1, 1923, the Goetheanum burned to the ground. At the end of the lecture of December 31, Rudolf Steiner said, "Next Friday I will speak further about the nature of this ritual in its relation to the knowledge of nature" (GA 219). He was referring to Friday, January 5, 1923.

This refers to the continuation of the presentations on the cosmic ritual given in the lecture cycle *Lebendige Naturerkennen* (GA 220). The lectures were held on Fridays, Saturdays, and Sundays, January 5–7, 12–14, 19–21, and 26–28, 1923 (see notes V, 2–3).

The overview of both of these lecture cycles, which were given to found and to make us conscious of the reversed, cosmic ritual, the anthroposophical ritual, shows clearly the great difference between this ritual and the Christian sacramental ritual.

The Christian sacramental ritual has the form of a closed, firmly disposed rite, even into the word formation. It has the form of a ritual decreed according to wording, gestures, implements, substances, altar, and space. Its elements are revealed out of the spiritual world. The sequence of its actions from word over to offering, transubstantiation, and communion occurs according to divine-cosmic order, and it is, on the whole, in this manner a gift of grace from the spiritual world itself. Its elements are formed down from the spiritual world into the world of Earth, in which the Mystery of Golgotha occurs, repeats, continues, and becomes real in the sphere of death for the cosmos, Earth, and humanity out of the creativity of the God Being, the Father, the Son, and the Spirit, in every concrete celebration of this sacrament. In such an execution, the sacrament forms out of its direct foundation of origin — that is, the resurrected Christ Jesus — anew every time. It creates itself in the full and free participation of the celebrating priest and the community present. It is, as such, a gift of grace that is woven into the spheres of death and in which the forces of resurrection carry the transformation of cosmos, Earth, and human being; it depends completely and totally on the inner attitude of the participating human beings — that means, on their free surrender and devotion.

In principle the reversed, the cosmic, ritual has such a form too. Rudolf Steiner made the observation that the earthly sacramental ritual is an image of the cosmic ritual. The cosmic ritual does not appear at first, however, as a closed form-structure, as wording — with the exception of such mantras as are given in the lectures quoted above. Its motifs and processes reveal themselves as anthroposophy founded on knowledge and, with that, as an execution in the individual and common efforts of human beings, which must be brought about ever anew. This ritual arises therefore as task, as mission. The initiates do not describe its stages in a systematic form in the sense of the sequence of execution of its primal form. The cosmic ritual has an esoteric character in contrast to the exoteric viewed sacrament. And already therein lies a part of the esoteric mission: to grasp the respective stages of this ritual in the corresponding presentation of anthroposophy, and also out of the whole of anthroposophy. In the foregoing, I was permitted to look at both of the first stages, the communion and the transubstantiation, in the light of Rudolf Steiner's indications. Where and how does the specific form of the third stage, the offering or offertory, appear in anthroposophy? How and where does the anthroposophist change from one who is communing and who is loving and transforming the self and the world in willing and feeling with wisdom to one who is offering? We are indeed already offering ones in the spheres of communion and transformation (transubstantiation). Where does the offertory step into the foreground of the ritualistic process in the cosmic ritual? Where does the offering become the leading principle in anthroposophy?

It is connected with its loving care in the human community, together in society.

CHAPTER V

THE REVERSED RITUAL IN THE SPHERE OF THE OFFERTORY

In the sphere of nature and world knowledge and human understanding in the form of communion and in the drawing together of "the heavenly being and deeds of the stars in the earthly activity" of the individuality in the form of transubstantiation in the physical and etheric bodies, the possibility matures in the anthroposophically striving human being of an attitude, a tolerance, a brotherliness, that allows what has been elevated to an inner ritual in communion and transformation to become an essential part of what becomes possible between one person and other human beings. What arises as motif in the three lectures of January 19, 20, and 21, 1923, leads toward an understanding of the question about the stage of the offertory in the reverse ritual (compare the quotation in note V, 3).

Human beings do not want to claim for themselves what they reached through communion, what they perhaps have attained through transubstantiation. And where is the help for that? Where is the help that summons us to become truly offering and selfless, in order to give what we have achieved and experienced? The help is our fellow human beings who stand closest to us — anthroposophically striving human beings. They are those with whom we pursue and nurture anthroposophy.

We can find communion in our relationships to nature. We can experience transubstantiation in the relationships we have to our own bodily nature. The offertory, however, as part of the cosmic ritual, can only come to pass between human being and human being. It cannot be otherwise.

Here now lie the problems, the difficulties, of our whole striving. Rudolf Steiner touched upon them in the letters he wrote to the members of the Anthroposophical Society after the Christmas Foundation Conference in 1923. They contain a kind of compendium of challenges to bring to light everything that arises as difficulties among and between people striving together and that threatens the true spiritual development (see note V, 4). The third stage of the reverse ritual can only take full effect when the human being has the attitude of offering. It becomes effective only when the human being goes from communion through transubstantiation to offertory, or offering. This occurs when we experience what we have received as an offering of the spiritual world and thereby now enkindle and ever again re-enliven and stimulate in ourselves the deep impulse to deal selflessly with what has been entrusted to us.

This thusly developed motif for the offering stage of the reverse ritual is something that plays a decisive role precisely in the Anthroposophical Society. Rudolf Steiner took this motif up again in February 1923 at the delegates meeting in Stuttgart (lectures of February 27 and 28, 1923) and in the lectures with the report of the delegates meeting on March 2, 3, and 4, 1923, in Dornach. One can find these lectures in *Awakening to Community* (GA 257).

The continuation of this motif is found in the contents of the letters mentioned before that Rudolf Steiner wrote to the members of this General Anthroposophical Society and to those members who wished to be active following the Christmas Conference for founding the General Anthroposophical Society in 1923/24. These were written from January 20 to March 23, 1924 (GA 26).

The themes of these lectures and letters have to do with a matter of the difference. The question is whether anthroposophy remains the same regardless of whether it is studied only in personal, individual study and striving, or is nurtured together in the branches of the society. In the latter case, whether existing writings, books, and lectures are studied and discussed together or whether individual people lecture out of their own work, anthroposophy is "born anew" every time.

This happens "when human being speaks to human being, and not through the 'thought' we have taken in" (second letter). "When human beings seek the spiritual together in inner honesty, then they find the way to each other along the paths that lead from soul to soul" (third letter). "Anyone who goes to anthroposophical meetings ought to have the feeling that he or she is finding more than when merely studying anthroposophy alone" (third letter). In a deepened form, the theme of the seventh letter arises where a spiritual view is spoken of that has gone through a spiritual conception of nature, but then, however, leads to an "awakening" in the nurturing of anthroposophy together in the society. "We feel that the common ground of human experience extends beyond the confines of the everyday." That is then enhanced in the ninth letter: "After all, from a certain point of view, anthroposophical truths are the most important things that people can communicate to one another." And then: "If we cultivate such conduct in anthroposophy, anthroposophy becomes the stimulus to human love." Then, the tenth letter says: "We sense, with the cultivating and especially with the presentation of anthroposophy, that what we bear in our soul is infinitely richer than what we can express in thought. And as we become more and more clearly aware of this, our reverence for the life of the spirit is enhanced. And this reverence must be present whenever anthroposophy is being presented."

The whole series of these motifs shows that we have now arrived at the spiritual place where the branch life can become the vessel or chalice for the reverse ritual.

Nowhere in the above presentations is the word "ritual" expressly spoken. "Living-nurturing" is spoken about. But if we combine these letters with the wording and contents of the above-mentioned lectures in Stuttgart and Dornach in February and March 1923, then we see immediately the connection of these contents, especially with the last letters of *The Michael Mystery* ("the awakening," "the human love," "the reverence"). In the lecture of March 3, 1923, in Dornach, the follow-up as it were of the lecture cycles on the spiritual communion and the intellectual Fall, the word "reverse ritual" is finally spoken again.

The offertory motif for the cosmic communion, taken up in the tenth letter to the members in 1924, was already fully disclosed a year earlier in the lectures mentioned from February and March 1923. The comparison of the Christian sacramental ritual with the reverse ritual with regard to the mystery of community building shows how the sacramental ritual prepares the way from heaven to Earth — the heaven of the Ascension is meant — for the cosmic-spiritual beings and forces. And the union or communion receives, as community, a kind of awakening of memories of life in common before birth, experienced in the widest sense as the presence of the community angel.

In contrast to this, the cosmic ritual leads to what Rudolf Steiner called the "awakening on the other human being," and the forces of meeting in this awakening present a lifting of the participants of a gathering in the branch life, cultivated in such a manner, into the spiritual world. This leads as it were from Earth to Heaven and, in this way, allows spiritual beings and spiritual forces to be present in the human community (see note V, 5).

This stage of the offering in the progress of the reversed, anthroposophical cosmic ritual must be looked at from three directions out of the totality of anthroposophy.

The "awakening on other people" is not possible if it does not go through a communion, which is brought about through the living reception of the thoughts of other people. I have already spoken about this. However, a subtle transformation of one's own being also comes about thereby. For I must overcome myself to the point of taking in thoughts of others that appear to me to be one-sided, misleading, false, foolish, absurd, and so on. In order to do that, I must open my soul. I must quiet my resisting ether body. I must order my physical body in correspondence to communion with the thoughts of the other person. This means a subtle transformation. The offering results from this. This offering consists in full recognition of other people as creators of their individual thoughts that are appropriate to them as the bearer of their individual karma. In this karma, however, also lies the relationship of the human being to the spiritual world; this means to the Hierarchies, especially to the Third Hierarchy of the Angels, Archangels, and Archai. The other human being as spiritual being, as bearer of karma, is as such a member of the spiritual world. The feeling for the fact that a karma bearer who is striving for spiritual idealism stands before us — that this person is, as we too are, anthroposophist — brings about a basic religious feeling in the sense of "Michael's thinking." Concerning the question of what Michaelic thinking is, Rudolf Steiner says: "The human being is invisible, truly invisible.... Michaelic thinking brings us to full consciousness of this in every moment of our waking life" (GA 194, lecture of 11/23/19, Dornach).

This spiritual consciousness for other people effects an awakening "on" the other person to the spiritual consciousness that relates to the angels — an awakening "to the spiritual world, a lifting up to the spirit."

This awakening "on" the other person effects secondly an awakening "to" the other person. It spiritualizes what I perceive through my I-sense as the invisible, spiritual fellow human being. I bow in reverence before the hidden Holy of Holies of the other person. The other, as you, as he, as she, becomes a mystery to me. I hear through the word to the other side of what is spoken and hear the speaker him- or herself. And I hear through the speaker right on through to his or her individual karmic connection with the beings of the spiritual world, of the Hierarchies, the Angels, Archangels, and Archai.

Only then does this create, thirdly, a community building that occurs as a lifting up to the angelic worlds and awakens a consciousness that is related to the everyday consciousness in the same way that the latter is related to our dream state: precisely an awakening "on" other people "to" a consciousness of community of anthroposophists, who are striving together, with spiritual beings (see notes V, 6–7).

Thus here is the place where we can speak of the anthroposophical branch as a vessel for the reverse ritual in the full sense of the word. For community building, as awakening on the other person, means precisely the transition from past karma to future karma. In the sense of individual and spiritual strivings for the future form of the cosmos, the earthly human community unites, working up into the spiritual world. It becomes obvious in the motif that runs through all the stages of the presentations of the cosmic, reverse ritual — it cannot be clearly enough envisioned again and again — that the actual ritual in these processes consists in the fact that through the human being something arises, is formed, that can then be given by the human being to nature, and it is something that nature no longer has. It is our independent living thoughts, our completing of the fragmentary character of the cosmos of nature. It is our reuniting of nature and humanity with the divine primal forces that work further only in the human being and the imbuing of these forces with the Christ (lecture of 6/11/22 in Vienna: "Anthroposophy as a Striving Toward the Christianizing of the World," in *The Sun Mystery and the Mystery of Death: Exoteric and Esoteric Christianity*, GA 211).

The awakening on the other person leads to that person's spiritual being: to the true I. It leads also, however, to a finer compassion for the karma of the other human being. But with this, it leads also to the sphere of that Hierarchy that is connected with the I, the folk, and humanity on the Earth and that helps to bear the karma of the individual human being. It is to the Angels, Archangels, and Archai that human beings who awaken on the other person, and therewith offer themselves, rise in the cultivation of anthroposophy together in the branch life. Anthroposophical community-building originates in the sphere of the Third Hierarchy and, with that, in the sphere of the Third Person of the Godhead itself. It is the sphere of the living, experiencing human soul, of the Anthroposophia, in the sphere of the Spirit God, the Holy Spirit. The third stage of the cosmic ritual takes place in the light of the

Holy Spirit. This is the stage of the offertory in the community building of people striving together anthroposophically to the spirit, into the Spirit God.

At this point, we must ask why this offering phase of the reverse ritual occurs only within the anthroposophical movement, in fact precisely within the branches of the Anthroposophical Society. Does not an element of the sectarian lie hidden here, an occurrence from which the non-anthroposophical human beings are excluded?

Here it can only be said that it is in principle absolutely possible for all human beings to seek anthroposophy and to join the Anthroposophical Society. Only they must find the way by themselves. The prerequisite for this is guaranteed in the fully public character of anthroposophy and the Anthroposophical Society. The finding and grasping of anthroposophy is, on the other hand, exactly also the condition for individual and communal cultivating of anthroposophy, and therewith, for the possibility of accomplishing the cosmic communion. And the being of this cosmic communion relates, precisely in its properly understood outcome, to all that pertains to the human and to the cosmic. However, individuals must unite, connect, and join in community with other people in freedom. They will experience that anthroposophy becomes something quite different through cultivating it together with others. It takes on a totally different power and form than when it is worked on or achieved on one's own.

CHAPTER VI

THE REVERSED RITUAL IN THE SPHERE OF REVELATION: OF THE LOGOS

In connection with this motif of the offering in the reverse ritual in the community of striving anthroposophists, we come finally to the question of the last stage of the reverse ritual. A possible guide can lie in how the ten letters to the members (GA 26), spoken of before, are continued by Rudolf Steiner, first in the five essays referring to branch life, which then change over between August 10 and 17, 1924, into essays on the Michael Age and the Michael Mystery, and then on to the Christmas contemplation on the Logos, of which we have already spoken. The further fifteen essays in the spring 1925, until Rudolf Steiner's death, are wide reaching in various directions.

Rudolf Steiner spoke of this fourth phase of the reverse ritual by pointing to the connection between the Michael Mystery and the Christ Mystery. This connection is presented in these essays in such a way that all four stages of the reverse ritual are taken up. In the essay on the "Michael-Christ Experience" it says: "Michael provides the proper orientation in those concerns where human beings approach the world around them in knowledge and action, whereas they will have to find an inner path to Christ." This indicates that the first, the second, and, perhaps to a certain extent, the third stage of the reverse ritual are concerned with the world. These stages have something to do with the world. The third phase already has something to do with the human being. Thus, Michael will give the proper orientation when the concern is the world that surrounds the human being. We must find the path to Christ within us. It is thoroughly understandable that, with the form that the knowledge of nature has taken today, a knowledge of a supersensible world has become necessary and that modern humanity can experience this through the leadership of Michael. But this nature has to be experienced as a remnant of a great past and as having the gods no longer present within it.

Through such a relationship to the world, human beings no longer experience themselves within it. We experience the world instead communicatively, as we let something flow from ourselves into this nature that it no longer has on its own — that is, the directly effective and present divine. With the human inner being, however, it is so that the cause is given not to let into its own inner being a way of knowing and living that is built up, as it is today, on outer nature. Then first come the ardent questions about the bonds of the anthroposophically striving human being with Christ. This means, however, it is the question concerning the spiritual effectiveness of the Christ Being himself. Then, out of the living together of the human beings and the Christ Being, there flows into the human souls what these souls should know about their own most inward, either Christ-less or Christ-connected I-being. Only then do we arrive at the Word, the Logos: thus the fourth stage of this reversed, cosmic communion. We can explore Dr. Steiner's lecture cycles again and again, anticipating the question of how he describes concretely what is intimated in *The Michael Mystery* in the sentence, "We must find the path to Christ within." What does Rudolf Steiner say concretely about this path, about how human souls can attain to the fourth phase of the cosmic ritual? They come, with their I, into a concrete, personal connection with the Christ Being, the Christ impulse, the Christ-I. And then they first gain the possibility to give to the cosmos what it no longer has — its future — and to awaken the seed impulse for this future in the "Christed" inner being of the human.

Various indications about this path of the soul to the Christ are given in a whole series of lectures and cycles. Out of these I am selecting a place (*Building Stones for an Understanding of the Mystery of Golgotha*, GA 175) where Rudolf Steiner speaks of Aristotle in a way that makes it clear that here we have to do with the pure, lonely, isolated human I itself and its experiences with itself and with the Christ Being. How does this appear tangibly in Rudolf Steiner's description? It is indicated briefly in the following. (See notes VI,1–16.)

This lecture relates how the human-I can go through experiences that essentially have a connection to the experience of loneliness and that can, in quite specific stages, lead to a relationship with Christ. This is the lecture of April 24, 1917. The first part of the lecture picks up the thread, in detail, of the most varied efforts and developments of Christianity, beginning from earliest Christianity. It also picks up on pagan cults that are connected with the whole cultic life that proceeded out of the old Mysteries.

It is shown how, for example, elements of the Mithras Mysteries and the Eleusinian Mysteries are contained in the Catholic Mass. And it is shown how this has led to the impossibility of understanding this ritual, unless it can be renewed from within, as took place in the founding of the Christian Community. The last part of the lecture, as already mentioned, describes a very specific path of the human I to the Christ Being. It becomes directly apparent from these descriptions that just through this Christ relationship of the human I, just from human beings who have Christ united with their I, something still quite different can stream out into the world than would be the case if this Christ experience did not occur. Rudolf Steiner also spoke in detail in *The Michael Mystery* about what it means to the world that human beings go through the phases of communion, transubstantiation, and offering with the Logos Mystery, with the connection of the human I with the Christ I. These human beings can radiate something to other people that would otherwise not be possible. What the human being carries out in this way as ritual, which can absolutely only be carried out by the individual alone, is shown in this description, especially in its last stage. Through both, it becomes possible that the human being can work out, let stream out, into the cosmos and into humanity to other individual human beings forces that are connected wholly with the future development of humanity, Earth, and cosmos. The Christed cosmic future, the new in which world evolution goes further from within, streams out from the human being into the dying outer cosmos, whereas nature in its whole glory of the past is consecrated to death and destruction in Earth existence. And what is the actual guarantor of this whole process? It is the deepest event inherent in all four acts of the reverse ritual. It is plainly and simply the quite personal Christ relationship of the human I; it is the consciousness soul. It is sought out of the ardent desire to place Christ in the midst, or it is sought out of a deep need for knowledge of all that is called Christology. It is grasped in freedom as insight; it is realized in love. It is then no longer the worlds or the beings, but rather "the Being, the source of creating love," that communes with the human being. It is a Pauline "Philosophy of Freedom." It is not simply "knowledge," but rather "festival of knowledge" (*Autobiography*, GA 28). And Paul says of this: "Now I know only piecemeal; then, however, I shall know even as I am known" (1 Corinthians 13:12). "So it is not I who live, but Christ lives in me" (Galatians 2:20). "Stand firm in the freedom into which the Christ has freed us" (Galatians 5:1). It is the most intimate divine-human happening.

The motif of the "need for the Christ," with which Rudolf Steiner (January 5, 1923) takes up the description of the reverse ritual from December 31, 1922, can draw our attention to a characteristic feature from which most of the descriptions of the Christ experience proceed. It is the inner situations of the I that can be characterized as loneliness, helplessness, weakness, need, consciousness of guilt, self-knowledge, and shock. The sphere of revelation in the reverse ritual has an apocalyptic character. It has the character of an apocalypse in the I.

Rudolf Steiner characterizes the causes within the soul — indeed the conditions — for such shaking circumstances quite concretely in the relevant descriptions. One can study the presentations in the Notes, especially notes VI,10 and 11.

CHAPTER VII

THE TOTALITY OF
THE REVERSED RITUAL

If we summarize everything that makes this reverse ritual understandable and executable from within, at least in an initial and anticipatory way, we see that it is actually an ideal. Rudolf Steiner set up an ideal in this cosmic ritual, a really true ideal, which each of us in our own way with our weak or stronger forces can try to strive for. We can try to touch it, can try ever anew, and to reach it in a beginning way. We see, however, that it works only when human beings are willing to have an exchange among themselves concerning these connections. This inner process is also expressed in a verse from Rudolf Steiner in Truth-Wrought Words (GA 40):

> To grasp the cosmic thoughts within:
> Wrests the soul from body
> And frees in it the spirit.
> The soul-will on cosmic-thought
> To enkindle, and in willing
> Turn back to the world,
> What it may give to thinking:
> Frees in love-creator-power
> The human being through the worlds,
> The worlds through the human being.

Rudolf Steiner's essay on "The Activity of Michael and the Future of Mankind" (GA 26) states this as follows:

> Nature is this divinely accomplished work of God; nature everywhere around us is an image of the divine working.
>   In this world of Sunlike divine glory, but no longer livingly divine, the human beings dwell. Yet as a result of Michael's working upon them, human beings have main-

tained their connection with the essential being of the divine and spiritual. They live as beings permeated by God in a world that is no longer permeated by God.

Into this world that has become empty of God, human beings will carry what is in them, what their being has become in this present age.

Humanity will evolve into a new world evolution. The divine and spiritual from which we originate can become the cosmically expanding human being, radiating with a new light through the cosmos which now exists only as an image of the divine and spiritual.

The divine being that will thus shine forth through humanity will no longer be the same divine being that once was in the cosmos. In its passage through humanity the divine-spiritual will come to a realization of being that it could not manifest before.

We can ask what this divine-spiritual is that takes on a new form when it penetrates and passes through the human being. The answer can be found by looking at the Christ Being that carries out this passage and permeation. It is the absolutely new cosmic love. The true cosmic capacity for love is no longer only a human capacity, but rather a Christ-permeated human capacity; it is the Christ-love capacity itself. And a brilliant light lives in this Christ capacity for love. This light can effect a radical ability to understand the world, the human being, our fellow human beings, and world evolution. A warmth force lives in it; it is a force that not only can have compassion for another being, but also can learn to feel the other being as one's own self. That is then the second thing. The third is that thereby an act of will arises, an act of will borne by love, just as it is expressed in the cosmic communion. This will-deed borne by love enables the human being not only to love other people but also to affirm them so that just through this affirmation the true being of the other, "the awakening on the other human being," can be experienced. That is the new thing that the anthroposophically striving human being can develop in the future. It is what was not yet present among the ancient gods, or rather was hidden behind their working as world creators.

Thus we have before us three primal phenomenal-ritualistic processes in their four-part nature. The first is the Mystery of Birth: an excommunion of the human being coming to Earth; a kind of transubstantiation, a transformation in becoming related with earthly materiality; a kind of offering in becoming clothed with earthly substance; and, finally, a revelation of the inner being of the human through the human word of the I. This process goes thus from communion through transubstantiation and offering to the Mystery of the Logos.

The reverse of that is the Christian sacramental ritual. This goes from the Gospel revelation, through the incense offertory, through the transubstantiation of bread and wine into the body and blood of Christ, on to communion with this Christ Being. This ritual is first and foremost a grace, a gift, and then only thereby a task, a responsibility. It flows ever new directly out of the continued working of the Mystery of Golgotha — from the Christ.

The opposite of that is the anthroposophical, the cosmic, the reverse ritual, which the individual striving person and the community of anthroposophists striving together can carry out. It is realized by starting from communion and going through transformation and offering to the primal Word: "Community among us, Christ in us" in the "Mystery of Death" (GA 159, lecture of 6/15/15).

This ritual is a task, an ideal, that stands before us, which anthroposophy has erected and continues to erect before us. Thus, this ritual also becomes a gift. With this, an element is given whose true realization means the achievement of humanity necessary for the continuation and progress of the evolution of humankind and Earth. This element, on which further progress depends, must necessarily be developed in addition to the Christian sacramental ritual.

We will go into the spiritual origin of the reverse ritual toward the end of this book. Here let it be pointed out that the four members of this ritual are intimately related to one another and mutually permeate one another. We can see how in each member all four join in. On the other hand, the element of personal freedom also lives in the whole of the ritual. Every person realizing this ritual can start directly with any of the four members or turn especially to any one of them. The element of freedom lives in a totally different manner in this cosmic ritual than it does, for example, in the sacramental ritual formed in ceremonial acts. (In notes VII,1–8, the motifs for the religious element in the reverse ritual are given, which also relate to the whole of the reverse ritual.)

CHAPTER VIII

THE COSMIC RITUAL:
THE HIERARCHIES IN THE SPHERE
OF HUMAN LIFE AFTER DEATH

The synopsis of the above-mentioned three ritual forms gives rise to the question of whether we have exhausted all the ritual forms or whether there are, out of the whole of anthroposophy, further forms of ritual.

The view of the reversal of the ritual of birth into the ritual of death and resurrection in the Christian sacramental ritual (a renewed form of which was made possible through Rudolf Steiner's mediation) brings us to ask how it is with the processes in the human being and the cosmos in the life after death — also in relation to the reverse ritual.

Anthroposophy answers this question to the effect that it is, here also, a matter of a ritual event that takes place in the spiritual world. Earthly humanity can participate in this in ritualistic form. This is related in a germinal manner in the lecture of July 4, 1924, in Dornach (GA 237, lecture 2). In this lecture, three mantric formulas are given, the first of which is called "a good, a beautiful, a glorious prayer." In these three prayers we find processes that take place in the supersensible world in connection with the dead. It is clear, however, that it is essentially a matter of the activity of the Hierarchies in this ritual after death. It is the stage of "conceiving" in the Third Hierarchy in ether weaving, the stage of "decaying" in the Second Hierarchy in the astral sensing of the cosmos, and that of a "resurrecting" in deed working in the First Hierarchy (See notes VIII,2–4).

We can easily recognize the stage of offering in the "conceiving," of a transformation, a transubstantiation, in the "decaying," and a communion in the "resurrecting." What however is offered, transformed, and communed through these three stages is the substance of the karma of the dead human beings. The gods are the religion of the human being. After death we have, in living together with them, a religious relationship to the Hierarchies. The substance of karma, on which the gods work and create, is the ritualistic object of the gods themselves. The "human being" is the religion of the gods (see note I,1).

Now this karma, this fabric of compensation effects and compensation forces, has a bearer, a producer, a recipient. That is the eternal I of the individual human being. And the revealing of this I, this eternal individuality, occurs already in the events of dying, of death itself. The after-death form of the disincarnate is the individual being of the human with its thought sheathing (its ether body), its feeling sphere (its astral body), and its will kernel of its I-being. It is the essence of the person, the very self. In various lectures Rudolf Steiner calls attention to the fact that there is actually a kind of unveiling, a kind of revelation, of the nature of that which is the feeling being — but, above all, of that which is the willing being — in the earthly human. In the description of the death processes given in the Vienna lectures on the inner being of the human after death, this self-revelation, this revelation of being, is described in the form of a soul-spiritual shining will-star (*The Inner Nature of Man*, GA 153; lectures of 4/6–4/14/14). These processes have to do with the first stage of the after-death cosmic ritual: the revelation of the dead human being as Word.

The cultic character of this first after-death stage of existence of the dead human being becomes clear through the fact that the dead experience this phase in living together with those spiritual beings that Rudolf Steiner calls the "primal teachers" of humanity. With them the first seeds of karma are planted in the form of an essential intention of the dead: to make possible the karmic compensation in a comprehensive sense through one's own individuality (GA 239, lecture of 6/7/24). If we compare the sequence of stages in the reverse ritual of the anthroposophically striving human on Earth, which goes from communion on to the permeation

of the I by the Christ, with the ritual of the after-death existence in the spirit world in the ritual of the Hierarchies that
goes from the revelation of the being of the I in death on to
communion in the First Hierarchy, we see that this ritual
after death is a kind of reversal in the spiritual world of the
ritual occurrence on Earth, a reversal of the reversed, cosmic
ritual (see notes VIII,1–4).

On the other side, this ritual of the life after death represents the reversal of the ritual of the life before birth. We
described this ritual at the beginning of this book (see notes
I,1–4).

CHAPTER IX

THE RITUAL OF THE GODS
UPON THE SLEEPING HUMAN BEING

The re-shaping and transformation of karma does not begin first in the life after death. There is an event in every twenty-four-hour period that corresponds to this ritual after death. It is a ritualistic event that does not take place first for the dead in the spiritual world, but rather happens already for human beings living on the Earth. This occurs in the condition of sleep. Every night in sleep, human beings are in the realm of the Hierarchies in the spiritual world with their I and astral body, which are outside of the physical body and ether body. In this condition every night the karmic events of the day are taken up by the Hierarchies in reversed order as past, present, and future karma and are prepared for the time after death. The ritual of after-death in the spiritual world sprouts in a ritual of the sleep condition every night. The initiate can see this. A description of what is seen there will not be gone into here. It can be found in the lecture given by Rudolf Steiner in Dornach on June 27, 1924 (GA 236; see notes IX,1–2).

In the view of this description, a magnificent imagination emerges in the realm of cosmic ritualistic events in the periphery of the Earth at night. The meaning of this process is pointed out also in the lecture of September 5, 1924 (*Karmic Relationships*, Vol. IV, GA 238).

With this picture of the administration of the sleep condition of the earthly human, a fifth ritualistic form is added to the four great ritualistic forms already discussed: the ritual within the sleeping human being every night.

The ritual of birth, with its pre-birth stages from excommunion to I-Word of the earthly human child, mirrors the ritual of death and the after-death events from I-revelation in death on to communion in the first Hierarchy. The ritual of the sleep condition is like a mediation between these two opposite processes. All of these cultic events originate from the great cosmic process of karma formation, of karma administration, of the central karmic law of compensation. In them there occurs the most comprehensive cooperation between the human being and the gods, between the gods and the human being.

CHAPTER X

THE PRE-CHRISTIAN CULTS
AND THE CHRIST IMPULSE

Here is a glimpse of the profusion of earthly ritual-forms of the pre-Christian cultures, whose more or less decadent offshoots reach into various regions of the Earth right to this very time. In connection with the description of the ritual for the sleeping human being in the above-named lectures (GA 236), Rudolf Steiner depicts a primal example of the origin of all these earthly cults. They are — in word, action, picture, and ceremony — earthly reproductions of what truly and really took place in the Mysteries as initiation processes in the spiritual worlds. The initiations of the old Mysteries are the reality. These were then presented in the ancient cultures for the people in such a way that the real processes arising between the gods and human beings in the initiations could be brought to humankind in general. Rudolf Steiner says that all of these cults contain both time-related and regional one-sidedness that were decisive respectively for the various Mystery centers and the cultures that proceeded from them.

As different as the pre-Christian earthly cults were from one another, they still all had the four stages of revelation, offering, transformation, and communion as earthly pictures of the initiation, more or less clearly, as a basis in their form (see note X,1–3).

These pre-Christian cults had the far-reaching possibility to contain, both in the initiation and in the earthly image, something of what the highest initiates experienced of the Christ Being proceeding out of the Sun in the ages before the Mystery of Golgotha and working into the guidance of humanity. Thus, they could, in a figurative sense, all be Christianized in different forms.

The Mystery of Golgotha brings together the realities of the one-sided pre-Christian initiations in the form of a divine-human earthly deed in the realm of the sphere of death. That did not exist in the pre-Christian initiations. The first result of this deed was the instituting of the Christian sacramental ritual through the Christ Being himself, beginning with his whole life-deed and continuing in the performance of the Last Supper and the further development of these processes through death, entombment, and resurrection, into the existing pre-Christian cults as the Christ impulse proceeding out of the Mystery of Golgotha. We can speak of the institution of the Christian sacramental ritual by the Christ Being himself in passing it on to human beings. The one-sided metamorphoses of this ritual appear then in that the impulse of the Mystery of Golgotha flowed into the already-existing pre-Christian ritual forms, which in turn have transformed and have gone over into the various Christian Mass forms during the history of Christianity.

In the beginning of the twentieth century (September 1922), through the renewal of the Mysteries, this cultic stream was given to humanity through the mediation of the initiate Rudolf Steiner in connection with the founding of the new Mysteries of the I through anthroposophy. A further result of the Mystery of Golgotha is, however, that the impulses and forces proceeding from it flow into the three karma-forming rituals of the Hierarchies spoken of above: those before birth, after death, and during the sleep condition of the earthly human. For the Mystery of Golgotha itself is the most central ritual in all of Earth existence. It is the working and coworking of the Son God into and out of the sphere of the Father and the Spirit. All of the Hierarchies participate therein.

Even so, it is also true of the reversed, the cosmic, ritual that this ritual of knowledge of anthroposophy in its four stages of communion through transformation and offering to the revelation of the Christ-permeated I can be Christed — is Christed. It is also the case here that in both the I and the community, the effective working of the Mystery of Golgotha continues in a totally new way.

This reverse ritual is not, as the Christian sacramental ritual is, renewed through the new Mysteries. Much more, it proceeded completely out of the new Mysteries of Anthroposophy, the Mysteries of the I. Therefore, it was not possible at all before the twentieth century.

However, before the twentieth century, the renewal of the Christian sacramental ritual was also not possible in the way that it could be realized in the founding of the "Movement for Religious Renewal." Only through the further development of the Michael movement and the Michael Mysteries since the end of the nineteenth century, and through the further development of the Christ impulse in the sense of his coming again in the etheric since the beginning of the twentieth century did the founding of the reverse ritual of the cosmic communion of humanity and also the renewal of the Christian sacramental ritual out of the spiritual world become possible. And only then did it become necessary for the evolution of humanity and the world. Both are intimately connected with world progress through the Christ impulse.

CHAPTER XI

THE COSMIC ORIGIN OF
THE REVERSED RITUAL

The spiritual-phenomenological comparison of the reverse ritual in its totality with the Christian sacramental ritual becomes apparent first of all in the reversal of the sequence of the ritualistic events. The sacrament flows from revelation to communion in a closed, self-contained form. The reverse ritual moves from communion over transformation and offering to revelation. Its form is open; the individual and the community can start from any of the stages or can cultivate any one stage in particular while maintaining its connection with the whole.

Over and above that, the starting point of each ritual is different. The sacrament proceeds out of the sphere of the Son, of the Mystery of Golgotha, from the proclamation of the Gospel. The reverse ritual, in every case, proceeds out of the sphere of the human being. What the human being has become in the age of the consciousness soul, of natural science, of the technological environment of machines, and of personal freedom — this closed earthly personality with a consciousness completely cut off from the spiritual world, this human being, becomes the starting point for the reverse ritual. This starting point is in the field of the life of knowledge (see note II,5).

But on the other hand, the reverse ritual is not possible without anthroposophy. The study of anthroposophy, the meditations as exercises for the individual and the cultivating of anthroposophy in community are: "... a path of knowledge, to guide the spiritual in the human being to the spiritual in the universe. It arises in the human being as a need of the heart and of the life of feeling" (GA 26, First Leading Thought).

With this, the question concerning the source of the reverse ritual opens before us. It unfolds only out of and with anthroposophy. But where does anthroposophy itself have its source?

Anthroposophy can offer an answer here too. It traces its own source back to events that are connected with the evolution of humanity both on Earth and in the spiritual world. These events took place through the centuries as a result of the Mystery of Golgotha, especially in connection with the destinies of the Sun Forces of the cosmic intelligence and its administrator, the Archangel Michael, in the progressing work of the Christ Being himself.

It is a matter of comprehensive events in the spiritual world and their results for the Earth, events with which specific streams of humanity are connected. Other events preceded the main occurrence, and others followed. In this realm the origin of the reverse ritual and, thereby of anthroposophy, can be found. It took place under the leadership of the Archangel Michael and with the participation of groups of human souls preparing for a future incarnation at the end of the nineteenth century and in the course of the twentieth century. It occurred in preparation of the beginning of the guidance of progressing humanity in 1879 through Michael himself, and spiritual beings participated who do not incarnate on Earth. There arose thus in the spiritual world a movement that Rudolf Steiner called in a lecture for youth the "Michael movement" (*The Constitution of the General Anthroposophical Society and the Free High School for Spiritual Science*, GA 260a, lecture of 6/9/24).

The description of the processes in the spiritual world that led to the Michael movement refers to several events. The first was the experience of the Christ event in the Mystery of Golgotha by the Michael community from the spiritual world. That gave the human souls within the Michael movement a first orientation for future incarnations.

The second was a gathering of human groups and spiritual beings in a kind of "supersensible school" at the beginning of the fifteenth century A.D. (GA 237, lectures of 7/24/24 and 8/1/24). The essential teaching content of this school was the protest of Michael against the powerlessness of human intelligence to raise itself to the divine through its own individual thinking activity. Michael gave the instruction that this human intelligence, which has become individual and at the disposal of the solitary I, can be made capable of rising to spiritual life in pure intelligence without illusion (GA 237).

The third event happened at the turn of the eighteenth to the nineteenth century. There were assemblies of souls who asked themselves: Why are we Christian? They drew the consequences of this Christianity in past Earth lives and condensed them to a common cosmic imagination, to pictures of a future existence that then should be sought during the next Earth existence (GA 237, lecture of 7/6/24). The deed of this imagination was a cosmic ritual in which the Sun Mystery of the Christ Being was celebrated in powerful pictures of a cosmic nature (GA 237, lecture of 7/8/24). One must, of course, accept that something from these spiritual events could also be taken up in earthly existence, indeed through something like the inspiration that Goethe received for his "Fairy Tale of the Green Snake and the Beautiful Lily." A reflection of this cosmic ritual can also be found in Schiller's *Letters on Aesthetic Education*.

In these three events lies the cosmic source of anthroposophy and, with it, of the reverse ritual for the anthroposophically striving human being (GA 237; see above).

The fourth event that belongs to the whole is the assumption of the Archangel Michael of the leadership of humanity, which began in 1879 and will last several centuries, and with it the possibility of the realization of anthroposophy and the reversed, cosmic ritual in Earth existence (see note XI, 5).

In all of these occurrences the origin of the reverse ritual can be seen. It can also be said that the renewal of the Christian sacramental ritual at the beginning of the twentieth century has the same source — though, indeed, not the founding, as that happened through the Christ Being.

The attempt at a synopsis of all that can be called ritual out of the whole of anthroposophy yields a peculiar picture. First, it is the totality of the variously formed ritual structures of the pre-Christian guidance of humanity in the Mystery centers and out of the Mysteries. Their differences were built up out of the progressing stages of humanity's evolution, as well as out of the regional impulses of the spiritual leadership of the respective peoples and cultures of pre-Christian times.

Then there is the ritualistic event that is connected with the fact of the reincarnation of the human being and karma formation. This means it has to do with the existence before birth and birth, with waking and sleeping on Earth, and with death and the existence after death. Two basic elements work in both of these powerful processes of birth and death. The foundational achievements of the whole of the Earth existence, the force of love and the force of freedom, are brought into connection with the processes of both birth and death in the lecture cycle *The Bridge Between the Spiritual World and the Physical World* (GA 202, lecture 7). This is just briefly indicated here.

From there we come to the two ritual events in the realm of earthly human existence, the Christian sacramental ritual and the anthroposophical, Christian-Michaelic ritual of knowledge, and to the attempt to look at the totality of this anthroposophical knowledge-ritual out of the presentations of Rudolf Steiner. To understand this ritual in its stages and to achieve, if ever so germinally, its realization, as well as to attempt to lift this ritual into total connection with other great ritual forms of the world, can be a contribution of knowledge to the mutual understanding among anthroposophically striving human beings.

CHAPTER XII

THE ORIGIN AND NATURE OF THE RELIGIOUS OF RELIGION

A spiritual life of human beings develops fully first when the whole human being is included in this spiritual life. It unfolds in three directions, which determine the fundamental activities of human beings out of their spiritual nature. The life of knowledge in everyday life on to the highest heights of every kind of science — also spiritual science — is the first branch of this tree of life. It stands under the ideal of truth.

The second branch is the artistic creating, experiencing, and appreciating of the simplest earthly activities in the household, handwork, technology, the art of cooking, the art of healing, in social life and conversation, and on to the highest heights of meaningful human artistic work in architecture, sculpture, painting, music, poetry, writing, and eurythmy. The spiritual life of the artistic moves under the ideal of beauty.

The third branch is the religious life. It is the ritualistic element. Its life is the connection of the human being to the beings of the higher worlds, the spiritual beings, and of the spiritual beings to the human being. The spiritual beings working in nature belong to it, as well as those working in and with human beings. The simplest daily routine no less than the highest social processes among people, and also what happens in the human beings themselves, can take on a religious, that is, ritualistic, character. They all stand under the religious-moral ideal of the good.

Anthroposophy is in the position to characterize the demeanor of the human being, the moods, the ways of thinking, and the whole attitudinal condition of the human being, in the religious-moral- ritualistic realm. It speaks of devotion ("The Mission of Devotion," in GA 58). It speaks of reverence (*How to Know Higher Worlds*, GA 10, chapter 5). Anthro-

posophy speaks of piety (content of the spiritual declaration of
the pink window in the north of the first Goetheanum in Dornach (*Designs for the Glass Windows of the Goetheanum*,
content of the pink window: "The World Wafts Piety"; "Piety
Works"; "Thus, He Becomes Pious"; in addition, Table 29). It
speaks of awe, reverence, harmony with the lawfulness of the
world, and surrender to the course of the world (*The World of
the Senses and the World of the Spirit*, GA 134, lectures of
12/27–28/11). It speaks of gratitude, love, and freedom (*The
Bridge Between the Spiritual in the World and the Physical in
the Human Being*, GA 202, lectures of 12/11/20 and
12/19/20).

Yet anthroposophy also speaks of how science and art,
through such demeanor of the whole human being, can take
on a religious and with it, precisely, a ritualistic character. We
have discussed this earlier in the book.

And it can also speak of where the religious element originates in the earthly human being.

We have also discussed the ritual that takes place through
the Hierarchies in and with the sleeping person during the
night. In the lecture cycle *Man's Being, His Destiny and World
Evolution* (GA 226, lecture of 5/18/23), Rudolf Steiner
describes what we experience in the first phase of sleep.

> We live in the general world ether. However, connected
> with this is the fact that, as souls, we feel ourselves to be,
> to a certain extent, without the ground under our feet.
> With this experience, a strong desire appears to be sup-
> ported by the divine…. And through our whole human
> constitution we bring this need for the divine with us into
> the waking condition. We have the sleep experience to
> thank anew every day for refreshing our religious needs.

The comprehensive founding of all the religious element out of
the whole of anthroposophy is found finally in the lecture
cycle that Rudolf Steiner gave in September 1922 in Dornach:
Philosophy, Cosmology and Religion (GA 215). Out of the

earthly and cosmic totality of the life of the ether body, all knowledge establishes itself as philosophy. Out of the totality of all the astral, cosmology develops. The root, the life, and the realization of all the religious element is the true life of the human I in living together with other human beings, with the Hierarchies, with the divine Trinity and in wrestling with the adversarial powers over the true evolution of the cosmos, Earth, and human being (see note XII.).

A powerful, full cosmic-ritualistic breath draws through the whole of human existence and the whole cosmos and makes us into what we truly are: beings in the universe and on Earth who, connected with and permeated by Christ, participate in connection with the Hierarchies in a taking and giving manner in the evolution of the world.

So a look at the cosmic events of the rituals before birth and after death, as well as at the cosmic ritual of the Hierarchies on the sleeping part of human beings around the Earth, belongs in an essential manner to a consideration of the reverse ritual. It is the karma-thought, the knowledge of karma, the cosmic event of karma formation. They appear in their religious components, because it is a matter of the working together of the gods, of the three Hierarchies, with the human being, whose life has a religious character.

The religious element is effective in the reverse ritual, especially in its third stage, the offering stage. Here human beings can, in awakening on the other person and in rising to community with the Hierarchies, have an experience of karma through which they can become devout. In the experiences in the reverse ritual, the reality of the creative time outside the body and, through it, also that of pre-birth and after-death enter all content of knowledge as basic religious feeling. For this reason, the view of the "karmic-ritualistic pictures" named above must be included with the examination of the reverse ritual (GA 236).

So how does the life of knowledge become religious in that comprehensive sense, as it must be understood anthropo-

sophically? How does cognition become "cosmic communion"? How does cognition become "cosmic ritual"?

The religious element does not sit in pure thinking. It
comes to life in a willing that deals with pure thinking in a
devout manner. Human beings want, while they think, also to
be thought themselves by the cooperating gods.

The religious element is not seated originally in willing. It
comes to life in the affirmation of the reviving cosmic will in
the enlivened thoughts. Human beings want, in affirming, to
be affirmed themselves by the will of the gods. There is the origin of religion.

The religious element does not live in pure perception. It
revives in a willing feeling that takes up the pure perception in
devotion. Thereby the sense world becomes a countenance out
of which past divine will, past divine feeling, and divine thinking look upon the human being. Human beings want, while
looking, to be looked at by divine deeds that were effective in
the world's past.

The religious does not have its seat in doing. It comes to
live in an active willing that creates what it and the world lack
out of moral intuition impulses, goals, and realizations.
Human beings want their free creating to be cocreated by
divine creating. The religious revives in thinking, feeling, willing, perceiving, and acting by allowing religion to come to life
again out of the divine existence and source of the human I.
Thus, the knowledge-religion of the reverse ritual forms itself
ever anew out of an ever renewed awakening. Religion is not
there. It can ripen and be awakened. It can be awakened and
can ripen. It can be brought to speech.

I will close with the verse that Rudolf Steiner gave to
Marie Steiner on December 25, 1922, just in connection with
the lecture cycle on spiritual communion (GA 40):

The stars spoke once to Man.
It is world destiny
That they are silent now.

To be aware of the silence
Can become pain for earthly Man.

But in the deepening silence
There grows and ripens
What Man speaks to the stars.
To be aware of the speaking
Can become strength for Spirit-Man.

CHAPTER XIII

LOOKING BACK — LOOKING FORWARD

The actual mystery of the lectures of both Friday and Sunday, December 29 and 31, 1922 (GA 219), is the exactness with which the communion nature of the reverse ritual, along with the transformation nature, the offering nature, and the revelation nature of the same, is expressed in a few accompanying sentences.

At the end of the lecture of December 29, 1922, Rudolf Steiner says:

"When we have found the physical and the soul and the spiritual cosmic forces working together in the inner center of our being, we can also behold them in the cosmos. Human willing rises to artistic creating and finally achieves a relationship to the world that is not merely a passive knowing but a positive, active surrender." (Something proceeds out of the human being.) "Human beings no longer look into the world abstractly, with the forces of their heads; more and more they look into it with their *whole* being." (The feeling and willing become "seeing" beyond the perceiving and thinking.) "Living together with the course of the cosmos" (through surrender in the course of the world) "becomes a happening different in character from their connection with the facts and events of everyday life." (The feeling and willing that confront the daily life transform themselves in human beings into cosmic forces that work in them, which are the same as those working in the universe.) "It becomes a ritual, and the cosmic ritual comes into being in which human beings can have their place at every moment of their lives." (Here for the first time the concept of cosmic ritual is found.)

"Every earthly ritual is a symbolic image of this cosmic ritual. This cosmic ritual is higher in comparison with every earthly ritual." (It develops, right into every word of the ritual, as a fully shaped image in the earthly ritual of what comprises the archetype of the cosmic ritual, which is forming more and more and becoming directly effective as a whole. The bodily-soul-spiritual event of the cosmic ritual is brought to appearance in a closed form in the earthly sacramental ritual in a sense picture in the earthly world. Thereby, it becomes a fact, as spiritual event, to the spiritual consciousness, which means to the direct religious experiencing. It is carried out in the sign of what happens in the spiritual. The earthly ritual becomes an image. The earthly ritual does not form in the way the higher ritual does through infinitely many individual efforts and exercises of the anthroposophically striving person as archetype of the ritualistic. As image it is finished, comprehensive, and presently effective. It is the earthly image of the highest cosmic-earthly world ritual as it was celebrated the first time and fully through the Christ Being in the whole of the Mystery of Golgotha and it works further directly through the earthly ritual; that means religiously, fully, essentially.)

In the lecture of December 31, 1922, the unfolding of the sanctity of the reverse ritual occurs again in a few sentences. There Rudolf Steiner says: "Concerning these creative thoughts I once said in my book *The Science of Knowing* that such thinking represents the spiritual form of communion of humanity." (Here Rudolf Steiner is apparently in error, because the actual formulation of "communing" does not appear in this book [See GA 2]. On the contrary, it is found in the introductions to Goethe's natural scientific works [GA 1; see note II,1] in the sentence: "The perception of the idea in the reality is the true communion of the human being." In spite of that, the indication is correct, because the title of the last general chapter of *The Science of Knowing* [GA 2] is "The Basis of Things and Knowing." This chapter has totally a communion character of the thinking, cognizing human spirit with the cosmic spirit in the things. Rudolf Steiner mixes up the introductions and *The Science of Knowing* in his memory.) Then it goes on: "For as long as human beings give themselves up to their mirror-thoughts about external nature, they do nothing but repeat the past. They live in corpses of the divine." (That is the situation of intellectuality and materialism of the modern consciousness.) "When they enliven their thoughts themselves" — (this comprises the beginning of thinking, of communion in thinking) — "then, communing" (in awe, reverence, harmony with the world lawfulness, and surrender in the course of the world from the objective side) "and receiving communion" (in the surrender of the world on the human being from the objective side) "through their own being, they unite themselves with the Divine Spirit that permeates the world and assures its future." (It takes place in the form of the thoughts; we make our own out of spiritual research, which are enlivened in Imagination, Inspiration, and Intuition as independently existing structures in earthly life.)

"Spiritual knowledge is thus a real communion" (the first part, the first stage), "the beginning of a cosmic ritual" — (cosmic: that raising itself to the divine-spiritual in the cosmos and the receiving within the human being of the divine-spiritual out of the cosmos) — "that is suitable for human beings today" (on the level of the free I of the consciousness soul), "who then can grow" (transition from communion to transubstantiation) "because they begin to realize how they permeate their physical and etheric organism with their astral and ego organism" — (the transubstantiation in the working of Earth with the beings of the starry heavens in the material copy in the physical body, transforming with love in willing within the astral body and the I; and the transubstantiation with the deeds of the starry heavens in the life of water in the material image in the ether body, transforming with wisdom in feeling within the astral body and the I) — "and how, as they quicken the spirit in themselves" — (the human being awakens the sleeping spirit that worked in the past in nature to its present and its future and makes it into a re-enlivened reality) — "they lay the spirit" — (it becomes the seed-force of the Jupiter condition, as revelation of the world, of the human being, of Christ in the human being; it is the revelation-stage of the reverse ritual) — "also into the dead and dying matter" (as mineral realm and plant realm) "that surrounds them."

Finally, at the end of this lecture the theme of the offering appears in connection with communion and transubstantiation. This occurs first in the I-form: "While I can see how in *will* the being and weaving of the stars change lovingly into the spiritual content of the future — (transformed with love for the beings of the zodiac, but also loved by the Seraphim, Cherubim, Thrones) — "I can also see how in *feeling* a wise change takes place when I receive into myself, in what permeates my fluid organism, an image of heavenly deeds" (the cosmic creating out of the plant nature and the guiding of these processes by the Kyriotetes, Dynamis, and Exusiai). "In this way, we can experience ourselves in willing and in feeling." (The human beings experience themselves being thought, felt, and willed in the Archai, Archangels, and Angels.) "Surrendering ourselves to the all-wielding power of the universe, of cosmic existence, that is all around us, we can experience what is carried out through us as transubstantiation in the great temple of the cosmos in that we stand within it as one who is celebrating a sacrifice in a purely spiritual way." (What does this very first, most subtle beginning of such a seeing, willing, and feeling actually look like for an honest consciousness of the striving, practicing anthroposophist?)

Finally, Rudolf Steiner says: "What would otherwise be mere abstract knowledge achieves a relationship of will and feeling to the world. The world becomes a temple; it becomes the House of God. When knowing human beings summon up powers of *will* and *feeling*, they become sacrificing beings." (Here the offering theme appears as the continuation of the motifs of communion and transformation.)

Rudolf Steiner then continues: "The fundamental relationship of the human being to the world rises from knowledge to *cosmic ritual*. The first beginning of what must come to pass if anthroposophy is to fulfill its mission in the world is that the human being's whole relationship to the world must be recognized to be one of cosmic ritual."

The basic relationship of the human being to the world is cosmic ritual. Spiritual science, as knowledge, is at first not yet anthroposophy. It takes place in perceiving and co-thinking the spiritual scientific contents in the intellectual consciousness. Only the human being struggling in feeling and willing, the human being transforming and offering him- or herself in the spiritual science, makes spiritual science into a ritual. Spiritual science as ritual, as cosmic ritual, as reverse ritual, is precisely the first beginning of what anthroposophy wants as mission in the world.

Finally, Rudolf Steiner says: "I have wished to say this to you, as it were, as a beginning. Next Friday I will speak further about the nature of this ritual in its relation to the knowledge of nature" (Friday, January 5, 1923, is meant).

We can assume that as these words were being spoken the torch had already been thrown into the roof of the south wing of the White Hall of the first Goetheanum. In this night, the building burned to the ground. The offering was there. It was the hardest sacrifice that the Anthroposophical Society had to make. The insufficient inner offering changed outwardly into a powerful cosmic sacrifice. Since then, the Goetheanum burns further as sacrificial flame in the hearts of anthroposophically-striving people. Out of this sacrifice, the shell is then removed from what was entrusted to the members in the lectures on the offertory stage of the reverse ritual in February and March 1923 for the life of the branches of the society.

It is ultimately significant to see how the continuation of the presentations on the cosmic ritual was actually taken up on the aforementioned Friday. There he speaks directly of the Christ and of the "need for the Christ," as the main feature of the spiritual situation of the human being today. In this it becomes clear how the reverse ritual as revelation contains the Christ Event that is deeply connected with the I of the human being (see note VI,1).

One year later, the Christmas Conference of the founding of the Anthroposophical Society took place (December 1923). We can find various spiritual events in it. From the ritualistic viewpoint, it is a kind of "consecration" of the Anthroposophical Society through the anthroposophical movement, of the Michael community on Earth through the Michael movement out of the spiritual world, the laying of the foundation stone out of the divine trinity for a new worth and dignity of the anthroposophically striving individuality. In it the shepherds and the kings are united with one another. It is the "priest ordination" of the anthroposophically-striving human being.

In the concrete earthly circumstances of humanity, the custodians, the bearers, those responsible for both of the fundamental ritual forms — that of the Christian sacramental and that of the reverse ritual — must live and work in clearly separated social structures. Between both of the lectures on cosmic ritual, Rudolf Steiner gave the lecture of December 30, 1922, in which he spoke very exactly and precisely about that separation. It was a world historical necessity.

If we compare both of these ritual forms once again, the closed form of the Christian sacramental ritual becomes apparent. Opposite of this stands the open form of the reverse ritual that permeates the whole of anthroposophy. The overview of the form of the sacramental ritual, even with all its infinite depths of mystery, can be attained with a glance. The organization of the reverse ritual consists of an infinite number of individual human deeds, which need to be grasped ever anew. These deeds are in effort to grasp ever again and to further more and more spiritual knowledge concerning cosmic-artistic enlivening and religious-ritualistic deepening. We see how comprehensively and deeply the tree of knowledge of spiritual science in all its branches is imbued with the tree of life of anthroposophy, the ritualistic-religious world event. Only then is it anthroposophically-oriented spiritual science.

A full understanding of the origin, nature, and realm of working of the Christian-Michaelic, of the reversed, cosmic ritual — and also a comparison with the earthly, Christian sacramental ritual — does not yet result when the approach for attaining this understanding is sought only in regard to the human being as the performer of this ritual, or in regard to the stages, contents, and spheres in which it is carried out.

It is possible only when the starting point for this understanding is seen where all ritualistic element ultimately originate. This includes the human and the divine, the earthly and the cosmic. It is the realm of the highest, deepest, and most comprehensive world reality in which the human being, the gods, and the world existentially weave, live, and are present. It is the realm of the Trinity: the Father God, the Son God, and the Spirit God.

For the earthly human being the experience of the highest divine unity is threefold. It is not just a passive thinking, feeling, and willing of an existing divine entity. It is an active, creative co-thinking, co-feeling, and co-willing of this divinity: an active inner thinking out, feeling, and willing, and with it, an active inner living or experiencing. This active experiencing with the Godhead is for this reason strictly differentiated.

1. Experiencing the full consciousness of one's own being as a real existing entity leads to the experience of the pure, existential ground of existence of the world; it leads religiously to the Father-experience. The substance, being, and existence of the human being is experienced as identical with the substance, being, and existence of the Ground of the World. Thereby, the human being can be experienced as arising out of this Ground of the World — as born out of him. Thus, the Ground of the World is the "Father," and the human being is the "Child" of this "Father": the human I coming into being in the World I.

However, the substance, being, and existence of the Father is in turn a creating, a becoming and transforming in being. It leads to an experience of the Son, inasmuch as he is born out of the Father as his Word. The Father experience becomes the Son experience through the creativity we can experience in ourselves.

But furthermore, because this experience is conscious, the source of this spiritual consciousness appears as shining forth out of itself, as independent being: as the Spirit God pouring forth from the Father God, as the divine spirit-light of the Father. Thus, the full experience of the Father God is indeed threefold and therewith complete.

Seen philosophically, here arises the concept of being of Plato and Hegel, the concept of substance of Aristotle and Spinoza, and, perversely, the concept of matter of Democritus, the materialists, and modern physics.

The Rosicrucians experienced the coming forth, emerging, in being. They summarized it in the words "*Ex deo nascimur....*"

2. The experience of the Son God becomes something quite different when it does not proceed only out of the Father experience, but rather passes over into the direct experience of the Son God himself. This is only possible, however, since the Son God fulfilled the Mystery of Golgotha. In Him, as born out of the Father God, as the Cosmic Word creating out of the Father God, his offering unites with the dying creation in the world and in the human being — permeating this dying, however, with the seed-force of the future and wresting this future out of the grip of the adversary powers. It is the deed of the Son I, which was willed by the Father God but fulfilled as a free offering.

For human beings, therefore, the experience of the Son God has the characteristic of a direct, quite personal meeting of the I of God and the I of the human being occurring in our most intimate inner being. It does not have — as the Father experience does — the character of gift and talent, of birth, but rather of present sacrifice, of redemption.

This meeting is always combined with the deepest shock or upset for the human being. For human beings come to the path to themselves and to their freedom only through error, illness, and death. Now, however, they experience a force living in the Son God that creates a new human being in the dying Earth existence. It is the force of divine love. In it downfall becomes ascent; weakness becomes strength; illness and evil become whole (healed); death becomes life, and falling away or estrangement becomes reconciliation.

The experiencing of the Son God is no longer philosophical in nature; it is mystical. It can never be completely conceptualized; it must be sensed, felt, experienced, and suffered or gone through. Thus, for example, Novalis speaks of the "heart of the heart" and of the "I of the I." They are, however, no longer philosophical, but rather mystical concepts. The Rosicrucians experience the shock or shake-up. They summarize it in the words, "*In Christo morimur....*"

The mystical character of the experience of the Son God in no way means that as such it is only feeling in the sense of a feeling mysticism. It takes place in the light of a totally new consciousness, a spiritual consciousness, which is at the same time a spiritual knowledge — of course, always only when the Son experience occurs as an experience that shakes one deeply. Before this, experience can only be sought, longed for, or hoped for — or avoided — in the subconscious soul life of the human being. If the Son experience emerges, a light is enkindled in the human being that immerses the whole experience in the light of knowledge, in faith, pondering, seeing, knowing, and being known. We could also say letting oneself be known. It is now the Spirit God pouring out of the Son God.

In this light the Son God makes the Father God understandable for the human being, because he reveals his substance, being, and existence as fatherly creative love. The philosophical substance concepts receive mystical-soul content, mystical-soul life.

The Spirit God poured out of the Son makes the Son God understandable for the human being in a knowledge that now no longer delivers a picture of God, world, and the human being; it is a cosmic process that takes place objectively in the human being. It is a process that conveys the past into the future through the power of the Son God in the light of consciousness of the Spirit God. The real mystical Son experience receives in faith, pondering, seeing, knowing, and being known a world-significant meaning; that experienced in the Son experience is meaningfully interpreted.

In this realm, spiritual knowledge becomes anthroposophy; it becomes Christology; it becomes a striving toward permeating the world with the Christ Being. Thus, also the Son-experience is threefold.

3. Sensing and experiencing the Spirit God is of a totally different nature. The Father God lives in being; the Son God lives in creating and transforming; the Spirit God shines forth from the Father and the Son as the essential, divine consciousness. The Holy Spirit pouring forth from the Father God appears in the Gospel in the imagination of the dove at the Baptism of Jesus through John in the Jordan. The Holy Spirit proceeding out of the Son God appears in the Gospel at Pentecost in the form of the flames at the heads of the disciples. It is not immediately noticed, but in both events the experience of the Spirit God is the result of preceding consents. The consent of Jesus and of John to the execution of the Baptism leads to the pouring forth of the Spirit God through the Father. The disciples consent to the fact that the Resurrected One withdrew from their direct beholding during the forty days of Easter through the Ascension, but then, however, He can work in the light of the knowledge of the Spirit God that poured forth from him — both in the most individual freedom and in the divine wisdom that unites the whole of humanity. And the Spirit God proceeding out of the Son leads ever anew to the meeting of the Son God with the human being.

The experiencing of the Spirit God must also be desired by the human being in freedom; it must be actively willed as it were. The spirit active in the human being must turn its conscious attention to and grasp and practice the spiritual consciousness and spiritual knowledge. Spiritual consciousness and spiritual knowledge must be enkindled ever anew, must be enkindled in a willingness of human beings to let themselves be illumined by, spiritually permeated by, and healed by the Spirit God. This happens then out of the Will of the Father in the Love of the Son. Thus also, the experience of the Spirit God is threefold.

This experience is the awakening to inner illumination. Here thinking is no longer philosophy, also no longer "pure thinking," but is rather "true thinking" of the divine goals. In it all ideas become ideals.

The Rosicrucians experience this content of the future. They put this into the words, *"Per spiritum sanctum revivicimus."*

4. If we survey the essence of the experience of the Trinity that is becoming knowable through anthroposophy, then we can also see that anthroposophy itself is woven into the sphere of the Godhead. It is poured forth from the Father God and from the Son God as the healing Cosmic-Wisdom-Light of the Spirit God, in order to be taken up by the human being in freedom and to be practiced, known, and accomplished. In this same realm of the Spirit God lies also the realization of anthroposophy in its religious form as the reversed, the cosmic ritual, as the spiritual communion of humanity. The experience of the Trinity in the sphere of the actively willed and actively practiced Spirit God is the religion within anthroposophy. In anthroposophy, in this sphere of the Spirit God, the Son God is the force of realization or fulfillment, and the Father God is the transforming substance of the future cosmos.

The Christian sacramental ritual flows directly out of the Son God, who fulfilled and continues the Mystery of Golgotha in the form of the healing streams of the seven sacraments. The working of the Father and the light of the Spirit are woven into them.

The knowledge ritual of anthroposophy forms out of the free spiritual activity of the human being in the consciousness sphere of the Spirit God.

An understanding of the common ground and of the clear discrimination of their differences can also be a contribution to a mutual human understanding of the spiritually striving individuals who are active in cultivating these two ritual forms.

5. The comprehensive threefold or trinitarian content of the cosmic ritual is found lastly in anthroposophy in that meditative ritualistic formulation that was given to the members at the Christmas Conference for the founding of the Anthroposophical Society on December 25, 1923. Rudolf Steiner called it the old Mystery Word renewed out of the signs of the present time: "Know Yourself." He referred to it as the "summary" of what wants to be placed before human souls as the most important result of the last years.

In the discussions of the individual parts of this ritual that followed during the Christmas Conference, Rudolf Steiner points ever again to the bodily-soul-spiritual rhythms that permeate the whole like a trinitarian or threefold fabric that differentiates the parts from each other and unites them into a unity.

This spiritual foundation stone, sunk into and spoken forth out of the hearts of the anthroposophically striving individualities also as members of the General Anthroposophical Society contains a fourfold Mystery, to which a fifth is added through further verses.

It is the Mystery of the threefold human being in limbs, breast, and head. The human being is the ground into which the foundation stone wills to be laid.

Secondly, it is then the Mystery of practice, of schooling, of meditation taken up in freedom in the active willing of the spirit in "spirit-recalling," "spirit-sensing," and "spirit-beholding" in the consciousness sphere of the Spirit God. It is the Mystery of the perpetual, free-willed "meditation," deepening and heightening. Here spiritual freedom is at home.

It is thirdly the Mystery of the macrocosm, of the heights of the starry worlds, of the depths of the earthly world, and of the Earth-Sun-Moon periphery of nature. In the latter of these the Son God leads to the Father God in sub-nature and to the Spirit God in super-nature and produces spirit-human in the earthly human being.

Fourthly, it is the Mystery of the transition of the foundation stone ritual into the world of the soul-spirits and of the elemental nature spirits in East, West, North, and South.

To this whole is added a fifth. It is the Mystery of the uniting of the age-long-separated mainstreams of humanity's evolution: the shepherd stream and the kingly stream through the Mystery of Golgotha in the person of every individual human being as the future form of spirit-human in the earthly human being.

Let us add these words here:

Human Soul!
You live within the limbs
That bear you through the world of space
Into the spirit's ocean-being:
Practice spirit-recalling
In the depths of soul,
Where in the wielding
World-Creator Being
Your own I
Comes into being
In the I of God;
And you will truly live
In human world-all being.

For the Father Spirit of the heights holds sway
In depths of worlds begetting life.
Spirits of Strength:
Let ring forth from the heights
What in the depths is echoed,
Speaking:
Out of the Godhead we are born.

This is heard by the spirits of the elements
In east, west, north, south:
May human beings hear it!

Human soul!
You live within the beat of heart and lung
Which leads you through the rhythms of time
Into the feeling of your own soul-being:
Practice spirit-sensing
In balance of the soul,
Where the surging deeds
Of world-evolving
Unite your own I
With the I of the World;
And you will truly feel
In the human soul's creating.

For the Christ-will encircling us holds sway,
In world rhythms, bestowing grace upon souls.
Spirits of Light:
Let from the east be enkindled
What through the west takes on form,
Speaking:
In Christ death becomes life.
This is heard by the spirits of the elements
In east, west, north, south:
May human beings hear it!

Human Soul!
You live within the resting head
Which from the grounds of eternity
Unlocks for you world-thoughts:
Practice spirit-beholding
In stillness of thought,
Where the gods' eternal aims
Bestow the light of cosmic being
On your own I
For free and active willing.
And you will truly think
In human spirit depths.

For the Spirit's world-thoughts hold sway
In cosmic being, imploring light.
Spirit of Soul:
Let from the depths be entreated
What in the heights will be heard,
Speaking:
In the Spirit's cosmic thoughts the soul awakens.
This is heard by the spirits of the elements
In east, west, north south:
May human beings hear it!

At the turning point of time
The Spirit-light of the world
Entered the stream of Earth existence.
Darkness of night
Had ceased its reign;
Day-radiant light
Shone forth in human souls:
Light
That gives warmth
To simple shepherds' hearts;
Light
That enlightens
The wise heads of kings.

Light divine,
Christ-Sun,
Warm our hearts;
Enlighten
Our heads;
That good may become
What from our hearts
We are founding,
What from our heads
We direct,
With focused will.

CHAPTER XIV

ADDENDUM:
THE PINK WINDOW IN
THE FIRST GOETHEANUM

The pink window in the north of the first Goetheanum: The high song of devoutness.

The starting point is the middle picture. It is the human being at all the boundaries of awakening. It is the awakening as child out of the incarnation sleep into the earthly consciousness. It is the waking up out of the sleep condition into the day waking consciousness. It is the awakening out of the day waking to the experience of the other human being. It is the awakening and the being awakened on all the boundaries and thresholds of the transformations of consciousness in knowledge. Lastly, it is the awakening in death to the beyond.

Two beings accompany every awakening. The one stands behind the human being. It is indistinct, shadowy but complete. The other being appears in front of the human being as a head, which, in the at-first profusely shining light of the new consciousness after every awakening, wants to become the content of this new consciousness.

This content is our own higher being, raying out of the light of the cosmos. In the awakening out of each preceding consciousness into each future consciousness, the world wafts devoutness for the human being as Sun, Moon, and stars of the heavens, as stones and plants of the Earth. "The world wafts devoutness" when the human being awakens in any manner. When the world is awakened in the human being, then devoutness sprouts in the human being.

And: "Human beings becomes devout" when we transform the arrogance and pride of Lucifer out of the Moon's past into wisdom.

And: "The devoutness works" when we wrest the Sun forces as seed of the world future from Ahriman, who wants to seize the past greedily for himself, and when we bind him with these Sun forces.

Both are possible only through the Mystery of Golgotha. That means devoutness comes about only when the wisdom out of the heights is offered, creating being, to the Mystery of Golgotha. The three crosses stand down low.

And: Devoutness works only when, in the depths of Earth, it leads, world creating, the past into the future in the sense of the Mystery of Golgotha. The three crosses stand high above.

All becoming is awakening. All awakening is metamorphosis, is actual transition. And in all that is real transition, there wafts the world devoutness.

It is always the same loving-humble-courageous primal gesture in the human being:

Devotion–Devoutness–Piety.

CHAPTER XV

AFTERWORD:
A TRANSITION TO THE NOTES

In looking back at the attempt to speak about the still very mysterious cosmic ritual, the cosmic communion, the mystery of the religious experience in anthroposophy, the writer of this book is assailed by a feeling of inadequacy in the face of such an attempt.

On the one hand, he met his own limitations. On the other hand, he met objective difficulties in transcribing spiritual experiences into words and intellectual content of thought. Misunderstandings arise all too easily when "what was said and what was meant" do not quite match.

Let me illustrate this problem with an example. We spoke of the four "parts" of the ritual. Just as fitting are these words: four processes, four levels, four events, four realms, four conditions, four basic happenings.

Every one of these conceptual descriptions by nature leads to separations, differences, and characterizations — to aspects.

But if we take a closer look, we will find that this is only the one side. The other side reveals itself more and more if we realize that in every one of the four events, the other three are also present and coworking.

The variety — however real it may be — has spiritually such an intensive life that in every part, in every realm, the whole works together with it. In the stage of revelation offering, transformation, and communion are really effective. Revelation works as it were in the foreground spiritually-spatially. Offering, transformation, and communion permeate it in the background. Also the temporal succession, the sequence of the stages is, spiritually-temporally, always with one another and in one another at the same time. Thereby the last is working in the beginning, and the beginning element is only complete at the end. One can attempt to find this in the details.

When, however, in the whole of the study we speak respectively of revelation, offering, transformation, and communion, we mean at the same time that in each of the four processes the others are present and working together (as religion between human being and human being, human being and nature, human being and cosmos, and human being and the Godhead, and in the human being him- or herself).

Etheric-soul-spiritual processes are spiritually unified even with all the differentiations. They are interdependent; the one is not possible without the other.

Thereby only the whole is living, real, and creating reality. So, an unspoken, unnameable element of reality is contained in all descriptions that characterize.

That is the one thing.

The other is the fact that the content of this attempt to find the religious in anthroposophy is made accessible completely through the revelation of anthroposophy. It lies in the lectures and writings of Rudolf Steiner. The credits are given in the Notes. One will not come to a complete experience of the theme through this book. Pictorially speaking, it may be compared to the outstretched finger of John the Baptist who stands beneath the cross in the painting of the Isenheim altar. If we make the effort to let the more that one hundred text formulations of Rudolf Steiner that are given in the notes work on our souls, we come only then to the reality of what this writing calls attention to. This book is meant only as a help and contribution to such a study.

September 1985
Friedrich Benesch

Notes

Steiner's works are collected in German in a Complete Edition or "Gesamtausgabe," also known as the "GA," published by the Rudolf Steiner Verlag, Dornach/Switzerland. Each Steiner title in the Complete Edition is assigned a number, the "GA number." Wherever possible, the English title and publication information are provided below in addition to the GA number.

The place and date referred to for each title indicate the specific lecture relevant to the note.

Note I

For the understanding of the earth ritual, in particular the renewed Christian sacramental ritual, also as inversion of the ritual of birth and pre-birth.

I.1. The Human Being: a polytheism

The Inner Being of Man and the Life between Death and New Birth, GA 153, Rudolf Steiner Press, 1994. Vienna, April 10, 1914.

I.2. Pre-natal excommunion

Theosophy of the Rosicrucian, GA 99, Rudolf Steiner Press, London, 1981. Munich, May 28, 1907.GA 153, n. I.1.Vienna, April 10, 1915.

Vienna, April 13; 1915. *The Bridge Between Universal Spirituality and the Physical Constitution of Man.*GA 202, Anthroposophic Press, Spring Valley, New York, 1979. Dornach, December, 10, 1920.

I.3. Pre-natal transubstantiation
GA 202, p. I. Dornach, December 11, 1920.

I.4. Pre-natal metamorphoses

See *The Spiritual Communion of Humanity*, this volume. GA 219.

I.5. Pre-natal sacrifice

Between Death and Rebirth, GA 141, Rudolf Steiner Press, 1975. Berlin, February 11, 1913; *Philosophy, Cosmology and Religion*, GA 215, Anthroposophic Press, Spring Valley, New York, 1984. Dornach, September 11, 1922.

I.6. The revelation of the earthly ego as the fourth stage of the ritual of birth, as "the word" "ego"

Theosophy, GA 9, Anthroposophic Press, Hudson, NY, 1994.

I.7. Spirit knowledge and spirit consciousness. Science and religion: contrast and correlation.

Building Stones for an Understanding of the Mystery of Golgotha, GA 175, Rudolf Steiner Press, 1972. Berlin, February 20, 1917.

I.8. The meaning of the holy communion in the past, present and future. The ritual and spiritual holy communion in juxtaposition and together.

From Jesus to Christ, GA 131, Rudolf Steiner Press, 1973.
Karlsruhe, October 13, 1911.

I.9. Religious ritual as a real symbol on the physical plane for its reality on the astral plane. Its social significance.

An Esoteric Cosmology, GA 94. St. George Publications, 1978
München, November 4, 1906.*At the Gates of Spiritual Science*, GA 95, Rudolf Steiner Press, 1970. Stuttgart, September 3, 1906.

I.10. Ritual and spirit knowledge: paths to the eternal being of the human soul. Metabolic knowledge in the ritual garb.

The Festivals and Their Meaning GA 211, Rudolf Steiner Press, 1981. Den Haag, April 13, 1922.

I.11. History of the ritual of the Freemasons and of the churches

Supersensible Impulses in the History of Mankind, GA 216, Rudolf Steiner Press, 1956.

a) The oldest rituals and the elemental beings of the sun and the moon. Dornach, September 22, 1922; b) The Egyptian and Chaldean rituals, the elemental beings of the moon, and the deceased, see a); c) The Greek rituals and the elemental beings of the air, see a); d) Post-Christian rituals and the elemental beings of the earth since the fourth and fifth centuries, Dornach, September 23, 1922; e) Post-Christian rituals as mummified pre-Christian rituals, Dornach, September 24, 1922; 1. The renewal by the Christ impulse of the mummified rituals, particularly the sacramental ritual, Dornach, September 29, 1922; 2. The teachings of the future adept to his pupils about the renewed sacramental ritual, Dornach, September 29, 1922; f) The resurrection of dead thinking by ritual and for ritual, Dornach, September 30, 1922.

I.12. The holy communion as preparatory stage for the mystical union with Christ

The Gospel of Saint John and its Relation to the Other Gospels, GA 112, Anthroposophic Press, 1982. Kassel, July 7, 1909.

I.13. Every earth ritual a symbolic image of the higher cosmic ritual

The Spiritual Communion of Humanity, GA 219, this volume.
Dornach, December 29, 1922.

I.14. The origin of the Catholic ritual

From Mammoths to Mediums...Answers to Questions, GA 350. Rudolf
Steiner Press, 2000. Dornach, September 10, 1923.

I.15. The renewal of the Christian ritual in the twentieth century

GA 350, see I.14. Dornach, September 10, 1923.

I.16. Rebuilding the sacramental ritual out of the innermost of man

GA 350, see I.14. Dornach, September 9, 1923.

I.17. The nature of sacramentalism

Pastoral Medicine: The Collegial Working of Doctors and Priests, GA 18.
Anthroposophic Press, 1987; Dornach, September 8, 1924; Dornach, September 15, 1924. I.18. Machine and ritual

Human Soul Life in Relation to World Evolution, GA 212, Anthroposophic Press, 1984 Dornach, May 7, 1922.

I.19. Ritual and scientific-technical experiment

"Naturbeobachtung, Mathematik, wissenschaftliches Experiment und
Erkenntniserlebnisse vom Gesichtspunkte der Anthroposophie," GA 324.
Stuttgart, March 21, 1921, pp. 89-95.

I.20. Temple architecture, ritual and karma
Karmic Relationships, vol. II, GA 236, Rudolf Steiner Press, 1974. Dornach,
April 27, 1924.

I.21. Earth as image of spiritual-ritual occurrences
GA 236, see I.20. Dornach, June 27, 1924.

I.22. Passage of a sacrament into the cultural stream

Christ and the Human Soul, GA 155. Rudolf Steiner Publishing House,
1956 Norrköping, July 16, 1914.

I.23. The sacramental-Christian-religious and the cosmic ritual in their
respective autonomous forms and in the independence of their supporting
bodies. Cosmic ritual and sacramental ritual. Anthroposophy and the
gospels. The anthroposophic movement and the movement for religious

renewal. The Anthroposophic Society and its branches. The Christian Community and its parishes. GA 219, see I.13. Dornach, December 30, 1922.

NOTE II

II.1. The fundamental philosophical descriptions of knowledge as communion.

a)Nature's Open Secret, GA 1, Anthroposophic Press, 2000.
The communion of thought
The communion of perception
The communion of knowledge

"Grundlinien einer Erkenntnistheorie der Goetheschen Weltanschauung," GA 2

The communion of perception.
The communion of thought.
The communion of knowledge.

b) Truth and Knowledge, GA 3, Steinerbooks, 1981.
The communion of perception: the directly given as partial communion.
The communion of thought as communion of being.
Knowledge as communion of reality.
Knowledge as communion in freedom.

Intuitive Thinking as a Spiritual Path: The Philosophy of Freedom, GA 4
Anthroposophic Press, 1995
The communion of thought as an exceptional state of consciousness in the form of thought observations and intuition. The communion of perception as observation: partial communion in the form of outer and inner observation. The communion of knowledge as a secular process in the human being. Tangible quickening of concepts by means of feeling as an artistic and religious Communion in knowing.

II.2. The communion of knowledge in the fully human artistic-religious social life with the course of the world as "world view"

The Spiritual Communion of Humanity, GA 219, this volume. Dornach, December 29, 1922.

II.3. The cosmic ritual als communion in the anthroposophical world view of knowledge.
This stage as a psychic-spiritual gift of the future of creative human thoughts to the dying mineral-plant world of the past is the beginning of the ritual. GA 219, see II.2. Dornach, December 31, 1922.

II.4. The beginning of sacramentalism through the Christian sacramental ritual and beyond to the future culture of humanity

The Karma of Vocation, GA 172, Anthroposophic Press, 1984.
Dornach, November 27, 1916.

II.5. What does the life of knowledge mean?

From Jesus to Christ, GA 131, Rudolf Steiner Press, 1973.
Karlsruhe, October 5, 1911.

NOTE III

The element of the religious/ritual in knowledge as communion.

III.1. The religious element in Goetheanism. Goethe as chief witness.
II.
Nature's Open Secret, GA 1.Chapter XI: relationship of Goethe´s way of thinking to other points of view.

III.2. Hegel and thinking in the awe of the divine

Spiritual Science as a Foundation for Social Formation, GA 199, Anthroposophic Press/Rudolf Steiner Press, 1979.
Dornach, August 27, 1920: the eternal in Hegelian logic. From thought to being *The Riddles of Philosophy*, GA 18, Anthroposophic Press, 1973.

III.3. Perception, conception, thinking and meditation in the religious region of wonder, admiration, awe, harmony, devotion and stillness

The World of the Spirit and the World of the Senses, GA 134, Steiner Book-Centre,Canada, 1979. Hannover, December 27, 1921; *How to Know Higher Worlds*, GA 10, Anthroposophic Press, 1994.

III.4. The abstract metaphoric nature and ineffectiveness of pure thinking GA 134, see III. 3. Hannover, December 28, 1911.

III.5. The *maya* nature of sense perceptions arises because "we have gone into the body."

The Karma of Materialism, GA 176, Anthroposophic Press/Rudolf Steiner Press, 1985. Berlin, September 4, 1917.

III.6. The thought-free nature of pure sense perceptions consists of twelve diffentiated unconscious will-streams of the ego passing through the feeling soul as feeling willing and willing feeling.

Theosophy, GA 9.*The Foundations of Human Experience*, GA 293, Anthroposophic Press, 1996. Stuttgart, August 1919, Lecture VII.

III.7. Sense perception as fusion of the will of worlds and sense-ego will. The reality content of the sense perceptions consists of twelve subjectified and specified streams of the governing will of worlds. Their thought content is suppressed by the will of perception. It remains behind the scene as governing wisdom.

The World of the Sense and the World of the Spirit GA 134, Steiner Book-Centre, 1979. Dornach, December 28, 1911.

III.8. The reality of thoughts as concept, idea, ideal is at first to be found only in their production, their creation as real spiritual activity, as human work. This reality can be made conscious by the observation of thinking. The product of this activity is the dead image, the corpse of the idea as pure abstract, intellectual thought, an impotent image with its own objective, conceptual content, conceived by real activity, whose original strength — in other words, will content — has been suppressed by the real activity of thinking itself. Only the intuited sense is communicated.

"Der Wert des Denkens für eine den Menschen befriedigende Erkenntnis," GA 164. Dornach, September 17, 1915, pp. 20-22.

III.9. Intellectualism as the modern Fall of man since the 15th century *Supersensible Influences in the History of Mankind*, GA 216, Rudolf Steiner Publishing House, 1956
Dornach, September 23, 1922; September 30, 1922.

III.10. Solemnity as a religious element in the study of Anthroposophy, as actual Michaelic impulse

Anthroposophic Leading Thoughts, G 26, Rudolf Steiner Press, 1973. The world thoughts in the actions of Michael and Ahriman

III.11. Conscious idealism in the study of Anthroposophy

Christ and the Human Soul, GA 155. Norrköping, July 7, 1915.

III.12. The mission of prayer in relation to thinking. Prayer as teacher of the consciousness soul

Metamorphoses of the Soul: Paths of Experience, vol. I, GA 58. Rudolf Steiner Press Berlin, October 28 1909, the mission of prayer.

III.13. What is thinking actually? Thinking and being thought.
Human and Cosmic Thought, GA 151, Rudolf Steiner Press, 1961. Berlin, January 23, 1914.

Note IV

The ritual element in knowledge as transformation in the physical and aetheric human being. Transsubstantiation by the stars in willing and feeling.

IV.1. The relationship of heart and mind to the cosmos: the zodiac and planets/sun

The Effects of Esoteric Development, GA 145, Anthroposophic Press, 1997. Den Haag, March 21, 1913.

IV.2. Metamorphosis of muscles, bones, sense organs
GA 145, see IV.1. Den Haag, March 22, 1913.

IV.3. Experience in the aetheric body by the temperaments

GA 145, see IV.1. Den Haag, March 22, 1913.

IV.4. The elements described in the Haag Cycle as ritual occurrence of the reverse ritual: as transformation of the stars in the human being, of the human being bz the stars in willing and feeling.

The Spiritual Communion of Humanity, GA 219, this volume.
Dornach, December 31, 1922.

IV.5. The effect of pre-natal life in world thoughts on the physical body and the aetheric body in sleep

GA 219, see IV.4. Dornach, December 31, 1922.

Note V

The reverse ritual as sacrificial stage in community formation.

V.1. In the human being something happens in the cosmic ritual which does not happen in nature

GA 219, see IV.4. Dornach, December 29, 1922.

V.2. The theme of awaking and waking for the Anthroposophic Society as the true esoteric

"Lebendiges Naturerkennen. Intellektueller Sündenfall und spirituelle Sünden-erhebung," GA 220, 1966 Dornach, January 14, 1923, p. 94, pp. 96-97, p.99.

V.3. Watchfulness *vis à vis* the hubris of knowing and of sectarianism as the starting point for sacrifice, the disposition to sacrifice of the human being

GA 220, see V.2. Dornach, January 21, 1923.

V.4. Fostering Anthroposophy in the individuality and the community
Anthroposophic Leading Thoughts, GA 26

V.5. The religious-ritual element in the fostering of Anthroposophy in community in the branches of the General Anthroposophic Society vis à vis the Christian-sacramental ritual

Awakening to Community, GA 257.
Stuttgart, February 27, 1923.
Stuttgart, February 28, 1923.
Dornach, March 3, 1923.
Dornach, March 4, 1923.

V.6. Awakening to the Other as karma experience
Karmic Relationships, vol. VI, GA 240, Rudolf Steiner Press, 1970. Bern, January 25, 1924.

V.7. Awakening to the Other through the Christ impulse

The Karma of Vocation, GA 172.
Dornach, November 27, 1916.

V. 8. The conversion of human earth-deeds into soul heaven-deeds, when, by means of people working together, holy spiritual actions are brought down into the physical sense world

Karmic Relationships, vol. III, GA 237, Rudolf Steiner Press, 1977. Dornach, July 4, 1924.

V. 9. The religious relationship to karma knowledge as awe

GA 237, see V.8. Dornach, July 6, 1924.

NOTE VI

The free relationship of the individual human being to Christ as a stage of the revelation of the reverse ritual. Knowledge as Christ-knowledge, as religion in knowledge.

VI.1. The Christ-permeated light and the Christ-permeated ego
"Lebendiges Naturerkennen, Intellektuaeller Sündenfall und spirituelle Sünden-erhebung," GA 220, 1966
Dornach, January 5 1923, pp. 18-20

VI.2. The path of thought and the path of will to Christ
The Inner Aspect of the Social Question, GA 193, Anthropsophic Publishing House, 1950. Zürich, February 11, 1919.

VI.3. Spiritual exaltation from sin means: truly understanding Christ GA 220, see VI.1. Dornach, January 21, 1923.

VI. 4. The practical idea of karma as the starting point for the Rosacrucian path of Schooling, which leads to the images of the Gospels
From Jesus to Christ, GA 131. Karlsruhe, October 6, 1911.

VI.5. The feeling of responsibility to Christ as light for the experience of Christus GA 131, see VI.4. Karlsruhe, October 7, 1911.

VI.6. The three exoteric paths to Christ
GA 131, see VI.4; Karlsruhe, October 7, 1911;Karlsruhe, October 8, 1911.

VI.7. The golden word for the esoteric path to Christ
GA 131, see VI.4 Karlsruhe, October 8, 1911.

VI. 8. The passage from the ritual to the spiritual holy communion Karlsruhe, October 13, 1911.

VI. 9. The inner path to Christ independent of any tradition
"Erfahrungen des Übersinnlichen. Die Wege der Seele zu Christus," GA 143,1970 Stockholm, April 16, 1919, pp. 119-122, pp. 124-125

VI.10. The path of self-inflicted loneliness to Christ-experience
Building Stones for an Understanding of the Mystery of Golgotha,GA 175. Berlin, April 24, 1917.

VI.11. Denial of God and weakness on the path to Christ

"Der Tod als Lebenswandlung," GA 182, 1976 Zürich, October 16, 1918, pp. 174-177."

VI.12. Earthly insignificance, personal freedom and the longing for cosmic Being as path to Christ

The New Spirituality and the Christ Experience of the 20th Century GA 200, Rudolf Steiner Press, 1988. Dornach, October 30, 1920. Dornach, October 31, 1920.

VI.13. The position of the anthroposophist on the mystery of Golgatha

"Das Sonnenmysterium und das Mysterium von Tod und Auferstehung,"GA 211, 1963 Vienna, June 11, 1922, pp. 212-216

VI.14. From the lectures on the aetheric return *The Reappearance of Christ in the Etheric*, GA 118, Anthroposophic Press, 1983; Karlsruhe, January 25, 1910;Düsseldorf, February 20, 1910; Stuttgart, March 6, 1910; Hamburg, May 15, 1910.

VI.15. Michael and Christ

Anthroposophic Leading Thoughts, GA 26:
Essay: The Michael-Christ experience of the human being

VI.16. The highest and deepest religious element in the fourth stage, the stage of ego-revelation of the reverse cosmic ritual GA 26, see VI.15.
Essay: World history and the influence of Michael and of Ahriman

VI.17. On the life of modern man in the age of science and the world of machines in the domain of freedom: forward to the philosophy of freedom or backward to Catholicism

The Human Soul in Relation to World Evolution, GA 212, Anthroposophic Press, 1984. Dornach, May 7, 1922.

VI.18. The personal relationship to Christ as the necessary religious correlate to the individualism of the moral intuition of the philosophy of freedom. Together the "philosophy of freedom" and "Christianity as mystical fact" make up the whole.

GA 212, see VI.17; Dornach, May 7, 1922.

VI. 19. The Christ experience of the occultist

Man in the Light of Occultism, Theosophy and Philosophy, GA 137, Rudolf Steiner Press, 1964; Kristiania, June 10, 1912; Kristiania, June 12, 1912.

VI.20. The Christ experience at the great guardian of the threshold *How to Know Higher Worlds*, GA 10.

NOTE VII

The whole of the cosmic, reverse ritual
The religious element in the whole of Anthroposophy.

VII.1. The transformation of thinking

Awakening to Community, GA 257, Anthroposophic Press, 1974. Stuttgart, February 6, 1923.

VII.2. Transformation of the will, GA 257, see VII.1. Stuttgart, February 6, 1923.

VII.3. The complete path of Anthroposophy

GA 257, see VII.1.Stuttgart, January 30, 1923.

VII.4. Anthroposophical formation of judgment

GA 257, see VII.1.Stuttgart, January 20, 1923.

VII.5. The three highest ideals of humanity GA 257, see VII.1.
Dornach, February 22, 1923; Religion; Art; Science.

VII.6. Reverse ritual and the world of the elemental beings

"Lebendiges naturerkennen, intellektueller Sündenfall und spirituelle Sündenerhebung," GA 220, 1966 Dornach, January 20, 1923, pp. 112-113, p. 119.

VII.7. The definition of human earth knowledge without religious admixture *Effects of Esoteric Development*, GA 145, Anthroposophic Press, 1997. Den Haag, March 27, 1914.

VII.8. Selflessness and love in knowledge. Transformation of feeling GA 145, see VII.7. Den Haag, March 27, 1913.

NOTE VIII

The ritual of worlds of the hierarchies in human death and life after death.

VIII.1. The first stage of life after death as cosmic ritual. The "ego" in death: the human being as "word". The stage of revelation.

The Inner Being of Man and the Life between Death and Rebirth, GA 153. Vienna, April 13, 1914.

VIII.2. The stage of sacrifice in the afterdeath ritual of the hierarchies

Karmic Relationships, vol. III. GA 237. Dornach, July 4, 1924.

VIII.3. The stage of transformation GA 237, see VIII.2. Dornach, July 4, 1924.

VIII.4. The stage of communion GA 237, see VIII.2. Dornach, July 4, 1924.

NOTE IX

The ritual of worlds of the hierarchies in the midst of sleeping humanity.

IX.1. GA 237, see VIII.2. Dornach, June 6, 1924.

IX.2. Temple architecture, ritual, and karma

Karmic Relationships, vol. II, GA 236 Dornach, April 27, 1924.

IX.3. The religious deepening of karma understanding to the fully human basis. Feeling by means of the Christmas idea, the Easter idea, the Pentecost idea GA 236, see IX.2. Dornach, June 4, 1924.

IX.4. The religious element in the karma experience GA 236, see IX.2. Dornach, June 29, 1924.

NOTE X

The origin of all pre-Christian rituals in the four stages of initiation. Their relationship to ritual and apocalypse in Christianity.

X.1. The four stages in Egyptian, Pythagorean, and Christian intiation

The Apocalypse of St. John, GA 104, Rudolf Steiner Press, 1977. Nuremberg, June 18, 1908.

X.2. The four stages of initiation in the Revelation of St. John
GA 104, see X.1. Nuremberg, June 18, 1908.

X.3. The Egyptian initiation
Egyptian Myths and Mysteries, GA 106, Anthroposophic Press, 1971
Leipzig, September 13, 1908.

NOTE XI

The origin of the reverse ritual of the cosmic communion in the Michael
movement in the spiritual world.

XI.1. The Michael movement in the spiritual world
"Das lebendige Wesen der Anthroposophie und seine Pflege." Vol. Nine:
"Die Konstitution der Allgemeinen Anthroposophischen Gesellschat und
der Freien Hochschule für Geisteswissenschaft," 260 a, 1966.
Breslau, June 9, 1924, pp. 257-258.

XI.2. Michael and the cosmic intelligence of the sun forces
Karmic Relationships, vol. III, GA 237. Dornach, July 28, 1924.

XI.3. The Michaelic school in the spiritual world and cosmic intelligence GA
237, see XI.2. Dornach, July 28, 1924.
Karmic Relationships, vol. IV, GA 238, Rudolf Steiner Press, 1965. Dornach, September 9, 1924.

XI.4. The cosmic ritual in the spiritual world GA 237, se XI.2.
Dornach, July 6, 1924;Dornach, July 8, 1924; GA 238, see XI.3. Dornach,
September 16, 1924.

XI.5. The final preparation for Michaelic leadership of mankind by
Michael´s victory over the dragon in the spiritual world in the forties of the
nineteenth century
The Fall of the Spirits of Darkness, GA 177, Rudolf Steiner Press. Dornach,
14, October 14, 1917; Dornach, October 26, 1917.

NOTE XII

Anthroposophy as the knowledge of religion, the knowledge of religion as
the path to religion, religion in Anthroposophy as its actual realization.

XII.1. The three steps of Anthroposophy

*Philosophy, Cosmology and Religion,*GA 215, Anthroposophic Press, 1984. Dornach, September 6, 1922.

XII.2. The path of knowledge to religion GA 215, see XII.1. Dornach, September 7, 1922.

XII.2. The origin of religion in sleep GA 215, see XII.1.Dornach, September 10, 1922.

XII.4. The origin of religion in pre-natal consciousness GA 215, see XII.1. Dornach, September 11, 1922.

XII.5. The origin of religion in the death experience and the Christ experience

GA 215, see XII.1.Dornach, September 12, 1922; Dornach, September 12, 1922; Dornach, September 12, 1922.

XII.6. Anthroposophy as a striving toward permeation of the world with Christ
"Das Sonnenmysterium und das Mysterium von Tod und Auferstehung," GA 211, 1963, pp. 203-207, pp. 212-217.

Note XIII
The secret of the trinity in the reverse ritual.

XIII.1. The most popular concept of differentiation in the trinity God the Father in the unknown, hidden underground places of nature, the cosmos and human nature;God the Son in the unconscious soul life of the human being; God the Spirit in the totality of all conscious soul and spiritual events in the human being; *From Jesus to Christ*, GA 131.
Karlsruhe, October 5, 1911.

The experience of the trinity

XIII.2. The anthroposophical-esoteric concept of the differentiation in the trinity

God the Spirit in Manas, God the Son in the Buddha, God the Father in Atma; *The Christian Mystery*, GA 96, Anthroposophic Press, 1998. Berlin, January 28, 1907.

XIII.3. The concept of the mysteries of differentiation in the trinity

The effect of the mystery of Golgatha as pouring out of the Holy
Ghost in the pentecost event as universal wisdom for the individual person

The pre-Christian mysteries of the spirit, the Christian ones of the Son, the
future ones of the Father GA 96, see XIII.2; Berlin, March, 1907; Berlin,
April 1, 1907.

XIII. 4. The dynamic-therapeutic concept of differentiation in the trinity

The Father in the subnatural, the Son in nature, the Spirit in the supernatural

The therapeutic process of doctor and priest in their polarity

Pastoral Medicine, GA 318, Anthroposophic Press, 1987.
Dornach, September 18, 1924.

XIII.5. The experiential concept of diffentiation in the trinity in the changing of the Times

Knowledge of reason, knowledge of Revelation and religion in Goethe and
Schiller;*The Mystery of the Trinity* GA 214, Anthroposophic Press, 1991.

On Goethe and Schiller: Dornach, July 29, 1922;The changing of the experience of the Trinity in the changing of the times: Dornach, July 30, 1922.

XIII.6. The Foundation Stone poem

The Christmas Conference GA 260, Anthroposophic Press, 1990. Dornach,
December 25, 1923.

Bibliography

Works by Friedrich Benesch

1. *The Ringworms* (Systems, anatomy, physiology and ecology) Publications of the Zoological Institute of the University Klausenburg 1931

2. *Power Struggle and the Church* (Kronstadt/Siebenbürgen) 1938

3. *The Hutberg Stronghold — A Neolithic Mixed Settlement —* Halle 1941

4. *The Energy Crisis: Limits to Growth?* Urachhaus, Stuttgart 1973 Floris Books, Edinburgh, 1983

5. *Ascension* Urachhaus, 1974/ Floris Books, 1979

6. *The Crisis of Consciousness of the Present* Urachhaus, 1975

7. *Pentecost Today* Urachhaus, 1976

8. *Easter* Urachhaus, 1978/ Floris Books, 1981

9. *Apocalypse — An Occult Mineralogie* Urachhaus, 1981

10. *Open Up the Door — Waldorf Pedagogy at Public Schools* Urachhaus, 1984

11. *Whitsun* Floris Books, 1979

12. *Der Turmalin: Eine Monographie* Urachhaus,1990

Part Three

Brotherhood and the Struggle for Existence

A Lecture by
Rudolf Steiner

Berlin, November 23, 1905

This is a revised translation of the German lecture: Bruder-schaft und Daseinskampf, which appears in Die Weltraetsel und die Anthroposophie, (GA Dornach 1966, B.-Nr. 54) published by the Rudolf Steiner Nachlassverwaltung who granted permission.

Today it is our task to speak about two impulses of the soul; one of them, brotherhood, is an ideal that has filled mankind ever since men have had the capacity to feel. The other one is the struggle for existence, which we meet with just at present wherever we look. Brotherhood and the struggle for existence! Those of you who have occupied yourselves even a little with the aims of our spiritual-scientific movement know our main principle: to create the heart, the kernel, of a brotherhood based on all-embracing human love that transcends race, sex, profession, religion, and so on. Thus, the Theosophical Society has placed this principle of general brotherhood foremost and made it the most important of its ideals. Of all these cultural endeavors that we need most at present the Society considers this great ethical striving towards brotherhood to be most closely connected with the ultimate aim of human development.

He who strives in the spiritual-scientific manner believes, and not only believes but knows quite clearly, that deep cognition, cognition of the spiritual world, when it really takes hold of man, must lead to brotherhood;[1] this brotherhood is the noblest fruit of deep, inner cognition.

Spiritual philosophy appears to contradict in this matter much that has appeared in recent times. Certain circles point time and time again to struggle as a force for progress. How often do we hear today that man's forces grow strong through meeting resistance, that man grows strong in will and in intellectual initiative by matching his strength against an opponent. One philosophy that grew out of a spiritual foundation, that of Friedrich Nietzsche, contains, among many other sentences inspired by struggle, the following: "I love the critic; I love the great critic more than the little one." We can find this sentiment ever and again in Nietzsche's work, in many different formulations; it is something that belongs completely to his view of life. According also to certain long-established economic theories, the struggle of all against all, as this takes form in economic competition, is a powerful lever for progress. How often has it been said that mankind would progress best if each person asserted and benefited himself, as much as he could. The word "individualism" has even become a catchword, mostly in connection with material life, to be sure, but also, and not without validity, in connection with the inner, spiritual life.

It is the belief of many economists and social theorists that man can serve his fellowmen best when he takes as much as possible from life, because if he becomes economically strong he can better serve the community. And we hear it asserted that a person should not fall into a routine, should strive for the all-round development of his powers, should live freely in self-expression, should unfold his inner being; and that by so doing he can best serve his fellowmen. There are many among us who are downright feverish in the pursuit of this latter principle, who cannot have enough of "doing their thing."

Spiritual science does not deny the necessity of this struggle for existence, especially in our tune; but is also conscious that just today, when this struggle is producing such powerful effects, the principle of brotherhood, in all its depth, must be brought closer to our understanding again.

The most important question will be: Is it actually true, as many believe, that man's forces grow best through encountering opposition, that above all it is struggle that makes man great and strong? Natural science has raised this idea of man's struggle for existence to a universal principle; and in the West particularly, it has been believed for some time that those creatures are fittest that have driven their opponents from the field, and so survived.

The scientist Huxley says: When we look at life, it looks like the combat of gladiators — the strongest is victorious, the others perish. If one would believe the scientists, one would have to assume that all creatures that now live in the world have driven out those who were here before them. There is even a school of social thought whose adherents want to make the principle of the struggle for existence into an actual doctrine of human development. In a book titled *From Darwin to Nietzsche*, Dean Alexander Tille tries to show that the happiness of mankind in the future will depend on man emblazoning this struggle for existence boldly and freely on the banners of his development, that we must see to it that the unfit perish, and that we must further only what is strong and forceful. We need a social order that suppresses the weak, because they impede man's progress.

I ask you: who is strong? He who has ideal, spiritual strength, but a weak body, or he who has less spiritual force, but a robust body? As you can see, general rules do not help much in this matter. It is difficult to decide who really should survive the struggle for existence; and if we were to deal with practical measures, this question would have to be decided first. Now we ask ourselves: What do we observe in human life? Is it brotherhood, or the struggle for existence, that has accomplished great things in mankind's development — or have both impulses contributed something?

Natural science does not occupy the same ground today that it did even ten years ago. The Russian scientist Kessler gave a lecture in 1880, in which he showed that the animal types most capable of development and truly progressive are not the ones that do the most fighting, but those that give mutual support to one another, that help each other. No one can maintain that struggle and combat do not exist in the animal kingdom. Certainly they are present but the question is: What furthers development more — warfare or mutual assistance? And which types survive? Those whose members constantly fight with each other, or those that have mutual service? Scientific investigation has already shown that it is not struggle but the rendering of assistance that truly promotes progress. Prince Kropotkin, in his book *Mutual Help in the Animal Kingdom and Human Life,* provides many beautiful contributions to the questions that occupy us here.

What has brotherhood achieved for human development? We have only to look at our own ancestors. One could easily gain the impression that it was the hunt and warfare that advanced them, that primarily molded their character. But when one delves deeper, it will be found that this first impression is not correct, that precisely those early Teutonic tribes prospered most that had developed the principle of brotherhood to an extraordinary degree. We find this principle of brotherhood expressed above all in the way property was managed, before and after the great migrations. Common ownership of land was the general rule. Each village owned common grounds, and — excepting those few possessions necessary for household use, and perhaps a garden — all other property was owned in common as well. From time to time the land was divided anew among the people. And it was these tribes, which practiced brotherhood to this extraordinary degree with respect to material goods, that became strong.

A few centuries later we find this principle bearing remarkable fruit. When the principle of brotherhood had manifested in earlier times, people went so far as to burn what somebody possessed on his own piece of land, at the time of his death, because one did not want to own the personal property of another after his death. This practice was abandoned for a number of reasons, but chiefly because some people had acquired large landholdings, forcing others into serfdom and feudal services. The idea of brotherhood then asserted itself in another striking form. Those who were oppressed by their masters, by their owners, wanted to free themselves. There was a great movement towards freedom throughout Europe in the middle of the Middle Ages. This movement towards freedom grew out of a spirit of the brotherhood of man, and from it arose a general culture, the city culture of the middle Middle Ages. Those who could not endure servitude on the land fled their masters and sought their freedom in the growing cities. People came down from Scotland, France, and Russia; from everywhere they came together and built the free cities. Thus, the principle of brotherhood developed and furthered culture to a high degree. Men of similar occupations joined in societies called oath-brotherhoods, which later grew into the guilds. These oath-brotherhoods were far more than mere societies of crafts or trades-people. Born of the practical, everyday life, these associations developed to moral heights. Mutual aid was the fundamental concern of these brotherhoods, and many aspects of life that are of nobody's concern today were occasions for such support. For example, members of such a brotherhood would help each other in case of illness. Two brothers were appointed to keep daily vigil at the bedside of a sick brother. Members who were ill received food and the fraternal spirit prevailed even beyond death: the responsibility for burying a brother member in proper fashion was considered a special honor. Finally, the care of widows and orphans was a duty of the oath-brotherhood. You can see from these examples how there grew up an understanding of the moral life of the community that modern man can hardly imagine. Present conditions are not being criticized in any way. They have become necessary; just as it was necessary that the conditions of the Middle Ages came to expression in their own ways. We must only understand that there have been other phases of development than the present one.

In the free cities of the Middle Ages people spoke of a 'lawful' price, of a 'lawful' market. What was meant? In the

early days, when produce was brought into town from the surrounding countryside, it was strictly prohibited during the first
days to sell these goods, except in retail. Nobody was allowed
to buy wholesale and to become a dealer. Then there was no
thought that price should be established according to supply
and demand: people understood how to regulate both. Groups
in the cities or in the guilds had to establish prices for the
products of members, after the members had explained what
was needed to produce the goods, to become a producer.
Nobody was allowed to sell at a higher price. Even when we
look at labor conditions, we see how profound was the understanding of man's needs at that time. When we consider the
wages, taking into account the entirely different conditions,
we must say that the laborer's wages could not compare with
those of today. This fact has often been interpreted quite
wrongly by researchers. These brotherhoods were organized
out of practical considerations, and therefore they developed
gradually along practical lines. They then spread from one city
to another, because it was natural that those in several cities
who had a common craft and common interests should unite
and support each other.

At that time, men were not united under police-enforced
law, but held together for practical reasons. This particular
phase of the deepening of the principle of brotherhood in the
cities of Europe can be seen vividly in its fruits. The immense
artistic accomplishments of the 12th and 11th centuries would
not have been possible without such deepening. Culturally, we
can only understand Dante's stupendous work, *The Divine
Comedy*, when we understand the impact of the principle of
brotherhood. Also, the arts of printing, copper-engraving,
paper-making, and watch-making, as well as the later inven-
tions, came about through the principle of brotherhood. What
we are accustomed to call the citizenry arises from the cultivation of this principle in the cities of the Middle Ages. Much
that has been created through profound scientific and artistic
activity would have been impossible without this principle.
When a cathedral was to be built-the one in Cologne or any

other—first a society was formed, a so-called building—guild, whose members joined in cooperative effort. One can see intuitively the expression of the cooperative principle even in the architectural style; one can see it expressed in almost every medieval town, whether you go to the north of Scotland or to Venice, whether you look at cities in Russia or in Poland.

The thing we must stress is this: The principle of botherhood arose under the influence of a current of the time that sought to enter decisively into the material culture. Therefore we see everywhere in the higher culture that arises, as well as in what remains to us as the fruit of that time, the material, the physical. Material existence had for once to be cultivated, and in order to cultivate it rightly, and work it through thoroughly, this brotherhood principle was at that time necessary. From the living spirit of brotherhood of the earlier time, arose the abstraction, and through this abstraction, through this intellectualistic kind of thinking, our life has been split so that now we do not rightly know, can no longer properly understand, just how the struggle for existence and the principle of brotherhood actually work together. On the one hand, spiritual life has become more and more abstract. Morals and justice, perceptions of political and other social relationships, have been reduced to ever more abstract maxims, and the struggle for existence has become more and more separated, as by an abyss, from what people truly have felt as their ideal. In the middle of the Middle Ages there was a harmony between one's ideal and what one actually did. If it has ever been shown that one can be an idealist and practical man at the same time, it was shown in the Middle Ages. Also, the relationship between Roman law and actual life was still harmonious. Today, however, considerations of justice float somewhere above the life of morals. Many will say: we know what is good, just and fair, but it is not practical. This divergence appears when thinking becomes separated from the highest principles of life. From the 16th century onwards, spiritual life develops more in accordance with the principles of the intellect. The guild-member who, together with the other twelve jurors, sat in judgment on an offense committed by a fellow member of the guild, was a brother to the man being judged. Life was connected with life. Everyone knew the other's work, and everyone tried to understand why, for once, the accused might have deviated from the proper path. One looked, as it were, into the brother, and actually desired to do so.

Nowadays a jurisprudence has developed in which both judge and lawyer are interested only in the law, so that both of them see only a 'case', to which they have to apply the law. Every moral thought has been divorced from the science of justice. We have seen this situation develop ever more explicitly during the last century. Under the feeling for brotherhood in the Middle Ages, however, there evolved the principles necessary for healthy progress: confidence and competence, both of which are falling by the wayside today. The judgment of the competent expert has given way almost entirely to abstract jurisprudence, to an abstract parliamentarianism. The average, the common understanding, the voice of the majority, has become the yardstick today, not competence. This preference for the majority had to come. But just as one cannot vote in mathematics to get the right result — because 3 times 3 is always 9 and 3 times 9 is always 27 — so it is here. It would be impossible to carry through the principle of competence, or expertness, without the principle of brotherhood, of brotherly love.

In life, the struggle for existence has its justification. Because man is an individuality who as a single being has to make his way through life, he is part of the struggle for existence. In a sense, the words of Rusckerts hold here: when the rose beautifies itself, it also beautifies the garden. If we do not make ourselves capable of helping our fellowmen, we shall be poor helpers. If we do not see to it that all our talents are developed, we shall be poor helpers. If we do not see to it that all our talents are developed, we shall have little success in helping our brothers. In order to develop these talents, a certain egoism is necessary because egoism is connected with initiative. The person who understands how not to be led, how not to be influenced by everything in his surroundings, but who descends into his own, inner being where the sources of strength are to be found, will develop into a strong and able person, and in him there will be a greater ability to serve others than in the one who conforms to all kinds of influences that come from his surroundings. Obviously, this principle which is necessary for man can be developed to an extreme. But this principle will bear the proper fruits only when it is combined with that of brotherly love.

The guilds in the free cities of the Middle Ages show how what is practical became strong precisely under the principle of the mutual, personal, and individual rendering of help. From where did the guilds draw this strength? They drew it from living in brotherhood with their fellowmen. It is correct to make oneself as strong as possible; but can we become strong at all without brotherly love? He who rises to a real knowledge of the soul must answer with a decisive NO.

In all of nature we see examples of the cooperation of single beings within a whole. Consider the human body. It consists of independent beings, millions and millions of, single, independent beings or cells. When one takes a part of this human body he will find that it consists precisely of such individual beings. But how do they cooperate? How has that which in nature must form a whole, a totality become selfless? None of our cells asserts its separateness in an egoistic manner. The miraculous tool of thinking, our brain, is also composed of millions of delicate cells, but each one operates in its place harmoniously with the others. What causes the cooperation of these small cells? What causes a higher being to express itself through these small living beings? Man's soul is the cause. But the human soul could never work on earth if these millions of small beings had not renounced their individualities, putting themselves at the service of this great being they have in common, which we describe as the soul. The soul sees with the cells of the eye, thinks by means of the cells of the brain, lives through the cells of the blood. There we can see what union, what association means. Association means the possibility for a higher being to express itself through the members when they are united.

This principle is general for all life. Five people together, who think and feel harmoniously together, are more than 1 plus I plus 1 plus 1 plus 1; they are not just the sum of the five, just as our body is not the sum of the five senses. Men's living together and within one another has the same significance as the living together of the cells within the human body. A new higher being is in the midst of the five-yes, even among the two or three. "Where two or three are gathered in my name, I shall be in their midst." It is not the one, or the other, or the third, but something entirely new that springs from the union. This new entity arises only when the one lives in the other, when the single individual person draws strength not only from himself, but also from others. But that can happen only when each lives selflessly in the other. Thus, human associations are the secret places where higher spiritual beings descend in order to work through the single individuals, just as the soul works through the members of the body.

In our materialistic time, what I have said will not be easily believed, but for spiritual science it is real in the highest degree. Therefore, spiritual science does not talk in abstractions when it speaks of a folk-spirit, or folk-soul, or a family spirit or the spirit of some other community. One cannot see the spirit who works through an association, but he is there; and he is there through the brotherly love of the people working within the association. Just as the body has a soul, so a guild or brotherhood has a soul; this is not just a figure of speech.

People who work together in a brotherhood are magicians, because they draw higher beings into their circle. One no longer has to call to witness the machinations of spiritism when one works out of brotherly love in a community. Higher beings do manifest themselves there. When we give ourselves over to brotherhood, this giving, this merging into the totality, is a steeling, a strengthening of our organs. When we then act or speak as members of such a community, it is not the single soul that acts or speaks in us, but the spirit of the community. This will be the secret of the progress of mankind in the future: to work through communities. Just as one epoch takes the place of another and each of them has its own task, so it is with the Middle Ages in relation to our own epoch, and so it is with our epoch in relation to a future one. The brotherhoods of the Middle Ages worked within the immediately practical life, when they laid the foundations for the useful arts. These organizations began to show a materialistic bias only after they had achieved their fruits. By then the foundations of their consciousness, namely brotherhood, had more or less vanished, as the abstract principle of the state, the abstract spiritual life, took the place of one person's entering into another with true feeling. The future will have the task of reestablishing brotherhoods, and of establishing them out of the spiritual, out of the highest ideals of the soul. The life of man has up to now given birth to a multitude of associations; it has called forth a terrible struggle for existence, which has just now reached its high point. Spiritual science, however, aims to advance mankind's highest ideals in the spirit of the principle of brotherhood, and thus you see that the worldwide movement of spiritual science replaces in all fields the struggle for existence with the principle of brotherhood. We must learn how to conduct community life. We must not believe that this or that scheme resting in anything less or other than the true feeling for brotherhood will be able to accomplish anything lasting.

Everyone would like to know how one unites struggle for existence with brotherhood. That is very simple. We must learn to replace struggle with positive labor, to replace combat with the ideal. What that means is little understood today. People do not know which struggle they are talking about, because they talk about nothing else: the social struggle, the struggle for peace, the struggle for the emancipation of women, the struggle about the soil, and so on. Spiritual science strives to replace struggle with positive labor. He who has immersed himself in spiritual science knows that in any field of life, struggle never leads to true results. Try, without fighting the opponent, to introduce into life, to assert, what you in your experience and through your cognition have found to be correct.

Of course, this can be only an ideal, but such an ideal must be there, so that it can be introduced into life as an axiom of spiritual science. The people who join with others and who put their strength at the disposal of all are those who will provide the foundation for healthy development in the future. The Theosophical Society† wants to be exemplary in this respect In this organization one works through the labor of each individual member. This idea must for once he really understood. He works best who does not want to push through his own opinion but seeks to support what he observes in the eyes of his fellow brothers — who searches the thoughts and feelings of his fellowmen and makes himself their servant. Within this circle he works best who in practical life does not regard his own opinions as important When we try thus to understand that our most valuable forces arise out of our society with one another, and that this society is not only to be adhered to as abstract principal but has to operate in every act, in every moment of life, then we shall progress. Only, we must not become impatient.

Spiritual science makes us conscious of a higher reality, and this consciousness will enable us to go forward in the application of the principal of brotherhood.

Today people still call us unpractical idealists. It will not be long, however, before spiritual scientists will prove to be the most practical people, because they take the forces of life into account. Nobody doubts that somebody will be hurt when we hit him on the head with a stone. What is not considered is that it is much worse to send somebody a hateful feeling, that the soul of man is much more hurt than when the stone hurts the body. Everything depends on the spirit or disposition with which we face our fellowman. But our strength for fruitful work in the future will depend precisely on our comprehending this truth. When we exert ourselves to live in brotherhood in this way, then we are putting the principle of brotherhood into practice.

To be tolerant in a spiritual sense is different from what is commonly understood. It means also to respect the freedom of someone else's thought. To shove somebody from his seat is the act of a lout, when this action, however, is committed in thought, nobody registers it as an injustice. We do speak a good deal in general about the necessity of valuing other people's opinions, but we are not inclined to apply this good advice to ourselves.

A word has for us, as yet almost no importance, it is heard, and yet it is not heard. We must learn, however, to listen with the soul. We must understand how to grasp the most intimate things with the soul. What later becomes physical reality always exists first in the spirit. Therefore we must suppress our own opinion in order to hear another's completely; not only the word, but also the feeling behind it even when the conviction arises in us that what the other person says is wrong. There is more strength in being able to listen as long as the other speaks than in interrupting him. Such listening produces an entirely different understanding. You will feel as if the other person's soul were filling with warmth, with light when you face him in this way with absolute tolerance. We should guarantee not only freedom of the person but complete freedom; yes, we must value even the freedom of the different opinion. This is only one example, but it can stand for much else. From the point of view of spiritual science, the person who interrupts someone else's speech does something similar to the person who would give him a kick. Once one understands that one commits a much more violent offense when interrupting someone's talk than if one were to kick him, only then can one really understand brotherhood with the soul, only then does it become a fact. Therein lies the greatness of the spiritual scientific movement: that it brings us a new faith, a new conviction of those spiritual forces that flow from man to man. That is the higher, spiritual principle of brotherhood.

Anyone can picture for himself how far mankind is removed from such a spiritual ideal. Everyone may develop himself to send his loved ones thoughts of love and friendship, if he can find the time. Generally, people consider such acts meaningless. But once you understand that thoughts are just as much a force as the electric current that flows from one apparatus to another, then you will also better understand the principle of brotherhood; then gradually our social consciousness will become clearer — and, finally, practical.

From this point of view it becomes clear how spiritual science considers the struggle for existence and brotherhood. We know quite well that many a person, having been placed in one or the other position in life, would simply perish if he did not howl with the wolves, so to speak; if he did not carry on his struggle for existence as cruelly as many others do. For the materialist there is almost no way to escape this struggle for existence. We must, to be sure, do our duty at the spot where karma put us. To do the right thing, however, we must be aware that we would accomplish much more, if we were to renounce the desire to see results immediately. A materialist will perhaps think that you do nothing when you make yourself send thoughts of love to him whom you might have hurt in the struggle for existence — perhaps, when you yourself stand with a bleeding soul. But after the foregoing explanations, you will understand that this act must have its effect later, because, as we know, nothing is lost that is done spiritually.

In this way we can take up the struggle for existence, disheartened in soul and with sadness in our hearts, and yet transform this struggle through our contribution. To work thus means to change the struggle for existence in a practical way. To accomplish this change from one day to another will not be possible, but that it will come is beyond all doubt. When we work on our own soul in the spirit of brotherhood, in serving ourselves we shall best serve mankind; for it is true that when we persist in our selfish separateness, our talents are uprooted like a plant that is torn from the soil. An eye is scarcely an eye when it has been torn from its socket and just so little is a human soul still a human soul when it separates itself from the community of man.

You will see that we develop our talents best when we live in a brotherly community, that we live most intensively when we take root in that totality. To be sure, we must wait till what has taken root in the totality ripens into fruitfulness, through silent inward meditation. And we must not lose ourselves in the world, because what the poet said is true in the highest spiritual sense: one has to be quiet within oneself that one's talents may unfold. Those talents, however, are rooted in the world. They strengthen us; but to improve our character, we have to live with and within a community. Therefore, if man lives in accordance with the real, true principle of brotherhood, he is strongest precisely within the struggle for existence; and he will find in the stillness of his heart his greatest powers, as he develops his entire personality, his entire individuality, in union with his other human brothers and sisters. It is true: a talent develops in tranquility. But the following is also true: character, and with it the entire human being and all of mankind, develops within the currents of the world.

† Editor's Note: Where "Theosophy" or "theosophical" is used in this text, Steiner essentially means the same spiritual science he later called "Anthroposophy."

[1] *Editor's Note*: Steiner's use of "brotherhood" and "man," conforming to the usages of his day, should not mislead us. His feminism was radical and prophetic. Interested readers should refer for example to his remarks in Chapter 14, "Individuality and Genus," in *Intuitive Thinking as a Spiritual Path: The Philosophy of Freedom* (Anthroposophic Press, 1995). It is left to the reader to exchange "sisterhood" for "brotherhood," or to make some other personally appropriate substitution.

Preparing
for the Sixth Epoch

BY

Rudolf Steiner

This lecture was given in Düsseldorf at the opening of Group II, on June 15, 1915. It was originally published in English with the title How Anthroposophical Groups Prepare for the Sixth Epoch.

We have come here today for the opening of the group founded by our friend, Professor C. This group wishes to dedicate itself to the spiritual life of the present and future in the way that is customary in our movement. On such an occasion it is always good to remember why we associate in groups and to ask ourselves why we found working groups and cultivate in them the spiritual treasure to which we dedicate our forces.

If this question is to be answered truly, we must realize that we make a distinction, even if only in thought, between the work we do in a group like this and our other work in the world. Those who are unwilling to enter deeply into more intimate truths connected with the spiritual progress of humanity. might ask if we could not cultivate spiritual science without forming ourselves into groups, but simply by finding lecturers and providing opportunities for people who may not know each other to come together and have access to the spiritual treasure of which we speak. We could, of course, proceed in this way. But as long as it is at all possible to establish, in the wider and narrower senses, associations of human beings who are known to one another and who come together in friendship and brotherliness within these working groups, we will continue to found them in full consciousness of the attitude of soul that is part and parcel of spiritual science. It is not without meaning that among us there are human beings who want to cultivate the more intimate side of spiritual knowledge and who sincerely intend to work together in brotherliness and harmony. Not only are relationships and conversation affected by the fact that we can speak quite differently among ourselves, knowing that we are speaking to souls consciously associated with us — not only is this so, but something else is also to be remembered. The establishment of individual groups is connected with the whole conception that we hold of our movement if we understand its inmost nature. We must all be conscious that our movement is significant not only for the existence known to the senses and for the existence that is grasped by our outwardly-turned mind, but that through this movement our souls are seeking a real and genuine link with the spiritual worlds. Again and again, in full consciousness, we should say to ourselves that by the cultivation of spiritual science we transfer our souls as it were into spheres that are peopled not only by beings of earth but also by the beings of the higher hierarchies, the beings of the invisible worlds. We must realize that our work is of significance for these invisible worlds, that we are actually within these worlds. In the spiritual world, the work performed by those who know one another within such groups is quite different from work carried on outside such a group and dispersed about the world. The work carried out in brotherly harmony within our groups has quite a different significance for the spiritual world than other work we may undertake. To understand this fully we must remind ourselves of truths we have studied in many aspects during recent years.

Earth evolution in the post-Atlantean age was sustained in the beginning by the culture of the ancient Indian period of civilization. This was followed by the ancient Persian epoch — the designation is only more or less appropriate but we need not go into that now. Then came the Egypto-Chaldean-Babylonian period of culture, then the Greco-Latin, then our fifth post-Atlantean epoch. On the one hand, each of these epochs has to cultivate a particular form of culture and of spiritual life primarily concerned with the external and visible world. But each epoch must at the same time prepare, bear within it in a preparatory stage, what is to come in the ensuing period of culture.

Within the womb, as it were, of the ancient Indian epoch, that of ancient Persia was prepared; within the ancient Persian culture, that of the Egypto-Chaldean epoch was prepared, and so on. Our fifth post-Atlantean epoch must prepare the coming sixth epoch of culture. Our task in spiritual science is not only to acquire spiritual treasure for ourselves, for the eternal life of the soul, but to prepare what will constitute the content, the specific external work of the sixth epoch of culture. Thus it has been in each of the post-Atlantean epochs. The centers of the mysteries were the places in which the form of external life belonging to the next epoch of culture was prepared. The mysteries were associations of human beings among whom other things were cultivated than those cultivated in the outer world. The ancient Indian epoch was concerned with the cultivation of the human etheric body, the ancient Persian epoch with the cultivation of the astral body, the Egypto-Chaldean with that of the sentient soul, the Greco-Latin with that of the intellectual or mind soul. Our own epoch, through-out its duration, will develop and unfold the consciousness or spiritual soul. But what will give to external culture in the sixth epoch its content and character, must be prepared in advance.

Many characteristics of the sixth epoch of culture will be entirely different from those of our age. Three characteristic traits can be mentioned, of which we must realize that they should be carried in our hearts for the sixth epoch of culture and that it is our task to prepare them for this sixth epoch.

Nowadays, we lack a quality that, in the sixth epoch, will be a characteristic of all those who reach the goal of that epoch and have not fallen short of it. It is a quality that will not, of course, be found among those who in the sixth epoch have still remained at a more primitive stage. One of the most significant characteristics of those who live on the earth at the peak of culture in the sixth epoch will be a certain moral quality. Little of this quality is perceptible in modern humanity. Today, one must be delicately organized for the soul to feel pain at the sight of others in the world in less happy circumstances than one's own. It is true that more delicately organized natures do feel pain at the suffering that is so widespread in the world. But this can only be said of the people who are particularly sensitive. In the sixth epoch, the most highly cultured will not only feel pain such as is caused today by the sight of poverty, suffering, and misery in the world, but such individuals will experience the suffering of another human being as their own suffering. If they see a hungry man they will feel the hunger right down into the physical, so acutely indeed that the hunger of the other man will be unendurable to them. The moral characteristic indicated here is that, unlike conditions in the fifth epoch, in the sixth epoch the well-being of the individual will depend entirely upon the well-being of the whole. Just as nowadays the well-being of a single human limb depends upon the health of the whole body, and when the whole body is not healthy the single limb is not up to doing its work, so in the sixth epoch a common consciousness will lay hold of the then-civilized humanity; and in a far higher degree than a limb feels the health of the whole body, the individual will feel the suffering, the need, the poverty or the wealth of the whole. This is the first, and preeminently moral trait that will characterize the cultured humanity of the sixth epoch.

A second fundamental characteristic will be that everything we call the fruits of belief today will depend to a far, far higher degree than is the case today upon the single individuality. Spiritual science expresses this by saying that in every sphere of religion in the sixth epoch, complete freedom of thought and a longing for it will so lay hold of men that what a man likes to believe, what religious convictions he holds, will rest wholly within the power of his own individuality. Collective beliefs that exist in so many forms today among the various communities will no longer influence those who constitute the civilized portion of humanity in the sixth epoch of culture. Everyone will feel that complete freedom of thought in the domain of religion is a fundamental right of the human being. The third characteristic will be that men in the sixth epoch will only be considered to have real knowledge when they recognize the spiritual, when they know that the spiritual pervades the world and that human souls must unite with the spiritual. What is known as science today with its materialistic trend will certainly not be honored by the name of science in the sixth post-Atlantean epoch. It will be regarded as antiquated superstition, able to pass muster only among those who have remained behind at the stage of the superseded fifth post-Atlantean epoch. Today we regard it as superstition if someone holds the view that no limb ought to be separated from the body at death because this would make it impossible to enter the spiritual world as a whole human being. Such a person still connects the idea of immortality with pure materialism, with the belief that an impress of one's whole form must pass into the spiritual world. This is to think materialistically while believing in immortality. Today, knowing from spiritual science that the spiritual has to be separated from the body and that only the spiritual passes into the supersensible world, we regard such materialistic beliefs in immortality as superstition. Similarly, in the sixth epoch all materialistic beliefs, including science, will be regarded as antiquated superstition. Men as a matter of course will accept as science only such forms of knowledge as are based upon the spiritual, upon pneumatology.

The whole purpose of spiritual science is to prepare in this sense for the sixth epoch of culture. We try to cultivate spiritual science in order to overcome materialism, to prepare the kind of science that must exist in that epoch. We found communities of human beings within which there must be no dogmatic beliefs or any tendency to accept teaching simply because it emanates from one person or another. We found communities of human beings in which everything, without exception, must be built upon the soul's free assent to the teachings. Herein we prepare what spiritual science calls free-

dom of thought. By coming together in friendly associations
for the purpose of cultivating spiritual science, we prepare the
culture, the civilization of the sixth post-Atlantean epoch.

But we must look still more deeply into the course of
human evolution if we are fully to understand the real tasks of
our associations and groups. In the first post-Atlantean epoch,
too, in communities that in those days were connected with the
mysteries, men cultivated what subsequently prevailed in the
second epoch. In the associations peculiar to the first, the
ancient Indian epoch, men were concerned with the cultivation of the astral body, which was to be the specific outer task
of the second epoch. It would lead much too far today to
describe what, in contrast to the external culture of the time,
was developed in these associations peculiar to ancient India
in order to prepare for the second, ancient Persian epoch. But
this much may be said, when those men of the ancient Indian
epoch came together in order to prepare what was necessary
for the second epoch, they felt: "We have not yet attained, nor
have we in us, what we shall have when our souls are incarnated in the next epoch. It still hovers above us." It was in
truth so. In the first epoch of culture, what was to descend
from the heavens to the earth in the second epoch still hovered
over the souls of men. The work achieved on earth by men in
intimate assemblies connected with the mysteries was of such
a nature that forces flowed upwards to the spirits of the higher hierarchies, enabling them to nourish and cultivate what
was to stream down into the souls of men as substance and
content of the astral body in the second, ancient Persian
epoch. The forces that descended at a later stage of maturity
into the souls incarnated in the bodies of ancient Persian civi-
lizations were like little children in the first epoch. Forces
streaming upwards from the work of men below in preparation for the next epoch were received and nurtured by the spiritual world above. So it must be in every epoch of culture.

In our epoch it is the consciousness or spiritual soul that
has developed in us through our ordinary civilization and culture. Beginning with the fourteenth, fifteenth and sixteenth

centuries, science and materialistic consciousness have laid hold of the human being. This will gradually become more widespread, until by the end of the fifth epoch its development will have been completed. In the sixth epoch, however, it is the spirit self that must be developed within the souls of men, just as now the consciousness soul is being developed. The nature of spirit self is that it must pre-suppose the existence in human souls of the three characteristics of which I have spoken: social life in which brotherliness prevails, freedom of thought, and pneumatology. These three characteristics are essential in a community of human beings within which the spirit self is to develop as the consciousness soul develops in the souls of the fifth epoch. We may therefore picture to ourselves that by uniting in brotherliness in working groups, something hovers invisibly over our work, something that is like the child of the forces of the spirit self — the spirit self that is nurtured by the beings of the higher hierarchies in order that it may stream down into our souls when they are again on earth in the sixth epoch of civilization. In our groups we perform work that streams upward to those forces that are being prepared for the spirit self.

So you see, it is only through the wisdom of spiritual science itself that we can understand what we are really doing in respect of our connection with the spiritual worlds when we come together in these working groups. The thought that we do this work not only for the sake of our own egos but in order that it may stream upward into the spiritual worlds, the thought that this work is connected with the spiritual worlds, this is the true consecration of a working group. To cherish such a thought is to permeate ourselves with the consciousness of the consecration that is the foundation of a working group within the movement. It is therefore of great importance to grasp this fact in its true spiritual sense. We find ourselves together in working groups which, besides cultivating spiritual science, are based on freedom of thought. They will have nothing to do with dogma or coercion of belief, and their work should be of the nature of cooperation among brothers. What matters most of all is to become conscious of the true meaning of the idea of community, saying to ourselves: Apart from the fact that as modem souls we belong to the fifth post-Atlantean epoch of culture and develop as individuals, raising individual life more and more out of community life, we must in turn become conscious of a higher form of community, founded in the freedom of love among brothers, as a breath of magic that we breathe in our working groups.

The deep significance of West European culture lies in the fact that the quest of the fifth post-Atlantean epoch is the consciousness soul. The task of West European culture, and particularly of Central European culture, is that men shall develop an individual culture, individual consciousness. This is the task of the present age. Compare this epoch of ours with that of Greece and Rome. The Greek epoch exhibits in a particularly striking form, especially among the civilized Greeks, a consciousness of living within a group soul. A man who was born and lived in Athens felt himself to be first and foremost an 'Athenian." His community, the city and all that belonged to the city, meant something different to the individual from what community between human beings means today. In our time the individual strives to grow out of and beyond the community, and this is right in the fifth post-Atlantean epoch. In Rome, the human being was first and foremost a Roman citizen, nothing else. But in the fifth epoch we strive above all else to be human in our innermost being, human and nothing else. It is a painful experience in our day to see people fighting against one another on the earth, but this, after all, is just a reaction to the perpetual striving of the fifth epoch for free development of the "human universal." Because the different countries and peoples shut themselves off today from one another in hostility, it is all the more necessary to develop, as resistance to this, the force that allows us to be human in the full sense, allowing the individual to grow out of and beyond every kind of community. But on the other hand the human being must, in full consciousness, make preparation for communities into which he will enter entirely of his own free will in the sixth epoch. There hovers before us as a high ideal a form of community that will so encompass the sixth epoch of culture that civilized human beings will quite naturally meet each other as brothers and sisters.

From many lectures given in past years, we know that Eastern Europe is inhabited by a people whose particular mission it will be in the sixth epoch, and not until the sixth epoch, to bring to definite expression the elementary forces that now lie within them. We know that the Russian peoples will not be ready until the sixth epoch of culture to unfold the forces that are now within them in an elementary form. The mission of Western and Central Europe is to introduce into men qualities that can be introduced by the consciousness soul. This is not the mission of Eastern Europe. Eastern Europe will have to wait until the spirit self comes down to the earth and can permeate the souls of men. This must be understood in the right sense. Understood in the wrong sense it may easily lead to pride and superciliousness, precisely in the East. The height of post-Atlantean culture is reached in the fifth epoch. What will follow in the sixth and seventh epochs will be a descending line of evolution. Nevertheless, this descending evolution in the sixth epoch will be inspired, permeated by the spirit self. Today the man of Eastern Europe feels instinctively, but often with a perverted instinct, that this is so; only his consciousness of it is, for the most part, extremely hazy and confused. The frequent occurrence of the term, "the Russian man," is quite characteristic. Genius expresses itself in language when, instead of saying as we do in the West, the British, the French, the Italian, the German — Eastern Europe says, "the Russian man." Many of the Russian intelligentsia attach importance to the use of the expression, "the Russian man." This is connected deeply with the genius of the particular culture. The term refers to the element of manhood, of brotherhood (or sisterhood) that is spread over a community. An attempt is made to indicate this by including a word that brings out the "manhood" in the term. But it is also obvious that the height to be reached in a distant future has not yet been attained, inasmuch as the term includes a word that glaringly contradicts the noun. In the expression, "the Russian man," the adjective really nullifies what is expressed in the noun. For when true manhood is attained there should be no adjective to suggest any element of exclusiveness.

But at a much, much deeper level there lies in members of the Russian intelligentsia the realization that a conception of community, of brotherhood must prevail in times still to come. The Russian soul feels that the spirit self is about to descend, but that it can only descend into a community permeated with the consciousness of brotherhood, that it can never spread over a community where there is no consciousness of brotherhood. That is why the Russian intellectuals, as they call themselves, make the following reproach to Western and Central Europe. They say, "You pay no heed at all to a life of true community. You cultivate only individualism. Everyone wants to be a person on his own, to be an individual only. You drive the personal element, through which every single person feels like an individual, to its highest extreme." This is what echoes across from the East to Western and Central Europe in many reproaches of barbarism and the like. Those who try to realize how things really are, accuse Western and Central Europe of having lost all feeling for human connections. Confusing present and future as they do now, these people say, "It is only in Russia that there is a true and genuine community of life among equals, a life where everyone feels like the brother or sister of the others, as the 'Little Father' or the 'Little Mother' of the others." The Russian intelligentsia say that the Christianity of Western Europe has not succeeded in developing the essence of human community, but that the Russian still knows what community is.

Alexander Herzen, an excellent thinker who lived in the nineteenth century and belonged to the Russian intellectuals, brought this to its ultimate conclusion by saying, "In Western

Europe there can never be happiness." No matter what attempts are made, happiness will never come to Western European civilization. There humanity will never find contentment. Only chaos can prevail there. The one and only salvation lies in the Russian nature and in the Russian form of life where humans have not yet separated themselves from community, where in their village communities there is still something of the nature of the group soul to which they hold fast. What we call the group soul, out of which mankind has gradually emerged and in which the animal kingdom still lives, that is what is revered by the Russian intelligentsia as something great and significant among their people. They cannot rise to the thought that the community of the future must hover as a high ideal, an ideal that has yet to be realized. They adhere firmly to the thought: We are the last people in Europe to retain this life in the group soul; the others have risen out of it; we have retained and must retain it for ourselves.

Yes, but this life in the group soul does not in reality belong to the future at all, for it is the old form of group soul existence. If it continued it would be a Luciferic group soul, a form of life that has remained at an earlier stage, whereas the form of group soul life that is true and must be striven for, is what we try to find in spiritual science. But be that as it may, the urge and the longing of the Russian intellectuals show how the spirit of community is needed to bring about the descent of spirit self. Just as it is being striven for there along a false path, so must it be striven for in spiritual science along the true path. What we should like to say to the East is this: It is our task to overcome entirely just what you are trying to preserve in an external form, namely, an old Luciferic-Ahrimanic form of community. In a community of a Luciferic-Ahrimanic character there will be coercion of belief as rigid as that established by the Orthodox Catholic Church in Russia. Such community will not understand true freedom of thought; least of all will it be able to rise to the level where complete individuality is associated with a social life in which brotherhood and sisterhood prevail. That other form of community would like to preserve what has remained in biological relationship, in brother- and sisterhood purely through the blood. Community that is founded not upon the blood, but upon the spirit, upon community of souls, is what must be striven for along the paths of spiritual science. We must try to create communities in which the factor of blood no longer has a voice. Naturally, the factor of blood will continue, it will live itself out in family relationships, for what must remain will not be eradicated. But something *new* must arise! What is significant in the child will be retained in the forces of old age, but in his later years the human being must receive new forces.

The factor of blood is not meant to encompass great communities of human beings in the future. That is the error that is filtering from the East into the dreadful events of today. A war has blazed up under the heading of community of blood among the Slavic peoples. Into these fateful times all those elements are entering of which we have just heard, elements that in reality have in them the right kernel, namely, the instinctive feeling that the spirit self can only manifest in a community where brother- and sisterhood prevails. It must not, however, be a community of blood; it must be a community of souls. What grows up as a community of souls is what we develop, in its childhood stage, in our working groups. What holds Eastern Europe so firmly to the group soul, causing it to regard the Slavic group soul as something that it does not want to abandon but, on the contrary, regards as a principle for the whole development of the state — it is this that must be overcome.

A great and terrible symbol stands before the eyes of the world. Think of the two states where the war had its starting-point. On the one side, Russia with the Slavic world in general declares that the war is based on brotherhood of blood, and on the other side, there is Austria, which comprises thirteen distinct peoples and thirteen different languages. The mobilization order in Austria had to be issued in thirteen languages because Austria encompasses thirteen racial stocks: Germans, Czechs, Poles, Ruthenians, Rumanians, Magyars, Slovaks, Serbs, Croatians, Slovenes (among whom there is a second and separate dialect), Bosnians, Dalmatians and Italians. Thirteen different racial stocks, apart from all minor differentiations, are united in Austria. Whether the implications of this are understood or not, it is obvious that Austria consists of a collection of human beings among whom community can never be based on blood relationship, for what its strange boundaries contain shoots out into thirteen different lineages. The most highly composite state in Europe stands in opposition to the state that strives most intensively for life in a group soul, or for conformity. But this striving for life in a group soul brings a great many other things in its train. This leads us to another matter, the significance of which we will think about today.

In the public lecture yesterday I mentioned the great philosopher Soloviev, one of the most significant thinkers of all Russia. Soloviev is an eminent thinker, but a thoroughly Russian thinker, a mind that is exceedingly difficult to understand from the Western European point of view. Anthroposophists, however, should study his work and try to understand him. I propose to speak from our more intimate standpoint about Soloviev's main and central idea. Soloviev is far too good a philosopher to adopt for himself without question the principle of life in a group soul. He has difficulties with it and he disagrees in many respects. But one idea predominates in him, not quite consciously it is true, but in such a way that one only wishes he were clairvoyant and could thus anticipate what his soul will have to wait to see on the earth when he is incarnated in the sixth epoch of culture. The following conception that is extremely difficult for the men of West and Central Europe to understand became the main and central idea in Soloviev's mind.

In Western Europe, as a preparation for the sixth epoch, we try among many other things to grasp the meaning of death, the significance of death for life. We try to understand how death is the manifestation of a form of existence, how the soul is transformed in death into another form of existence. We describe the life of a man within his body and the manner of life between death and new birth. We endeavor to understand death, to overcome death by realizing that it is only semblance, that the soul in very truth lives on when it has passed through death. It is an essential aim with us to overcome death through understanding. But here we come to one of the points, indeed to one of the most vital points, where spiritual science deviates altogether from the central idea held by the great Russian thinker, Soloviev. His idea is this: There is evil in the world, wickedness in the world. If we, with our senses, behold the evil and wickedness, we cannot deny that the world is full of both. This, says Soloviev, refutes the divinity of the world, for when we behold the world with our senses, how can we believe in a divine world, since a divine world can certainly not exhibit evil! But the senses perceive evil everywhere and the extreme evil is death. Because death is in the world, the world is revealed in all its evil and wickedness. The arch-evil is death!

Thus does Soloviev characterize the world. He says (and I am quoting almost word for word): Look at the world with your ordinary senses; try to understand the world with your ordinary mind. You can never deny the existence of evil in the world, and to desire to understand death would be absurd! Death exists. Knowledge acquired through the senses reveals a world of wickedness, a world of evil. Can we believe, asks Soloviev, that this world is divine when it shows us that it is full of evil, when it shows us death at every step? Nevermore can we believe that a world that shows us death is a divine world. For in God there can be no evil, no wickedness, above all, not the arch-evil death. In God there cannot be death. If, therefore, God were to come into the world (I am repeating what Soloviev says practically word for word) — if God were to appear, should we be able immediately to believe him to be

God? No, we should not! He would have to establish his identity first. If a being claiming to be God were to appear, we should not believe him. He would have to prove his identity by producing something of the nature of a world document that would enable us to recognize him as God! Nothing of the kind exists in the world. God cannot prove his identity through what is in the world, for everything in the world contradicts the divine nature. By what means, then, can he prove his identity? Only by showing, when he comes into the world, that he has conquered death, that death can have no power over him. We should never believe Christ to be God if He did not prove his identity. But Christ did so, inasmuch as He has risen, inasmuch as He has shown that the arch-evil, death, is not in Him.

This is what Soloviev says. It is a consciousness of the divine that is based solely upon the actual, historical resurrection of Christ, Who, as God, proves His identity. Soloviev goes on to say: Nothing in the world, with the single exception of the Resurrection, enables us to realize that a God exists. If Christ had not risen, all our belief would be vain, and everything we could say about a divine nature in the world, this too would be vain. Soloviev quotes these words of St. Paul again and again.

This, then, is the fundamental outlook of Soloviev. If we look at the world we see therein only evil, wickedness, degeneration, senselessness. If Christ had not risen, the world would be meaningless, therefore Christ has risen! Note this sentence well, for it is a cardinal saying of one of the greatest thinkers of Eastern Europe: "If Christ had not risen the world would be senseless, therefore Christ has risen." Soloviev has said: "There may be people who think it illogical when I say, if Christ had not risen the world would be senseless; therefore Christ has risen — but this is far better logic than any you can adduce against me."

In this curious example of a document for proving God's divinity, which we find in Soloviev's writings, I have given you a concrete instance of the strange ness of thought in Eastern

Europe. Curious thoughts crop up in the attempt to understand by what means God reveals indisputably that he is God.
How different it is in the West and in Central Europe! What is
the aim of spiritual science? Try to review and to compare
what we try to cultivate in spiritual science. What is its aim
and direction? It is our desire and aim to recognize out of
knowledge that the world has meaning, significance and purpose, and that the world is not filled merely with evil and
degeneration. It is our aim to realize through direct knowledge that the world has meaning. By this realization we try to
prepare for actual experience of the Christ. We desire to comprehend the living Christ, accepting all these things, of course,
as a gift, as grace. We realize the portent of the words: "I am
with you always even unto the end of the world." We accept
all that the Christ unceasingly promises us. For He speaks not
only through the Gospels; He also speaks within our souls.
That is what He means by the words: "I am with you always
even unto the end of the world." Always He can be found as
the living Christ. We want to live in Him, to receive Him into
ourselves. "Not I but the Christ in me!" Of all St Paul's sayings this is the most significant for us. "Not I but the Christ in
me." For thereby we realize: Wherever we may turn, meaning
and purpose are revealed. Faust expressed the same truth
when he clothed his philosophy in the following words:

> Spirit sublime, thou gav'st me, gav'st me all
> For which I prayed. Not unto me in vain
> Hast thou thy countenance revealed in fire.
> Thou gav'st me Nature as a kingdom grand,
> With power to feel and to enjoy it. Thou
> Not only cold, amazed acquaintance yield'st
> But grantest, that in her profoundest breast
> I gaze, as in the bosom of a friend.
> The ranks of living creatures thou dost lead
> Before me, teaching me to know my brothers
> In air and water and the silent wood.
> And when the storm in forests roars and grinds,

The giant firs, in falling neighbor bough
And neighbor trunks with crushing weight bear down,
And falling, fill the hills with hollow thunders;
Then to the cave secure thou leadest me,
Then show'st me mine own self, and in my breast
The deep mysterious miracles unfold.

These words indicate a spiritual understanding of the outer and the inner worlds, of universal purpose, of the meaning of death itself and the realization that death is the passage from one form of life to another. In seeking the living Christ we also follow Him through death and through the Resurrection. We do not, as the man of Eastern Europe, take the Resurrection as our starting point. We follow the Christ, letting His inspiration flow into us, receiving Him into our imaginations. We follow the Christ until death. We follow Him not only by saying: *Ex Deo Nascimur*, Out of God we are born; but by also saying: *In Christo Morimur*, In Christ we die.

We scrutinize the world and know that the world itself is the document through which God expresses His divinity. As we try to experience and understand the weaving power of the spiritual, we in the West cannot say that if God were to come into the world we would need a document to establish His identity, but rather we seek for God everywhere, in nature and in the souls of men.

So this fifth post-Atlantean epoch of civilization needs what we develop and cultivate in our groups. It needs the conscious cultivation of the spiritual aura that still hovers above us, cherished by the spirits of the higher hierarchies, and that will flow into the souls of men when they live in the sixth epoch. It is not our way to turn as in Eastern Europe to the group soul life that is dead, to a form of community that is a mere survival of the old. Our efforts are to cherish and cultivate a living reality from its childhood — such is the community of our groups. It is not our way to look for what speaks in the blood, calling together only those who have blood in common, and to cultivate this in community. Our aim is to call together human beings who resolve to be brothers and sisters, and above whom hovers something that they strive to develop by cultivating spiritual science, feeling the good spirit of brotherhood hovering over and above them.

At the opening of one of our groups, this is the dedicatory thought we will receive into ourselves. Hereby we consecrate a group at its founding. Community and quickening life! We seek for community above us, the living Christ in us, the Christ Who needs no document nor has first to be authenticated because we experience Him within ourselves. At the foundation of a group we will take this as our motto of consecration: Community above us; Christ in us. We know furthermore that if two, or three, or seven, or many are united in this sense in the Name of Christ, the Christ lives in them in very truth. All those who in this sense acknowledge Christ as their Brother, are themselves sisters and brothers. The Christ will recognize as His brother that man who recognizes other men as brothers.

If we are able to receive such words of consecration and carry on our work in accordance with them, the true spirit of our movement will hold sway in whatever we do. Even in these difficult times, friends from outside have associated themselves with those who have founded the group here. This is always a good custom, for thereby those who are working in other groups are able to carry to other places the words of consecration. They pledge themselves to think constantly of those who have undertaken in a group to work together in accordance with the true spirit of the movement. The invisible community, which we should like to found through the manner of our work, will thus grow and prosper. If this attitude, uniting with our work, becomes more and more widespread, we shall put to good account the demands made by spiritual science for the sake of the progress of mankind. Then we may believe that those great masters of wisdom who guide human progress and human knowledge will be with us. To the extent to which you here work in the sense of spiritual science, to that extent I know full well that the great masters who guide our work from the spiritual worlds will be in the midst of your labors. I call down upon the labors of this group, the power and the grace and the love of those masters of wisdom who guide and direct the work we perform in brotherhood within such groups. I call down the grace and the power and the love of the masters of wisdom who are directly connected with the forces of the higher hierarchies. May there be with this group the spirit of good that is in you, great masters of wisdom, and may there also prevail and work in this group the true spirit of the movement!

Appendices

Appendix 1

Sacramental and Spiritual Communion

Dietrich V. Asten

Spiritual Communion

In Earth-activity there draw near to me
(Given to me in substance-imaged form),
The heavenly Beings of the Stars.
In Willing I see them transformed
with Love.

In Watery life there stream into me,
(Forming me through with the power of substance)
The heavenly Deeds of the Stars.
In Feeling I see them transformed
with Wisdom.

To meet or not to meet the Christ is very much a matter of individual human destiny. This statement is not meant in the sense that we are predestined to find or not to find the Christ, because destiny is both something that happens to us and that we make happen. We are subject to the strokes of destiny, but we also have the possibility to shape it or create it. We struggle to find our destiny, and in this struggle the encounter with the Christ enables us gradually to overcome the effects of the Fall of Man, through which we became "earth-bound."

The individual now yearns to raise himself from the Fall and to *reunite* with the Divine, from which he was separated. To reunite means *"religere,"* not only in spirit and soul, but with one's entire being. It is from this deep human striving that the reality of religion originates.

On the basis of these introductory thoughts, let us ask: What is the connection of Anthroposophy to Religion? How can reunion with the spirit world be accomplished by the Anthroposophist? How does his approach differ from that of the churches, and, specifically, from the Act of Consecration of Man?

We will try to find answers to these questions about the relationship of Anthroposophy to Religion by dealing with the reality of Sacramental Communion as offered by the Christian Community, and the reality of Spiritual Communion, which is based on the anthroposophical path of inner development. It is not a question of determining which of the two communions is more right than the other. They both liberate and heal the human being from the effects of the Fall of Man, but they have distinctly different forms. They take different points of departure, and take place in different realms of human striving. The important task is that we become as conscious as we can of the nature of both communions, so that we can find our own proper orientation toward them. We have to discover the approach that is most compatible with our own personality.

In order to come close to what lives in Sacramental and Spiritual Communion we cannot use definitions. We can only give descriptions. These will be like the veils of a watercolor painting which are superimposed one upon the other, whereby a meaningful picture will gradually appear.

First, however, let us examine the meaning of the word communion. The prefix *com* in com-union has two meanings. We find it used, in companion, communication, commiserate, compassion, commune, to denote "together with." Here *com* points to the *mutuality* of actions or concerns. There is quite another quality to the *com* when it expresses the *intensity* and the fullness of actions or concerns. We find the second meaning in words like commitment, compression, compactness, and many others. Both meanings are part of communion.

Here are two brief stories which in imaginative form can help to introduce Sacramental and Spiritual Communion:

Picture someone who left his homeland and lives in a foreign country. One day he receives the *message:* that a friend or relative from his homeland will visit him. Perhaps it is a person he respects and loves. This expectation leads to careful *preparations,* so that a warm welcome may be offered to the visitor. Then the moment of fulfillment arrives. The door opens and the guest enters the room. A real *encounter* takes place. The guest is surrounded by the atmosphere of his country. He brings it with him. An intense conversation ensues during which the host gratefully receives the many gifts that the visitor has brought along. Their mutual concerns and their exchange establish a sense of mutuality, of belonging together and they share a true *sense of community,* a real communion. The guest leaves after the encounter has taken place, and both have gained something from their joint experience.

The second story has a similar beginning. Someone has left his homeland and lives in a foreign country. However, he is filled with a deep *longing* for his homeland and so he makes the resolve to start out on a journey in order to find it again. He *prepares* his physical and mental baggage and sets out on a long road of trials and adventures. After a long and eventful pilgrimage he finally reaches his true homeland and feels *reunited* with it. Then he departs again to the foreign country from which he came, and to which he must return, until he has fulfilled his tasks there. He leaves with the awareness that he has learned anew and more consciously who he is and what his homeland stands for.

In these two pictures we meet the guest who comes *from* and the pilgrim who is on his way *to* the promised land. The story of the guest who arrives is a picture of Sacramental Communion. It describes a human encounter that can be experienced on four levels, in four phases:

1. The announcement, the message.
2. Preparation for the visit.
3. The encounter, when the guest enters.
4. Communion, becoming one, com-union.

These four stages are clearly visible in the four parts of the Act of Consecration of Man, in which a relation is established to the one who comes to us from our true homeland as our friend and bringer of light. The letter or the message from the friend corresponds to the *reading of the gospel*. It is a personal message to us from the Christ. The response to the message about the friend's visit, for whom a warm welcome is being prepared, reminds us of the *offering* in this service. In this context "preparation" does not mean an external setting of the stage only, but also an inner activity: the awakening of the soul, the quickening of our feelings of reverence and love, which are extended to the guest as an offering. They are all raised like a golden cup. Then the guest enters. He is no other than the Christ. The mystery of transubstantiation, of *Christ's presence*, takes place. He brings something of the air of his spiritual home, which is also man's real home. Finally, the guest and the host unite in *communion*. Man receives the being of the Christ, he takes the Christ into himself. But more takes place. Something of man's being unites with the Christ. He receives man's good will and thus takes upon Himself the ill effects of human errors, failings and shortcomings.

In our time, Sacramental Communion has found a new expression in the ritual of the Christian Community. We can discern characteristic elements in this ritual:

- Sacramental Communion is the highlight of the Act of Consecration of Man, which proceeds in the realm of sense perception. The events of the Act of Consecration of Man can be seen, heard, smelled, felt and tasted.
- The service takes place at a particular time and at a particular location.
- The vestments of the priest, the setting of the altar, and the different colors, make visible what is spiritually present during the yearly course of Christian Festivals.
- All the elements of the earth are included in the action: matter in the bread, water in the wine, air in the smoke that ascends and in the voice of the priest, fire in the light of the candles.

- The spiritual works down into the physical sphere, into physical space.
- The human being receives material substances of the earth, that are consecrated by the proceedings of the ritual.
- As the body receives, drinks, chews, swallows, it is healed by the spirit of Christ that has been imparted to the substances he receives.
- The body is healed and with it man's soul and spirit.

Thus the Act of Consecration of Man has a therapeutic effect on the earth and on those who partake in it. For through this ritual of the Christian Community the spirit world speaks directly to the modern ego consciousness of Man.

We return to our second story, the story of spiritual communion, which describes the pilgrimage that someone makes from the foreign country, to which he has been exiled, back to his homeland. Again the pilgrimage has four visible phases:

1. The longing for the far distant land.
2. Inner preparation and setting out on the road.
3. The experience of getting there.
4. The reunion.

We have before us an outline of the road to the spirit. It begins with the perception that there is another world than that of mere sense existence. We yearn for this world, we thirst for it. Blessed are we if we have this *deep-seated longing*. When we prepare ourselves we create an awareness of what we are and want to be. We form images of the world we are to rediscover. We create *imaginations*. The distant land appears in the form of pictures. Now we must set out to find the spirit land. The actual journey to the spirit unfolds like a symphonic drama. All stages along the way are experiences in time. We reach the level of *inspiration* through which we come in touch with the deeds and movements of the spirit world. Finally, we find the promised land. We are reunited, we become one with it. We have reached the level of *intuition*.

If we place the two kinds of communion side by side we can now see some additional differences:

- Sacramental Communion, as we have described it, is very concrete. It has its specific forms and rhythms and grows on the practitioner as he participates in the cultic life. Spiritual Communion is much less tangible. It cannot be described in one all-encompassing picture.
- In Spiritual Communion several specific probations have to be undergone. There are many different trails, or paths, all of which represent different approaches to the spirit land. The constant danger exists that one may get lost on a trail, that one may lose direction and the sense of self. This is a tough and unpredictable experience. As mountaineers know, climbing is exhilarating, but on many a trail there is a sign of warning:
- Attempt this trail only if you are in excellent condition. Be prepared for sudden and unpredictable changes. Many have perished from exposure.

It is necessary to study and prepare for Spiritual Communion and it is instructive to deal with several variations of the basic theme of Spiritual Communion. We will try to show how this theme resounds repeatedly in the spiritual research biography of Rudolf Steiner.

One aspect, which already occupied Rudolf Steiner in his early years, and which was deepened throughout his life, is related to the resurrection of thinking. He was very much concerned with the question of the nature of knowledge. How does it work? How reliable is knowledge to convey to us the real truth of things? Can it be objective, or does it merely reflect our subjectivity? Before Steiner could describe actual results of knowledge, he had to have an understanding of the *process* of knowledge and develop the proper instruments for knowing. He concluded that through thinking the human spirit can penetrate the maze of sense perception, pierce through it and become one with the spiritual content of the world. As early as 1886, in the introduction to the second volume of Goethe's scientific works, he writes:

> When thinking takes hold of ideas, it fuses together with the ground of existence; that which works outside enters the spirit of man: he becomes one with the world of reality on the highest level of potency. Becoming aware of the idea in the world of reality is the true communion of man.

These sentences carry many levels of meaning. What is outside enters the spirit of man. He becomes one with reality on its highest level. At this level the dangers of untruth and misrepresentation are overcome. The human being does not just understand, he *merges* with the truth. This is communion in the realm of thinking. Here world-thoughts overflow (Weltgedanken schenken).

In thinking the world outside enters the spirit of man, and as we experience thought we also experience a response of our soul. This response is our capacity of feeling. If we now examine our feeling life we find that it is really the response to what comes to us as impressions from both the outer and our inner worlds. At first we can recognize our response to what we encounter as subjective. Our feelings usually say much more about our individual make-up than about the things felt. We would not be human if it were otherwise. At least that is the situation in the beginning. If, however, we attempt to redeem our faculty of feeling from this dependence upon our subjective nature, we can transform our purified feeling into a new organ of perception. In such a state, feelings no longer express how *we* feel; they become true messengers of the very things that we have feelings about. They perceive the world in a different way. They are true feelings because they are true to that which is perceived. In this way the human soul can relate to the world in quite a different manner. The real encounter with the world takes place through this inner readiness to receive, because the involvement of the soul with itself has been overcome. In such a state of soul a real work of art can be born.

The greatest art originates from the encounter of a soul that has overcome all self-centeredness, all subjective limiting involvement, with other things and beings. Such encounters are an empathetic intercourse creative of new beings; creative of something new that now becomes visible and audible.

The deeper and more intensively this relationship between the soul and the world can be felt, the more truthful is the resulting work of art. The receptive and creative attitudes of the artist expand into the objective and cosmic environment. As Rudolf Steiner describes in his essay of 1888 on "Goethe as the Father of a New Aesthetics," a real artist is the one who gives to the world of matter and substances another dimension. He does not bring the divine or the spirit down into material manifestation by making it visible or audible through artistic achievement, but he raises matter, he lifts it upward, into the sphere of the divine or the spirit. In this essay Steiner proclaims:

> The beautiful is not the divine in a visible garment, but, quite to the contrary, it is visible reality in a divine garment.

We can understand this to mean: as man produces works of art, he connects and stands in relation with the world through his feelings. In other words, when he cleanses his feeling life from all subjectivity, vanity and conceit he can *relate* to the world. Thanks to these redeemed powers of feeling, man can become a creative artist and when the artist raises the materials he uses on to a higher level of being, he achieves another kind of communion, a communion in the realm of feeling. He can recognize the meaning of "to feel is to unite" (Fühlen = Vereinen).

When we ask how can the will be redeemed, we are asking questions leading to the resurrection of our willing. We are so constituted that our will, to begin with, is very much involved with fulfilling the needs of existence. However, the nature of the will changes when it is no longer exercised for the sake of self-serving initiatives, when it acts in order to serve the needs of nature, of the earth's creatures, and of other people. When we serve in this way, we connect our own will, that is directed toward the spirit, with the world will. Our individual will merges into universal will so that increasingly we do what needs to be done. As the will changes, we follow our personal needs less and less.

This is particularly clearly stated in the last chapter of the book *Knowledge of the Higher Worlds and Its Attainment.* Only when we can renounce our own development and serve the earth and human development do we move from the Lower to the Greater Guardian. There Rudolf Steiner describes how the Lower Guardian confronts man as a counterpart of his twofold nature, in which the eternal and the temporal values of his being are blended. This Guardian demonstrates how far the person is still removed from attaining his true spiritual and moral potential. Indeed, it can be said that the redemption of the human will is really the main subject of the book, *Knowledge of the Higher Worlds.* The book reaches its climax when man has recognized all the elements from which he must liberate himself. He is then ready to meet the Greater Guardian, who speaks to him in words that are related in the book:

> You have attained your present degree of perfection thanks to the faculties you were able to develop in the sense world. But now a new era is to begin, in which your liberated powers must be applied to further work in the world of the senses. Hitherto you have sought only your own release, but now, having become free, you can go forth as the liberator of your fellows. I shall therefore bar your entry into the higher regions of the supersensible world, as long as you have not applied all the powers you have acquired to the liberation of your companions.

Rudolf Steiner goes on to describe how the union with the Greater Guardian looms as a far distant ideal before the soul's vision. But it becomes equally clear that this union will not be possible until all the powers afforded by this earthly world are applied to the tasks of its liberation and redemption. The student in this state is aware of new laws coming from the higher Light Being; laws which can be experienced as demands. By fulfilling the demands placed on him, the student will contribute to the liberation of the human race. He lays his gifts on the sacrificial altar of humanity. Through such deeds he can become one with the Greater Guardian who is, as we know, no other than the Christ. This union with the Greater Guardian, of which the book so clearly speaks, is in reality a communion of man with Christ through human acts of will. We can take this to mean that through his redeemed will man lets flow Christ's will into the world. This new redeemed will finds expression in good deeds and in social practice.

In the last phase of the life of Rudolf Steiner anthroposophy was introduced as a new impulse in many fields of human endeavor like education, science, medicine and therapy, social and economic life, art and the care of the earth. He gave many direct indications as to how such activities could be renewed. During this phase of his work he gave guidance to a group of young theologians for the renewal of religious life. The rituals of the Christian Community grew out of this effort and the Act of Consecration of Man culminates in Sacramental Communion. In order to cultivate a clear sense of discrimination in spiritual matters. Rudolf Steiner took great pains at that time to explain the difference between Sacramental Communion as celebrated in the service of the Christian Community and the Spiritual Communion that can be achieved by someone who is engaged on the anthroposophical path of inner development.

Ultimately, the path of Spiritual Communion leads to the cosmic ritual. It is difficult to speak about this subject in mental pictures, partly because in every process of communion, be it sacramental or spiritual, the unspeakable, the unutterable takes place. We must therefore try to feel what lies beyond the words we can utter in describing these events. Let us attempt to place before our inner eye a person who has developed some dispositions for imagination, inspiration and intuition. In this state he no longer approaches the world in an abstract way with the power of intellect. Instead he beholds the world more and more with his entire being; he *participates* in the world with his entire human potential. This situation brings about a completely new relationship to all experience, aspects of which were described by Rudolf Steiner on December 29th, 1922, in his cycle "The Spiritual Communion of Humanity." He says:

> Living together with the course of cosmic life becomes a happening different in character from his connection with the facts of everyday life. It becomes a ritual, a cult, and the *cosmic ritual* comes into being, in which man can have his place at every moment of his life.

He then went on to describe Spiritual Communion. Everything that is mirrored in matter in our being is related to the *resting stars,* which stand still in the signs of the Zodiac. We are connected in our physical organism with these constellations in space. In like manner, we are also traversed by streams of fluids. The etheric organism lives in the fluids and juices of the body. Through them we are connected with the deeds of the stars. These deeds are the *movement of the planets.* Two days later, the content of this reality was expressed by Rudolf Steiner in the mantra entitled "Spiritual Communion." He gave this mantra a few hours before the first Goetheanum burned down.

The experience of the connection of the solid substances with the fixed stars and that of the fluid substances with the wandering stars can become the equivalent of "receiving" bread and wine. Thus the mantra points to the earth substances and watery life in our physical organism and how, through the effect of our meditations, they can be transformed into *love* and *wisdom* just as bread and wine are transubstantiated in the Act of Consecration of Man.

It is important to recognize that our meditations transcend our intellect and quicken the life of feeling and willing, as Steiner indicated on the same evening when he described the cosmic ritual:

> What would otherwise be mere abstract knowledge is transformed into a relationship of will and feeling toward the world. The world becomes the Temple, the House of God. When man as knowing man summons up also powers of will and feeling, he becomes a sacrificing being. His fundamental relationship to the world changes from knowledge into *cosmic ritual*. The first thing that must come to pass if anthroposophy is to fulfill its mission in the world is that man's relationship to the world must be recognized to be one of cosmic ritual.

It is obvious that this cosmic ritual, which is communion in pure meditation, can be attained only after persistent practice. We have to work on the content, and work meditatively on it over and over again.

We can receive considerable help in this work from the *Calendar of the Soul*[1] and the *Foundation Stone.*[2] Anyone living intensively with the *Calendar of the Soul* will experience how he can draw ever closer to the cosmic surrounding in which he lives. This morning we cannot go into details. Suffice it to say that these verses, also, can lead to a communion with the forces and the spirits in the cosmos around us.

The transformation which takes place through communion is a process. Every act of communion is an event whereby something that is infinitely higher than we are ourselves works into our physical being, and, in homeopathic fashion, transforms it. What takes place is the redemption of the physical. During the early stages of Earth Evolution, spirit was turned into matter by the divine creator forces. And now, beginning with our age, matter can be once again turned into spirit. Matter can be spiritualized whenever and wherever communion is experienced. As earthbound matter that makes up our organization is spiritualized, transubstantiation can take place.

This process is expressed in the most concentrated and succinct way possible in the second verse of the *Foundation Stone Meditation,* where it is shown how our own I unites with the World I. The words are like seeds with unfathomable germinating power:

Where the surging Deeds
Of the World Becoming
Thine own I
Unite
With the World I
And thou wilt truly feel
In the Soul-Weaving of Man.
For the Christ Will in the encircling Rounds holds sway
In the Rhythms of Worlds, bestowing Grace on the Soul.
In Christ Death becomes Life.

Our own I unites with the World I, and the World I is the Cosmic Christ. As the human I unites with Christ, through Him death is transformed into life. This is the process of

Spiritual Communion with Christ. Here we are given the possibility of transubstantiation and the experience of Cosmic Ritual through the *Foundation Stone.*

The emphasis on the *Cosmic* Christ and the *Cosmic* ritual can give rise to an important group of questions which must be asked: If anthroposophy leads the esoteric student to Spiritual Communion by enabling him to transcend the limits of ordinary knowledge and by having his being transformed, is man thereby not overemphasizing his *own* development? Is he not led away from the responsibilities toward the earth and his fellow men? Does Spiritual Communion estrange us from daily life, or can it help to make this life more meaningful? Is the earth included in the sphere where communion takes place?

The very thought of transubstantiation is meaningless if the earth and its substances were excluded from this process. But more is required than the assurance that Spiritual Communion does make daily life more meaningful, and that the responsibility towards the earth and towards his fellow men is increased when the limits of knowledge are transcended. These questions require an examination of attitudes, and it is proper to speak of a new sacramental attitude.

In his later years Rudolf Steiner repeatedly urged that a new *attitude of reverence* should be developed with regard to how man treats the substances and processes of nature. Mankind must learn to deal with nature the way the creative Gods have dealt with it. Nature must not be exploited for its cash value but in accordance with the laws of its growth. Steiner makes the drastic statement: that the *laboratory workbench* must become an *altar*. For anyone working in research today, this is a most challenging call. The research and development bench turns into an altar! What does this mean?

Unless we feel real reverence for the substances of nature, unless we live with the awareness that we are not entitled to the so-called raw materials of the earth, but rather, that they are *given* to us, our scientific and commercial endeavours will pursue only selfish and special interests. However, if we practice a reverential attitude, the laboratory workbench can become an altar. And so it can be with the desk top or the conference table when we deal with other human beings in a socially responsible and therapeutic way.

Such human striving, in which the Christ impulse can be active, leads to what Steiner calls the *New Sacramentalism*. This kind of sacramentalism should not be practiced in secluded sanctuaries, it must not remain a lofty ideal. It must and it can, so I believe, become practical reality. We must make every effort that, at least in part or selectively, in our modern world of economic necessities and political constraints, communion in the sphere of work comes about. As a matter of fact, all the various communal experiences described in spheres of activity and in the realms of knowledge, in the arts, and in human development, are preparatory stages which make the esoteric student a good servant of the earth. Without question, Spiritual Communion must be related to the earth and serve the earth in order to be real.

In the time remaining to us let us examine some additional questions about communion as related to community. Is the road to communion one that the individual must tread alone and in inner isolation? Can he join others? Can he feel united with them in the same striving? The answer to these questions is twofold: Man is indeed alone as an individual human being on this road, yet he feels inwardly connected with others who are struggling along the same road.

Is the experience of community different when man is engaged in Sacramental or Spiritual Communion? The community experience engendered by the ritual on the one hand, and the path of inner development on the other, are different in the way and sequence in which they occur, but not in substance. A different movement was illustrated by the two stories told earlier. The one showed how in the religious ritual the supersensible is brought down from the spirit world to the assembled congregation through the intervention of the priest. The process is witnessed by the active participation of those present. A bond of common experience is formed: a Christian Community. Consciously or unconsciously, this experience is a reflection of pre-earthly life. The archetype of the Act of Consecration of Man is something everybody has seen in the pre-earthly life. It is now received and shared as a religious experience in the world of space, color and time.

For the one who pursues the spiritual path rather than the cultic path, the movement of spiritual action flows the other way. On this path, which is the counterpart of the ritual, man's striving. begins in the physical world and reaches out to the spiritual world. The direction is from below upward. On this path also unconscious memories of pre-earthly experiences in the spirit world provide the stimulus for seeking the recovery of this world.

We know that many souls have participated in the Michael School before the descent into their present incarnation, and as we search and struggle here along the way, we wake up in the mutual encounter with other human beings. The direct encounter with our fellow men stimulates an

enlarged sense of wakefulness and alertness. We build com-
panion-ships in the quest for truth and enlightenment. When
we have discovered the possibility that human souls wake up
in the encounter, sometimes even in the collision, with other
human souls, we begin to grow together with others. Human
spirits wake up in the encounter with other human spirits. A
real community spirit is attracted by our common experiencing when we study the science of the spirit together.

Thus, the religious cultus brings the supersensible down
into the physical world, while in anthroposophical groups the
thoughts and feelings of the assembled individuals are raised
into the supersensible. When the content is experienced in the
right frame of mind, souls wake up in the encounter with each
other. Where this really exists and groups of this kind make
their appearance in the Anthroposophical Society, we have the
reversed cultus, which, although it moves in the opposite direction as compared with the religious cultus, sets off a powerful
community building force. Rudolf Steiner spoke about this in
the sixth and ninth lectures of *Awakening to Community* and
in "Preparing for the Sixth Epoch."

Now let us draw some final conclusions: Spiritual Communion, as we have seen, can be achieved on several levels of
human activity. It can be attained in pure thinking when we
become aware of the idea in reality. The transformation of
thinking then becomes living knowledge. Creative endeavors
in the realm of the arts can raise and transform the materials
of the earth to a point where they become the garment of the
Gods. In this transformation of feeling, through the arts, matter is raised from its fallen state. Through our working fruit-
fully in the world there is also a way to experience communion
with Christ. This requires a transformation of willing, which
means becoming one with the Greater Guardian of the
Threshold. Communion in the will brings about social deeds.
We reviewed the mantra "Spiritual Communion" through
which we can experience—as a result of our patient and dedicated meditating—the transubstantiation of the solid and the
fluid elements in our body. We approached the Cosmic Ritual.

We drew attention to the center part of the *Foundation Stone,* which describes the communion that our own I can have with the World I. Then we saw how our life can become an offering to the divine creator powers, to whom we owe our existence. Our work turns into a service to heal social ills, and to restore the balance of nature. Our work receives the power to transubstantiate that which is corrupted and decayed. Thereby work performed in all spheres of human life has a redeeming effect. Through such work we can stand in communion with spirit beings. We can experience the New Sacramentalism.

Finally, we highlighted the community building aspects of communion, how we awaken as individuals in the mutual encounter with one another and how we then feel united in our search for the spirit.

In its broadest sense, Spiritual Communion encompasses *all* human creative activity. It can be attained in the world of pure thought, in all the arts, in the care of nature and its creatures, in therapeutic work, and in group meetings dedicated to the science of the spirit. The point is that Spiritual Communion can be experienced over the entire range of creative human deeds into which it is possible to carry our humanity and which are subject to transformation. This is a range which begins in the lofty realm of intuitive knowledge and reaches all the way down into the sphere of work. Moreover, Spiritual Communion can be achieved with many beings: spirit beings in nature, in the cosmos, with living and departed souls, with the beings of the hierarchies, and with the Christ Being.

In contrast to this, Sacramental Communion lives within the forms and sequences of the archetypal religious ritual, whereby bread and wine are transubstantiated. Moreover, this ritual highlights the Communion with Christ.

Both kinds of communion are spiritual and religious. A priest of the Christian Community can practice what we have described as Spiritual Communion in addition to Sacramental Communion. Likewise, someone who is an esoteric student, or a member of the School of Spiritual Science, can participate in and support the Act of Consecration of Man. Such a person will, if he takes his schooling seriously, find Spiritual Communion quite naturally in accordance with his interests and inner dispositions.

There are thus considerable differences with regard to form and sequence, with regard to physical location, and the beings we commune with, when we compare Spiritual with Sacramental Communion. Yet, it seems to me, that one thing is the same in both Spiritual and Sacramental Communion. In both instances the Christ Impulse, and the Christ Impulse alone, makes it possible that communion takes place.

This could be said in different words: Our description has shown that we can stand in Spiritual Communion with many different spirit beings here, and in the spirit world, as well as with the Christ Being Himself. We can gain access to several of these beings through communion. The one power that makes this access possible, the one power of grace that enables us to relate to these beings, this Power is the Christ Impulse. The Christ Impulse makes transubstantiation possible in both Sacramental and Spiritual Communion. He is the great Facilitator. The Christ Impulse provides the magic spark that enables human beings to enter into communion with other spirit beings and also with the Christ Being Himself.

Our perception of and involvement with the Christ Impulse is very much a question of personal destiny. It is our very personal destiny whether or not and *how* we can be united with Him, the Christ, who can redeem us from the effects of the Fall of Man. The Fall was the destiny of Humanity. It happened to us. Finding or not finding the Christ is very much a matter of our individual destiny. It happens; we make it happen. As we began, so shall we close with movements of visible speech which will express the Question of Destiny.

[1] Rudolf Steiner, *The Calendar of the Soul*, Hawthorne Press, 1990.
[2] Rudolf Steiner, *The Foundation Stone*, Rudolf Steiner Press, 1996.

BIBLIOGRAPHY

GA *Goethe's Scientific Writings*
Introduction to the second volume, 1886

GA 10 *Knowledge of the Higher Worlds and its Attainment*
Chapter 10, 1905-6

GA 30 "Goethe as Founder of a New Science of Aesthetics"
An essay, 1888

GA 40 *The Calendar of the Soul*
1918-1919

GA 112 *The Gospel of SL John (Kassel)*
Lecture of July 7, 1909

GA 118 Single lecture: "Buddhism and Pauline Christianity"
Lecture of February 27, 1910

GA 131 *From Jesus to Christ*
Lecture of October 13,1911

GA 160 Single lecture: "Preparing for the Sixth Epoch"
Lecture of June 15, 1915

GA 172 *Karma of Vocation*
Lecture of November 27, 1916

GA 198 Single lecture: "Heilfaktoren fuer den sozialen Organismus" Lecture of July 17, 1920

GA 212 *The Human Soul and the Evolution of the World*
Lecture of May 5, 1922 21

GA 216 Supersensible Influences in the History of Mankind
Lecture of September 29, 1922

GA 219 Man and the World of the Stars. The Spiritual
Communion of Mankind. Lectures of December 29, 30, 31, 1922

GA 236 Karmic Relationships
Lecture of June 29, 1924

GA 257 Awakening to Community
Lectures of February 27 and March 3,1923

GA 260 *The Foundation Stone*
1923-1924

F.W. *Zeylmans van Emmichoven*. Rudolf Steiner Verlag Frejes
Geistesleben 1961

Hagen Biesantz. "Anthroposophie und religioese Erneuerung"
Was in der *Anthroposophischen Gesselschaft* vorgeht. 58.
Jahrgang Nr. 23/24

Eberhard Kurras. "Die Kommunion im Kultus und Geistesstreben"
Mitteilungen, Jahrgang 35, Heft 4, Nr. 138 Christmas 1981

Hans-Werner Schroeder. "Vom Erleben der Menschenweihehandlung"
Verlag Urachhaus 22

APPENDIX 2

HUMAN ENCOUNTERS AND KARMA

by Athys Floride

TRANSLATED BY
CHRISTOPHER BAMFORD

Foreword

Knowledge of the laws of karma and reincarnation is becoming increasingly important. The new age of light, which human beings entered at the end of the Kali Yuga, urgently demands of us an awareness of the living reality of karma, which must be understood as penetrating even the facts and details of daily life.

A consequence of this is a greater awareness of one of the most characteristic events of human life: the meeting of human beings with each other. Such meetings do not occur arbitrarily at the whim of "chance," but reflect, hidden beneath a veil, the realities of karma.

The new spiritual path of karma demands that we awaken to what is veiled and unveiled in these encounters and participate consciously in the processes that bring them about. We can no longer remain passive before this person or those persons but must ask: Why is this meeting taking place? What does it mean in my life? How can I become fully conscious of a bond with this person or that? Such questions can only receive answers through the inner activity of those taking part in the meeting. We must become, more and more, collaborators in this area. This is what the new spirituality, the new Light, asks of us.

Introduction

No religion exists yet. If you believe religion to be possible, it must be made and brought forth out of the union of several individuals.— Novalis

What is an encounter with another human being? What does such a meeting mean for a person's life? What is revealed when two or more people meet together? What is the connection between an encounter and the knowledge of karma and destiny?

Questions like these arise when we become interested in meetings between people. We have the powerful feeling that we're touching on an intimate matter involving not only human beings, but other beings, especially the gods, as well. Is not every meeting in fact a moment in the evolution of humanity as well as of the gods? Is not every meeting actually a critical moment in the world's evolution? After all, we know that it is human beings who make history, and who thereby also shape the evolution of the world. Such are some of the questions that we shall try to shed light on here.

Human encounters can be looked at from different points of view. We could, for instance, adopt the scientific point of view and proceed as follows: "Suppose a young person — not an infant, but someone who's already about fourteen — is asked to solve consciously the problem of how to make a decisive encounter with another person occur when he or she is fifty years old. Just imagine what a problem it would be — what an effort it would take — if you had to solve this by calculation, like a problem in arithmetic!"[1] In this example Rudolf Steiner draws our attention to the enormous complexity involved in human encounters; and he adds that the first hierarchy must apply the highest mathematics or resort to science to solve so difficult a problem. Steiner states: "Even the superficial details of human life can be fitted into calculable laws." We could also consider human encounters from an artistic point of view: people meeting each other then would act like artists, freely forming the substances born between them. In this book, however, we will deal with human encounters from the point of view of religion.

In pre-Christian times, science and art were the prerogative of the temple and the priesthood. The evolution of the human spirit, however, successively liberated first science (thanks, for example, to Socrates, Plato, and Aristotle) and then art (thanks to Giotto), placing these activities more and more in the hands of particular human beings, free individualities. Today it would seem to be the turn of religion to realize itself in daily life. We shall try to show here that religion has not become decrepit and dried up, but has been placed in the hands of each one of us, so that our task is now to cultivate it responsibly and knowledgeably. This knowledge can be deepened by the study of anthroposophy, which can make us conscious of perspectives that will renew the experience of encounter.

From the religious point of view every meeting between people includes three basic stages:

1. the period before the encounter
2. the encounter itself
3. the period after the encounter

This is the structure that we shall adopt in order to illuminate this most important part of human life. In the course of our existence, each of us meets innumerable other human beings. Some of these meetings are brief, evanescent, others are more important, some are decisive. Some are limited to a look, a casual word in the street, others take on dimensions that transform our lives.

To conclude, let us note that we find in human biography, without our being conscious of it, the activities of science, art, and religion. That is to say, human biography completely fulfils what anthroposophy aspires to, namely, the reunion of these three great domains. Our task is to become conscious of them by penetrating them with our cognitive powers.

From Before the Encounter
Up To the Encounter

Anyone who views life other than as an illusion that consumes itself is still entangled in life. Life should not be a novel given to us, but one written by us.— Novalis

A human being in the physical world structures space in such a way that we can distinguish a center and a periphery. At the center is the human being, while at the periphery is everything that the person perceives by means of the senses. When the person moves, this spatial configuration moves along with him or her.

Everything that appears in this space, arising within it through the senses, is more or less clearly perceived. Human encounters also take place here. As long as a second person has not yet appeared within this circle (see diagram), no encounter has taken place. This does not mean that the first person has no connection to the second, but only that the connection has not yet penetrated to a conscious level. However, the forces that will bring about a meeting between the two are already at work.

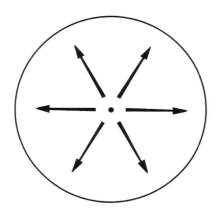

In his lecture of January 25, 1924, on the two gates of the Sun and the Moon, Rudolf Steiner described how lunar and solar forces penetrate and work in human lives. Lunar forces surround human beings with an iron necessity; solar forces grant them the possibility of freedom. Before people meet each other, before they find each other in earthly life, they have worked on each other without knowing it.

> If two people meet, let us say, when one is twenty and the other twenty-five, they can look back on everything they have experienced up to that point. It will become clear to each of them that every single detail in their lives has been urging them on towards this meeting. Both the twenty-year-old and the twenty-five-year old can look back over their lives and see how they came from different directions to meet each other in this particular place. In shaping our destiny, everything depends on two people setting out from two different parts of the globe and then meeting as if brought together by an iron necessity directing them towards the point in which they meet.[2]

Before two people meet, they are led toward each other by necessity; and the point where they meet lies within the space I have mentioned. As soon as the two people perceive each other within this space, as soon as their circles interpenetrate, something remarkable happens: they enter their field of mutual vision, and solar forces begin to work.

Is there an event in human history which illustrates an important encounter and confirms Rudolf Steiner's description? The Baptism in the Jordan gives us a primordial image. First, John the Baptist and Jesus of Nazareth, both of whom belonged to the Hebrew lunar culture, met. Then the Baptism was performed, allowing the solar forces to bind themselves with the being of Jesus. The forces of necessity, of Jehovah, had penetrated Hebrew culture and sternly led this people.

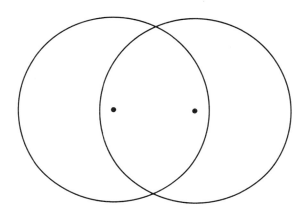

Within it, St. John and Jesus unfolded their destinies to the point of their historic meeting. Then the moon gave way to the sun, to the impulse of freedom for humanity. And we can see how after this important meeting the forces of the moon, which had guided these two great spirits with the hand of necessity, had to diminish, while the forces of the sun, the Christ forces, had always to increase. The words of John the Baptist — "He must increase but I decrease—take on quite another resonance, and seal the universal nature of this meeting. Ancient, lunar karma must be trans-formed, metamorphosed by means of the forces of the sun, of Christ. These must undergo dying and becoming, sacrifice. For this reason John the Baptist was beheaded while the I of Jesus made way for the solar God. All of humanity can see this meeting at the turning point of the ages as an archetypal image, a model, and a source of life.

The question arises: How can this powerful impulse be realized on the level of the individual in daily life? It seems to me that here lies a task having to do with the liberation of religion. Rudolf Steiner deals with the question in his lecture "The Work of the Angels in Man's Astral Body." He draws attention to the fact that human encounters will become more and more of an enigma and that we must learn to approach others with an ever-deepening interest.

> Yes, there will come a time when human beings will not be able to live as though asleep, but will receive an impulse to action from the spiritual world through their angels. This impulse will demand that they develop a much deeper interest for every human being, deeper than we can imagine today. This heightened interest in our fellow human beings will not simply be something subjective that people can develop comfortably and at leisure, but will happen all of a sudden. The spiritual world will instill in human beings a sense of the specific mystery of what the other person is. I mean this very concretely, and not just as some kind of theoretical consideration. People will experience something of interest to them in each and every other human being.[3]

When the destinies of two people (the action of the lunar forces) bring them face to face, each one of them is at a specific stage in his or her biography. Since a biography never stops developing, this means that a process is set in motion between the two people. Then it is a question of giving a different meaning to daily life, of cultivating our meetings with others from another perspective, with different intentions; in a word, it is to live daily life religiously.

A being can help us in this task — he of whom Rudolf Steiner said in his last address, "His magical and poetic idealism enables him to resurrect even the most insignificant material thing and let its spiritual glory shine forth."[4] This being is the poet Novalis.

> *There is only one Temple in the world and that is the human body. There is nothing more sacred than this higher form.* — Novalis

Religion and Daily Life

During the Encounter
First Stage: The Proclamation

Our whole life is an act of worship.
In ordinary life, we serve like priests at the altar. — Novalis

Meeting another person can be a double experience. On the one hand, we may find ourselves confronted with forces from the past; then again it may be that we must prepare ourselves for some future task. In any event, a future task for each of us must be to know ourselves and work in harmony with evolution, that is, to realize what we really want through this encounter, what we ourselves have decided upon before birth.

The moment of encounter can become a sacred moment in our lives if we try to put into effect something Rudolf Steiner spoke about when he said: "In the future each human being will see the divine concealed in every other human being." And "In the other human being, a revelation from the divine foundations of the world presents itself to us in flesh and blood." [5]

Such knowledge of oneself and the other may be discovered in the course of a process:

1. Learning to know each other outwardly;
2. Gaining a deeper insight into the being of the other person;
3. Recognizing the karmic forces at work in the encounter, through which
4. A new stream of forces comes about.

Let us consider this evolutionary process. We become aware that people participating in a meeting in this way experience something which otherwise takes place during divine service, during the Mass. We know that the Mass unfolds in four main stages:

1. Proclamation;
2. Sacrifice (Offertory);
3. Transubstantiation;
4. Communion.

To awaken in this way to what really happens between two or more people who meet each other — to perceive in depth the unfolding of an encounter — is to turn Rudolf Steiner's prediction into reality in our daily life:

> Any truly religious feeling developing within humankind in the future will be based on recognizing the image of the divinity in every human being as a matter of immediate daily experience, and not merely in theory. There will be no need to force people to be religious because then, right from the onset, every meeting of person with person will be a religious act, a sacrament.[6]

Here the gods' intention is clearly expressed: religion, the connection between human beings and the gods, is to become a free act, an intentional activity leading to the cultivation in daily life of a conscious bond with the spiritual world. For "at the source of angelic impulses lies the intention to pour out over human beings the possibility of complete freedom in religious activity." [7] That is true esotericism. It is our task, even our obligation, not to sleep through this reality. Awakening in our encounters in this way, we are on the way to performing the same sacrament as that of the Mass.

When someone appears in our field of perception we feel the need to know who this person is. This is the first stage: an exact knowledge of who this person is on the physical plane. A being is announced, full of mystery: Who is it? We see him or her for the first time. What secret does he or she bear? We learn the person's name and where he or she comes from; we learn something about the outer circumstances of the person's real life in his or her present incarnation. The stage can appear banal; it is often seen this way; but there is nothing banal about it. We should not forget Rudolf Steiner's words:

> The first stage in the formation of a human community is when we awaken to the outer appearance of another person. Usually we are asleep before the other. How can we wake up? We awaken thanks to the outer world — its light, sound, warmth — thanks to all that comes to us from the world of the senses. We awaken also — at least in our daily life — through the outer, natural appearance of other human beings.[8]

This statement makes it clear how important our sensory perceptions are. Therefore let us develop this attention and interest for the outer appearance of our neighbor. Faced with our neighbor, we are usually inattentive and dreamy, with little interest in this side of his or her being. This is why it is often difficult to remember these outer appearances. But we have been given our senses in order to perceive, and in order to perceive ever more consciously. When another human being enters the circle of our perceptions, we are not permitted to go on dreaming, but must wake up to who he or she is physically.

This attention to the other sets in motion the four-stage process we are considering. The powers of destiny, human forces, have sent me this person whom I see on the physical plane. An event in my destiny announces itself. At the moment when I meet him or her, the solar forces begin to work, bringing freedom. What will become of this meeting? How will it continue? What will I make of it? All this is no longer subject to necessity. I must take hold of this instant of freedom, I must live this first stage consciously. From now on it is up to me to decide to guide this process through the next three stages.

The True Image of the Human Being

Second Stage: The Sacrifice (Offertory)

I am Thou. — Novalis

Human beings are immersed in the flow of evolutionary time. As soon as we are born, we enter into the quality of change. Only death ends this situation; until then human beings never cease to become. Thus we are faced with the following questions: How can we take part consciously in this becoming? Is it altogether possible? We have seen how in the moment of meeting, when our partner enters the circle of our perceptions, the solar forces, the forces of freedom, begin to work. The hour of freedom rings out. What does this mean? Nothing less than the possibility of participating consciously from that moment on in the evolution of the relationship born of the encounter.

Once the first stage has been completed, a space has opened toward the future. We can feel the need to go further on the path, to deepen this new connection. But of course the process can also be broken off at this point, either because the person we met disappears from our lives or because, not noticing the importance of the moment, we do not seize it consciously, we let it slip away. It is comforting to know that usually the forces of destiny bring us together again and again, until eventually we wake up. But if we take hold of the process deliberately and consciously, we are ready to take a second step that will lead to a deepening of the connection with the other person.

However, there is a condition attached to taking this step. How are we to pass beyond the veil of the physical? How can we enter more deeply into the other? A sacrifice becomes necessary. We must be able to open and give ourselves devotedly to whatever seeks to show itself in the encounter. Many are those who, unconsciously renouncing any deepening of the relationship, remain at the first stage and are satisfied with a purely external bond. Such people shut themselves off, as it were, from the inquiring gaze of the other. "Hell is other people": here fear, indifference, egotism are in full command.

The second step, the stage of the offertory, as we would like to call it, is taken only with difficulty. There is no doubt that one could go further and open oneself devotedly to the other. Indeed, when the ego has been sacrificed on the altar of encounter, something important happens. By virtue of this sacrifice, the true image of the other arises to the one who has sacrificed him or herself. The external, physical, natural aspect, which one came to know with such interest during the first stage, is overcome; it is no longer an obstacle. "What, then," we ask, "is the true image of this human being?"

At this point we need to heed a warning from Rudolf Steiner. As a general rule, people do not perceive each other with sufficient awareness. The usual reaction — simply to find the other person sympathetic or unsympathetic — is superficial; for the existential human condition is to be thrown into the conflict between the opposing forces of Lucifer and Ahriman.

In former times, pagan peoples lived in myths, in a world of images, while the Jewish people strove toward abstraction in the form of the Law. Steiner therefore warns us to "put aside our current way of looking at things with its remnants of 'Thou shalt not make any graven images' and find our way back, this time consciously, to the soul's old image-forming capacity."

In the future, it will only be possible to organize society appropriately by means of images and imaginations. The next opportunity to restructure society will depend on our ability to apply consciously the same strength that was present, unconsciously or only semiconsciously, in the old myth-making ability of the human race.... Once people have arrived at this pictorial ability, this conscious myth-making, through their worldview, the possibility will be opened for social forms to evolve out of interactions between human beings.[9]

The quotation that follows can be taken as an exercise in developing this capacity of approaching the true image of the human being, as required by the spirit of our time.

> If you look at an image such as this statue of the Representative of Humanity with Lucifer and Ahriman on either side,[10] you are face to face with what is actually at work in each human being as a totality, because human beings are in fact in the state of balance between the Luciferic and Ahrimanic forces. If the impulse to confront people in this way, to concretely see this trinity in each individual, permeates your daily life, then you will begin to understand your fellow human beings. It is essential that we cultivate this ability now in the fifth post-Atlantean epoch, so that we do not just continue to pass each other by like ghosts, defining each other by means of our abstract concepts without being able to form any images of each other. What we do now is nothing more than pass each other by as if we were ghosts. One ghost comes up with the thought, "That person's a nice fellow," the other, "That person's not such a nice fellow": "that's a bad man," "that's a good one"—just a lot of abstract concepts.[11]

But what do people want in the depths of their being? What do they want to accomplish?

The fact is, as Steiner says, that an image "radiates out from deep within each human being, an image that expresses the person's unique state of balance. When two people come face to face, each one should perceive the image welling up Out of the other." But in order for this to happen, we must "develop the heightened interest I have often described to you as the basis of human society, the powerful interest each human being should feel when in the company of another human being."[12]

In Rudolf Steiner's lecture cycle, *The Mission of the*

Archangel Michael, we find the epistemological basis for this perception or image that we seek to find in the other:

> We must learn to look at people as they will be in the future, that is, to think Michaelically. Let me describe this Michaelic thinking more precisely. Although you may not be saying it out loud or even thinking it, in the intimate depths of your consciousness you're saying to yourself, "This is a person of flesh and blood, an earthly material human being." But you don't really see the actual being who pulls this material together. The right train of thought would be, "I see before me particles of matter accumulated by a spiritual human form in order to make this invisible being visible." Real human beings are actually invisible. If in every waking moment we are fully conscious of this fact, and cease to regard a human being as the conglomerate of mineral particles he or she arranges in a particular way, then we are thinking Michaelically. To know that we are in the company of invisible human beings — that's what thinking Michaelically means.[13]

Another of Rudolf Steiner's exercises also helps in this second stage. This exercise asks of those who would practice it a great love of and trust in the other. Steiner calls it the way to Christ through thinking:

> Instead of taking an interest merely in my own way of thinking, and in what I consider right, I must develop a selfless interest in every opinion I encounter, however strongly I may hold it to be mistaken. The more people pride themselves on their own dogmatic opinions and are interested only in them, the further removed they are from Christ at this moment in world evolution. People must develop a brotherly, social interest in the opinions of others, even if they think they're mistaken. They must allow the opinions of others to shed light on their own

thinking and take the same interest in the possibly mistaken thoughts of others as they do in thoughts of their own which they hold to be true. The more they're able to do so, the more they'll feel in their soul of souls one of Christ's sayings, which today must be interpreted in the sense of the new Christic language. Christ said, "Inasmuch as ye have done it unto the least of these my brethren, ye have done it unto me." The Christ never ceases to reveal Himself anew — even unto the end of earthly time. And thus He speaks today to those willing to listen: "In whatever the least of your brethren thinks, you must recognize that I am thinking in him; and that I enter into your feeling whenever you bring another's thought into relation with your own, and whenever you feel a fraternal interest for what is passing in another's soul. Whatever opinion, whatever outlook on life, you discover in the least of your brethren, therein you are seeking Myself." [14]

At the first stage we saw that a lack of interest could hinder us from truly awakening to the physical appearance of the other, to his or her natural aspect. Similarly, at the second stage, we must avoid being so in love with our own thoughts and opinions that we are unable to be objective about them. If we take up allowing ourselves to be permeated through and through with the opinions and thoughts of another, sacrificing our own opinions for the moment, as a spiritual exercise or path, then the other person can express what he or she is.

Everything that the other person expresses in words emanates from that person and may be thought of as a substance radiating toward us. When this is so, we become a vessel for the other: we create a free space for the other's being. To do this is to perform a sacrifice, but through this sacrifice some of the obstacles between human beings may be overcome, leaving the way open for the next stage.

DESTINY:

PERCEPTION OF THE FORCES OF KARMA
THIRD STAGE: TRANSUBSTANTIATION

We will understand the world once we understand ourselves, since we and it are integral halves of the same whole. We are God's children, divine seeds. At some point we will become as our father is. — Novalis

Receiving another person's thoughts into oneself and letting them unfold within one's own soul prepares one to attempt the next stage. This stage, which corresponds to the Transubstantiation, must be willed; to do so will take all the strength we possess. The perception of the other, of the true image of the other, of our bond with the other, now becomes deeper. We enter the realm where the forces of karma are at work. Now we can strive to understand the impulses, the currents bringing us together with other human beings.

The previous stage, which we called the stage of sacrifice, corresponds to the Offertory. It allowed us to open ourselves up to another being coming toward us. Yet a certain mystery still remained — the reasons for this meeting. Why has this person come to me? What aspect of our past unites us? What will we have to do together in the future?

In order to get to the bottom of this mystery, to lift the veil of Maya, we must allow forces to work in us that will transform us so completely that they let us see beyond the bounds of our present incarnation. These forces are solar forces that have united themselves with the earth, the solar forces of Christ Jesus, which are connected with karma. They are the forces that bring freedom, and we must individually decide by our own deeds to allow them to take effect.

At this point we can turn to and consider in this light the karma exercise given by Rudolf Steiner on May 9, 1924.

Practicing the exercise will perhaps lead us to a perception of the forces that shape destiny and help explain what occurs in a meeting.

Let me describe the exercise briefly. It takes three days to carry out. On the first day, you must recall as intensely as possible a situation you experienced a short time ago. You must "paint" the image of this experience in your soul as livingly as possible and in every detail. You see the person you have met, his or her physical aspect, gestures, behavior, as well as the environment where the meeting took place — all this with the greatest possible intensity. This is how the exercise begins, and it should be done with great care, for it sets in motion a stream of forces that will evolve over the next three days.

In the course of the three days and nights, the image is worked on by the different members or "envelopes" of the person practicing the exercise, undergoing a veritable transformation on its journey from the astral body to the ether body to the physical body. When you wake up after the third night, that is, on the morning of the fourth day, if the exercise has been successful, you will perceive a new image revealing the karmic context of the situation you pictured in your original image. At this point you see a scene from a past life where an event occurred that "provoked" the meeting in your present incarnation — the meeting preserved with an effort of memory at the beginning of the exercise.

Rudolf Steiner summarizes this process as follows:

1. Day One, Night One — Outside of the sleeping physical and ether bodies, the astral body works formatively on the image of the lived experience. The external ether impregnates the image with its own substance.
2. Day Two, Night Two — The image is impressed on the person's ether body by the astral body. During the following night the ether body works on and elaborates the image.
3. Day Three, Night Three — The image is impressed on the person's physical body by the ether body. During

the following night, the physical body works on and elaborates the image.

4. The morning of the Fourth Day—This image, totally transformed by now into an image of a past life, the "cause" of the scene represented on the first night, is the one you wake with.[15]

Rudolf Steiner comments that this exercise can help one recognize karmic relationships more quickly. However, all things being equal, a very strong will is required to carry it out. He emphasizes that this exercise must be done, not just 10 or 20 times, but 50 to 70 times before one can count on results. The process of the transformation of the image breaks down again and again. A power emanating from Ahriman, a being who does not want people to realize the possibility of looking into karma, repeatedly provokes this breakdown. Thus Rudolf Steiner speaks of the courage required to continue this exercise as long as is necessary.

The battles on this most important field of life, the struggles against the forces opposing human progress — opposing the knowledge and the practice of karma — raise the question of whether and where aid and protection are to be found. After the Christmas Conference of 1923, in the course of which he laid the Foundation Stone of the General Anthroposophical Society, that fundamental meditation, in the hearts of the members, Rudolf Steiner took up the question of karmic connections and of karma in general in an entirely new way. From that moment on, he explained, it was possible for him to speak freely of this eminently esoteric subject. As Ita Wegman puts it in her book *An die Freunde,* "The laws of karma were revealed. Before the Christmas Conference, it had not been possible to speak in such detail about karma and the laws governing it. . . . Revealing the mysteries of karma always calls up the greatest possible opposition from the Ahrimanic powers who want karma to remain veiled in mystery. This resistance had to be overcome if the Anthroposophical Society was not to be cut off from the youthful forces, the impulses of Michael."[16]

We are left to dwell on the question how is it possible to overcome the Ahrimanic forces. During the Christmas Conference of 1923, Rudolf Steiner entrusted the Anthroposophical Society's members with a meditation, the Foundation Stone,[17] planting it like a seed in the hearts of those present and those who have taken it up since then. The circle of radiance surrounding this seed — its influence — protects spiritual work as, for example, research in the field of karma. Again, Ita Wegman: "When karma is understood by means of heart and head forces, when repeated earth lives are looked at and understood without undue emotion or frivolity but in full earnestness, then it will be possible to overcome even the last anti-Michaelic demons, and the Age of Michael will find its continuation in the coming Christ-event." [18]

With all due caution, let us now look at the Foundation Stone in relation to Steiner's karma exercise of May 9, 1924. The Foundation Stone meditation consists of four parts. The first three parts address the human soul, asking it to carry out particular exercises. In the first part, we are asked to practice "spirit remembering," going all the way to the point of perceiving this memory. This activity of remembering ascends to the recognition of humanity's divine origin. After this exercise, students on this path "know that the supersensible was there first, with everything sense-perceptible developing out of it. They know that they themselves belonged to a supersensible world before they entered this sensory world for the first time".[19] Correspondingly, the first thing we do in the karma exercise of May 9, 1924, is to remember a personal karmic situation and picture it inwardly in an image, which then forms the point of departure for the exercise. Here too then we have the activity of remembering.

In the second part of the Foundation Stone, the exercise called for is to "practice spirit-mindfulness" — concentration of the spirit. Doesn't this mean that in the course of this meditation we must try to allow the spirit to penetrate ever deeper within us and that in this way our "feeling will be true"? In the karma exercise the second day is characterized by the fact that the image of the memory is impressed on the etheric body by the astral body, the seat of feeling.

Finally, the third exercise of the Foundation Stone brings us to the point of beholding: the soul must "practice spirit-beholding" — spirit vision. The soul is led to contemplate something — something spiritual.

What precisely do we contemplate thanks to the Foundation Stone meditation after this third exercise? It is said that our will becomes free; that our thinking becomes true. What do we perceive with these forces? We must take the next step and examine the fourth part of the Foundation Stone meditation.

In the first three parts the meditator recalls the spiritual history of human evolution, including the Fall from grace and the being bound to matter, while the fourth part spreads before his or her spiritual gaze the incarnation of the solar forces at the turning point of time. He or she becomes aware that "The spiritual light of the world has entered the stream of earthly existence." The deed of Christ becomes an experience for the meditator. Uniting Himself with a human body, the Christ canceled out, balanced the Fall from grace. He took upon himself the karma of humanity. He bore the sins of the world. On the fourth day of the karma exercises, corresponding to the fourth part of the Foundation Stone, the person practicing them sees in an image the karmic relation that provoked the original event. That morning, on awakening, one sees an image that "explains" the memory that was formed on the first evening.

Through meditative work with the Foundation Stone, we attain an exact vision of the cosmic karma of humanity's evolution in which the descent into matter (the Fall) is compensated for by the sacrifice of the solar being of Christ — the Light of the World. Thus there opens before us through this inner work an immense path that we can travel on a small scale in relation to our own personal karma with the karma exercise described above. Revealing the intimate relationship of Christ Jesus to the karma of the human being, the radiant aura of the Foundation Stone supports and protects the work we need to do in order to penetrate personal karma; it provides a spiritual basis for objectifying this work and placing it in the greater context of humanity's evolution.

This third stage of encounter, then, the stage of transformation or transubstantiation, is the moment of truth. A meeting, a human connection, becomes something else. It receives a new dimension. In order to work through this stage, we must truly transform ourselves so as to achieve a true relationship with another human being.

If we do not succeed, if we stop short at one of the preceding stages, no further progress is possible, and the crises which follow bring about not metamorphoses but repeated misunderstandings, painful struggles, and insoluble problems between the people in question. To conceal this tragedy of evolution, this failure to become aware of the profundity of an encounter, we cover up our inability with words like "That's life" or "That's karma," phrases — unfortunately all too common — in which an undertone of negative fatalism and resignation may be heard. If, on the other hand, we accept our own freedom, if we recognize the immense, sacred task of liberating religion, of sanctifying human encounters and feeling responsible for the course of a relationship, then this decision will give us courage and strength, and our meetings with others will become divine service, for "every meeting of person with person will be from the beginning a religious act, a sacrament." [20]

Fragmentation and Unity
Fourth Stage: Communion

Only through religion do people become one. — Novalis

The requirements of evolution meant that humanity had to lose its unity in favor of the development of personality, but the impulse towards personality left humanity atomized, fragmented. The original language common to all human beings was lost, and humanity was split up into different peoples. This most important event has come down to us as an image in mythological consciousness: the story of the Tower of Babel.[21] After this event, the more humanity has progressed, the more evolutionary conditions forced individual human beings to confront themselves. In this way real spiritual progress set each human being the task of developing his or her own powers. Therefore isolation increases, accompanied by a feeling of solitude. At the same time, however, we must now take up and evolve a direction counter to this development. Since the fifteenth century, the development of the consciousness-soul — stimulated by scientific consciousness and technological achievements — has brought humanity to a point which allows individual personalities to unfold completely, but isolates them as a result. To forge a path to a new unity now seems a vital necessity, but there are two conditions attached to this way:

1. People must actively choose this way: the will must be involved (this is a corollary of freedom).
2. The way must be clearly defined.

The goal of the new unity is called Communion.

In the fourth part of the Mass — the Communion — bread and wine are shared out. Members of the congregation wishing to do so come to the invisible table and are unified through this common repast. Through the priest's Offering and through the Transubstantiation, bread and wine have become the body and blood of Christ. The bread, the Holy Host, has the shape of a little sun, and the sun forces taken up through it serve to unify the members of the congregation. There is a mystery here, however, with regard to the solar forces of the Christ — they work on a general human level and yet have access to single individualities.

The Christic solar forces have, in fact, a double quality: they are objectively universal, and yet they support the development of free individuality. As Rudolf Steiner writes:

> We do not owe our individuality to the sun. The sun shines on the good and the evil, on men of genius and on fools. As far as earthly life is concerned the sun has no direct connection with our individuality. In one instance only has the sun established connection with earthly individuality and this was possible because at a certain point in the earth's evolution, a sublime sun being, the Christ, did not remain on the sun but came down from the sun to the earth and became a being of the earth in the body of a man, thus uniting his own cosmic destiny with the destiny of earthly humanity. Thus, through becoming an earthly being, the Sun-being of Christ gained access to single human individualities.[22]

The solar beings who remain on the sun lack this particularity of the Christ; they have only general access to humanity as a whole. However, Christ did retain one attribute of sun-beings which can be a source of great blessing for the human race, namely, that His activity does not discriminate among human beings:

> What remained in Him was and is that his power knows no differentiation among human beings. Christ is not the Christ of this or that nation, of this or that rank or class. He is the Christ for all human beings, without distinction

of class, race or nation. Nor is He the Christ of particular individualities, inasmuch as his help is available alike to the genius and the fool. The Christ impulse has access to the individuality of human beings, but to become effective it must take effect in the inmost depths of human nature. It is not the forces of the intellect but the deepest forces of the heart and soul which can receive the Christ impulse; but once received this impulse works not for the benefit of the individual-human but of the universal-human. This is because Christ is a solar being. [23]

The powers of Christ can solve the following problem connected to the existential situation of human beings in their relation to each other: how can I fully develop my individuality in a community of individuals? Transposed to the field of human encounters, this question reads, "How can I intimately relate my individuality to that of another human being without losing it?" The first three stages of an encounter, as we have described them above, constitute a first attempt at an answer: Mutual recognition on the physical plane, proceeding through sacrifice and the recognition and understanding of a common destiny, can provide a new basis for meeting forged from the spirit.

A new community forms thanks to a spiritual impulse. What really unites people shows itself clearly: the spirit that brings us together reveals itself. We commune in Christ, the Lord of destiny. He wants people to rediscover each other so that what is universally human can prevail anew among them. It was for this that He came down among us.

This is the final stage of encounter. After a process that can last hours, days, and even years, those who have met each other are permitted to experience the forces of communion. Grace descends upon them, and they sense the flames of the Holy Spirit forging them into a new unity.

This fourth stage, Communion, may also therefore be called a Pentecostal event. The process of the encounter passes through several metamorphoses, so to speak, and then ends with the mystery of what occurred at Whitsun or Pentecost:

the participants in the encounter form a new unity, but without losing their essential individuality.

How should we understand Pentecost in the light of the new — Michaelic — mysteries? Again, some of Rudolf Steiner's thoughts can provide enlightenment. What he has to say in the lecture cycle *The Easter Festival in the Evolution of the Mysteries* about the real significance of the seasons or festivals of the year is quite foreign, even shocking, to the way we look at things today. [24] Of Easter, for instance, he says the following:

> For Christians Easter commemorates the Resurrection. The corresponding pagan festival taking place at approximately the same time of year as Easter in a sense celebrated the resurrection of nature, the reawakening of what, as nature, had been asleep throughout the winter. However, the similarity ends there. It must be emphasized that with regard to its inner meaning, the Christian Easter festival in no way corresponds to the pagan equinox celebrations. Rather, a serious examination of ancient pagan times reveals that Easter, in the Christian sense, is related to the festivals that grew out of the mysteries that were celebrated in the fall. This most curious fact demonstrates what serious misunderstandings regarding matters of the highest importance have occurred in the course of humanity's development. In the early Christian centuries, nothing less happened than the confusion of Easter with a completely different festival, with the result that Easter was moved from fall to spring.

The ancient festival Rudolf Steiner speaks of here is the festival of Adonis or Attys. Adonis represents "all that manifests itself in human beings as vigorous youth and beauty.... Many indeed took the image of Adonis to be the actually present god, the god of beauty and youthful strength, of an unfolding seminal power that reveals in splendorous outer existence all the inner nobility and grandeur of which humanity is capable." In autumn, in the course of religious festivities, the image of this god was plunged in the sea, then brought up out of the water after three days. Then "the laments gave way to songs of joy and hymns to the resurrected god, the god who had come back to life."

This ritual took place in autumn, when the earth loses its mantle of plants and leaves, at the moment when nature is dying. In the lectures quoted here, Rudolf Steiner explains how the understanding of resurrection can be found and expanded at that time of year, autumn, when the forces of nature offer no support. "Humanity was to contemplate the dying of nature in order to recognize that human beings die as well, but that in accordance with their inner nature they arise anew in the spiritual world. The purpose of these ancient pagan Mystery festivals was thus to reveal the true meaning of death." [25]

The Mystery festivals taking place in the spring on the other hand confronted people with the beginning of life, the mysteries of birth and of the descent into matter. Candidates for initiation into these spring mysteries were also led into the mystery of how the forces of nature experience resurrection at this time of year. This is in stark contrast to the autumn mysteries, as Rudolf Steiner shows: "If we look back in time, we see that human beings' descent from pre-earthly to earthly existence was recognized in certain mysteries, while other mysteries, the autumn mysteries, recognized their ascent to the spiritual." [26]

The Mystery of Golgotha took place in spring. Rudolf Steiner indicated April 3 as the date of Christ's death on the cross. In *The Calendar of the Soul,* published in 1912, we find him writing: "April 3, 33 A.D., is the date of the Mystery of Golgotha, according to spiritual-scientific investigations."[27] What candidates for initiation in the spring Mysteries were allowed to experience — in advance as it were — this actually became reality through Christ's deed. Again, as Rudolf Steiner has indicated, a historical misunderstanding resulted in Easter being confused with a completely different festival. The reason was that human beings were no longer capable of experiencing resurrection in the autumn; to understand resurrection they needed the support of the burgeoning nature forces of spring. Summing up his lecture of April 21, 1924, Steiner says that for human beings, but not for nature, the true festival of Easter is clearly related to autumn. For nature, Easter occurs in spring when the spirit causes the natural world to sprout and spring forth out of the earth:

Resurrection of the human being: autumn
Resurrection of nature: spring.

For human beings, Easter is an autumn mystery. "At the time when nature declines and dies away, human beings should think about their ascent, their inward elevation, their resurrection in the spirit."[28] Novalis, for whom this mystery was transparent, wrote in one of his fragments: "When a spirit dies, it becomes a human being; a human being who dies becomes a spirit. A free death of the spirit, a free death of the human being."

Since the beginning of the new Age of Michael in the last third of the nineteenth century (1879, according to anthroposophical research), it has become possible, even necessary, thanks to anthroposophy, to distinguish between these two Easter festivals, at first theoretic-ally and then as a matter of experience. The festival of Easter, bound up with the mysteries of spring and the resurrection of nature, that is, of physical and etheric forces, is followed by the Feast of Pentecost, celebrated seven weeks later. But what is there in the Easter Festival that is connected with the autumn mystery? Is there a connection? And if so, where to find it, how to understand it?

The experience we have in the fall when we perceive the forces of death taking hold of nature and we penetrate these forces of death consciously — this experience leads us to a more profound understanding of the forces of resurrection. We awaken to the spirit. Such would be the experience of Pentecost in relation with the mystery of autumn: to awaken to the spirit, to the individual spirit reborn in every soul. At what moment of the year can this happen in the new Mysteries? Undoubtedly, at Christmas.

Rudolf Steiner often spoke of the need for a new under-standing of Christmas. For instance, in his lecture cycle *The Spiritual Communion of Humanity* he said:

> Eventually the human race will not be content with sim-ply looking back over biblical accounts of Christ Jesus' spiritual journeying on earth, but will understand that since that time, Christ has united with human beings in earthly life and still reveals Himself to them, if they only listen. In our own time, humanity will be able to come to the insight that, just as the festival of Christmas follows Michaelmas in the cycle of the year, the new revelation of Michael which began one autumn in the last third of the nineteenth century will need to be followed by a festival of consecration, a Christmas, which will enable us to acquire an understanding of spiritual birth, of the birth in the spirit humanity needs in order to continue on its earthly journey so that the earth can be spiritualized and transformed in the future. It is not simply that we are now in the autumn of the year and that the annual Christ-mas is coming. We are living in a time when we should comprehend the Michael-revelation which began in the last third of the nineteenth century, comprehend it in the very depths of our souls and out of our own human nature, and when we should also be looking for a way towards a true Christmas festival, a festival of the indwelling of the spirit we strive to recognize. [29]

To understand this passage correctly is to realize that a new Christmas festival needs to accompany any new Michael festival in the fall. The festival of Easter in the spring, as festi-val of resurrection, and the event of Pentecost some weeks lat-er, provide forces that save the physical and etheric aspects of the natural world, and thereby also human beings, insofar as they are natural creatures, from death. Christ's deed on Golgotha and his Resurrection at Easter have made it possible for nature and humanity to continue to live. Thus the danger has been avoided of a physical and etheric hardening that have made it impossible for human souls to find bodies on earth into which to incarnate.

But ever since humanity received the consciousness-soul, each individual human being must personally want to undergo death and resurrection in relationship to Michael. The possibility of doing so is open to all human beings every autumn, the Michaelic moment of the year. The Michaelic impulse of autumn, a force of resurrection, can surmount a second, new danger — the danger of the human soul shutting itself off more and more within itself until it no longer provides a dwelling place for the spirit. Christ Jesus rose living from the grave: this is Easter in spring. Living individual human beings must descend of their own free choice into the grave: this is Easter in autumn. Such individuals will have a conscious experience of the forces of resurrection and for them Christmas becomes a new Pentecost: a festival of the birth of spiritual individuality in the soul. "The time has come when we need to find a way from Michaelmas to a mid-winter celebration which includes a sunrise of the spirit."[30]

These considerations point to an essential aspect of the Christmas Conference of 1923. Laying the Foundation Stone, the fundamental meditation that unites the new community, laying it in the depths of the human heart, Rudolf Steiner "baptized humanity anew"[31] with the fire of the Holy Spirit. In the course of this celebration of a new humanity, each participant was able to experience the birth of individuality, linked by virtue of the Foundation Stone with other individualities, and so a community was born where the flame of the Holy Spirit united human beings in a common task. From this point of view, the Christmas Conference can be seen as a Pentecost event — Christmas understood in the sense of the new Michaelic mysteries: Christmas as a spiritual birth. This is the new communion in which human beings feel connected through the spirit. Now roots must be sought in the spirit, no longer in the blood. No longer blood brothers and sisters, we are brothers and sisters in the spirit. The spiritual bond is now as strong as was the blood-bond. And surely what Rudolf Steiner said in conclusion to those gathered for the laying of the Foundation Stone on December 25, 1923, sounds like the message of Pentecost:

And if you hear this resounding in your own hearts, my dear friends, then what you will establish here will be a true union of human beings on behalf of Anthroposophia, and will carry the spirit which prevails in radiant thought-light around our dodecahedral stone of love out into the world, where it may shed light and warmth on the progress of human souls and the progress of the world.[32]

The thoughts on communion — the fourth stage of the process of encounter — developed here in relation to the Christmas Conference, that is, to the new mysteries, indicate the special quality of this communion. We can consider the Christmas Conference as a meeting of, an encounter between, 800 people brought together by their destiny for a common act. On several occasions during the Christmas Conference, Rudolf Steiner insisted that the participants' deed was what mattered — that an action accomplished by the participants themselves was required.

What came to pass in this December 1923, on the level of humanity as such in relationship to the cosmos, is a seed for communion as the fourth stage in any meeting of two or more people. The process of human encounter leads to communion, to the participants' finding a new relationship to each other, a new bond, whose roots are purely spiritual. Lunar forces lead us toward each other. The process of encounter completed, solar forces radiate between us. A community founded in the spirit has been born.[33]

Transformation of Consciousness During an Encounter

Mary Magdalene Meets the Risen Christ

How do we see physically? No differently than we do in our consciousness — means of the productive power of imagination. Consciousness is the eye and ear, the sense for inner and outer meaning. — Novalis

Our consideration of encounters has shown us that what happens during the process of meeting another person is linked to a transformation of consciousness. As the archetype of the human forces that lead people toward each other, we chose the meeting of John and Jesus at the Baptism in the Jordan. Another archetype exemplifies the process of transformation of consciousness during an encounter: the meeting of Mary Magdalene with the Risen Christ, as recounted in the twentieth chapter of St. John's Gospel.

Mary comes to the tomb on Easter morning and discovers the absence of Jesus' body. The body that she loved so dearly on a human level has disappeared: it is not there. We have already shown how, in the course of the first stage of an encounter, the physical body of the other as perceived by the senses must be met with great interest and love. The physical appearance of another human being, when it is perceived with sufficient interest, sets the whole process in motion. We wake up to the other. We may say then, without fear of being wrong, that Mary Magdalene had awakened fully to the external, physical aspect of Christ Jesus. But in order to go any further, in order to move to the second stage, it is necessary to look for the other person's true image. A person's outer appearance, the point of departure for the entire process, despite its importance, is after all merely Maya, an illusion: it must be overcome, it must disappear, yielding its place to something higher.

Here, the physical having disappeared, Mary Magdalene awakens to another stage of consciousness by "turning around." This transformation of consciousness enables her to see the etheric. She sees the true image of Christ Jesus: the "gardener" who now wants to cultivate the earth, to tend it so as to receive its true fruits. That is, she finds herself in full consciousness before the etheric Christ. But she has not consciously grasped the real relationship between them. Her consciousness must be raised again in order for her to understand Him. Christ Himself prompts her, aids her in attaining the necessary degree of consciousness. He calls her name, "Mary." Then her consciousness is raised, as signified by these words — "and she turned around again."

Obviously, this "turning around" is not meant to be taken literally for she turns around twice, which is absurd from a physical point of view. Rather, what is meant is that different forces of cognition, different states of consciousness are in question — first imagination, then inspiration. Thus this encounter becomes gradually clearer by a process of cognition. The karmic relationship to the Risen One becomes conscious. "Rabbi, Master!" she says. This is the third stage: she recognizes him fully.

The final stage, Communion, total union one with the other, is not yet possible at this point in evolution: "Do not touch me!" says the Risen One.

HUMAN BEINGS AND
THEIR RELATIONSHIP TO
THE GODS WHO SHAPE DESTINY

In any case this world is the result of an interplay between myself and the divinity. Everything that exists, everything that comes about, comes from being touched by the spirit.
— Novalis

Rudolf Steiner has drawn our attention to two important points concerning anthroposophy:

1. Anthroposophy must fructify life;
2. Europeans must seek the spirit through the senses, through sense perceptions.

In *The Work of the Angels in Man's Astral Body,* for example, Steiner says: "The anthroposophical grasp of the spirit should not be merely theoretical philosophy. It should be the constant content and vital force in our daily lives. Only when we are in a position to empower the anthroposophical grasp of the spirit, so that it really becomes fully alive in us, only then will it actually fulfill its task."[34] And in *The Mission of Folk Souls,* Steiner states that: "The European race in particular, with its strong sensory orientation, must apply itself to the task of finding a way to the spirit through the senses."[35]

Is there an example in which the anthroposophical grasp of the spirit can become a content of life, a vital force? Is this not the case when we seek to permeate our daily lives with some religious substance? Certainly; and the foundation, the basis of any permeation of daily life with religious substance, is to strive to know as an experience that "through flesh and blood something appears in each human that reveals itself as coming from divine cosmic depths."[36] The angels pursue a goal, that of weaving into human souls this ideal: "In the future each human being will see hidden in his neighbor a divine being." Such words give us an idea of what could come into play between people when they try to live their encounters as religious acts, as "acts of consecration."

To put it differently, an activity we perform in everyday life becomes religious if it establishes our connection to the gods. Remember what we said at the beginning: that human encounters are the affair not of humans alone but also of the gods. In a lecture given soon after the Christmas Conference, Steiner expressed some thoughts concerning human encounters considered from the point of view of anthroposophical knowledge. If we wanted to give a title to this passage we could call it: *On the importance of Human Encounters for the Gods.*

> The gods have already lived through what happens to us when we meet another person. They went through this experience in advance as a consequence of what we did with the person in question in a previous earthly life. . . . Thus the activity of these divine beings of the first hierarchy, of the seraphim, cherubim and thrones, was determined by their human creatures on earth. And then, in turn, they experienced in advance the destiny they were preparing for us for a lifetime still to come.[37]

Consequently we must realize that *the forces arising during an encounter derive from a divine substance.* The gods have lived *this*, and we can come into relation with the gods if we are able to seize *this* consciously and render it transparent. The situation is depicted in the accompanying diagram.

Our path toward the divine in the other human being, in humanity, begins through the senses. (This is the first stage of the encounter.) Our task then becomes to return this divine element to the gods. This is the "reverse ritual."[38] It is the stage that follows the encounter. Finally, after death, in recapitulating our life, we re-experience the encounter in the spiritual world, but much more consciously. In communion with

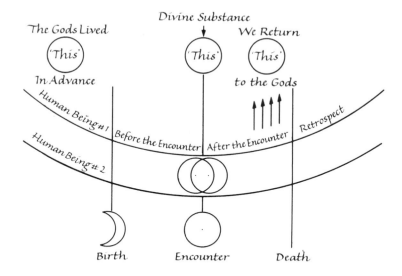

the gods, and in the full light of consciousness, we prepare the divine element for our next incarnation. In our next life, we will encounter the other person again, but under the star of the new Mysteries, that is, knowing what we decided between death and rebirth. We shall then understand the meaning of this encounter. Although this understanding may seem an ideal distant from our present lifetime, we must nevertheless strive for it consciously so that in subsequent incarnations we will be able to experience human encounters as "free religious acts."[39]

Rudolf Steiner was in full possession of this awareness, as the following description by Zeylmans van Emmichoven reveals.

I went to Dornach in December, 1920. My relationship to anthroposophy had grown to the point where I had a strong desire to meet Rudolf Steiner, and it was indeed a decisive experience. The details were as follows: On the evening of December 17, 1 was sitting in the lecture hall with my fiancee, who was studying eurythmy in Dornach. We were waiting for Rudolf Steiner's lecture to begin. It was bitterly cold outside, and Dornach was covered with snow. All of a sudden the blue curtain at one side of the stage opened and Rudolf Steiner, whom I recognized from photographs, walked up to the lectern. At that moment I had an undeniable experience of recognizing someone I had known before, to the point where a whole series of pictures hinting at earlier situations appeared before me as if I were looking at a man who had been my teacher down through the millennia.[40]

After the lecture, Zeylmans von Emmichoven was introduced to Rudolf Steiner, who said to him, "I've been expecting you here for a long time." Zeylmans took this to imply that he had already been in Dornach for some time and therefore replied, "But sir, I only arrived late this afternoon!" Rudolf Steiner smiled happily and said, "I didn't mean it that way at all."[41]

Thus, for an initiate, an encounter is completely transparent. And for us? Is not the substance that we can perceive arising during an encounter a divine substance? Yes, it is a divine substance, since human beings are the thoughts of the gods[42]

The gods think, and human beings arise. True communion occurs when we perceive a human being as a divine thought in the reality of karma.

Epilogue

Over the years significant steps have been taken in many areas to rise to Rudolf Steiner's challenge to fructify our daily life by means of anthroposophy — for instance, in education, agriculture, medicine and many different artistic, social and economic fields. In this context the reality of human encounters occupies a central place. Human encounters are moments in the evolution of the world. They affect individual human acts in relation to other human beings — the teacher meets the students, the doctor meets the patients — in such a way that consciousness of what happens during these meetings becomes ever more important.

There are still two questions of general interest to be discussed. The first one is whether each of the four stages must be brought to a conclusion before one can move to the next stage:

Proclamation,
Sacrifice (Offertory),
Transubstantiation,
Communion

Obviously, each stage needs to be brought to some kind of ripeness before we can proceed to the next. However, in reality, the stages overlap. Attending to the physical elements of the other (Proclamation) can go on for a long time before it is experienced fully. It is important that our interest in the external aspect of the other person not diminish, that our interest be constantly renewed. We must not stop after acquiring some knowledge, as if it were final. Likewise, the sacrifice of our own personality (Offertory) is something that must happen repeatedly, and for the sake of progress, our willingness to make this offering must never fade, we must never stop practicing active tolerance. When we are in search of transformation and the perception of real karmic relationships

(Transubstantiation), patience, suffering, and constancy are the prerequisites of progress. And finally, Communion allows humility and gratitude to be born in the soul. Thus each stage is sustained by its own moral qualities, and there are different levels to be passed through at each stage.

The second question is whether all participants in a human encounter must progress at the same pace. We need to know whether the two people in question are both unfamiliar with anthroposophy, whether one is an anthroposophist while the other knows nothing about it, or whether they are both anthroposophists. In the first instance, both people can go through the process quite involuntarily. This corresponds to what Rudolf Steiner called "initiation through life." In the second instance, it is natural that the person who has some knowledge of anthroposophy should feel responsible for the situation and its development. For anthroposophy helps one to understand and aid the other. In the last instance, both persons are responsible. If one happens to notice that the other does not follow what is happening, that one should endure this delay patiently and, without interrupting his or her own development, try to advance the process, always making an effort to accompany the other person attentively.

A striking example of this situation is given by the incident between Rudolf Steiner and Zeylmans van Emmichoven related at the end of the last chapter. Rudolf Steiner was in possession of a consciousness which permitted him an overview of all karmic relationships. With infinite patience he tried, through lectures, meditations and exercises, to widen the awareness of members of the Anthroposophical Society — and of all in the twentieth century — to the point where Communion can be consciously experienced. The Christmas Conference is a seed for this. What Rudolf Steiner experienced at the level of humanity is valid for all of us in our own domains.

Of course, many questions remain to be answered. The ideas developed here are meant to serve as a stimulus for deepening this important theme of human encounters. But this deepening can also be attained by practicing what has been described — in the sense that Novalis means when he says, "We know only to the extent that we do."

ABOUT THE AUTHOR

Athys Aimé Floride was born April 15, 1924, in Cayenne, French Guyana. He was trained as a figher pilot in North Africa at the end of World War II; by the end of 1945, he was in occupied Germany in the French zone (near Lake Constance). From 1946 to 1952, he was in Paris, studying philosophy at the Sorbonne and ethnology at the Faculté des Sciences de Paris (Musée de l'Homme). He was then a teacher of philosophy at various French schools and colleges. In 1956-58 he helped in the founding of the Waldorf Movement in France. In 1958, he went to Germany as teacher of languages in Benefeld. He returned to France in 1965 for the founding of an institute for curative education (St. Martin in Normandy) where he worked for a few months. At the end of 1965 he moved back to Germany to teach in the Waldorf School in Kassel, from which he became a language consultant for the German Waldorf Schools. From 1970 to 1980 he was a member of the Board of the Anthroposophical Center in Frankfurt-am-Main. Since 1982, he has been a member of the Board of the Anthroposophical Society in France.

NOTES

1. Rudolf Steiner, *Karmic Relationships*, vol. 1, lecture of 2/17/24, Rudolf Steiner Press, London, 1981.

2. Ibid, lecture of 1/24/24.

3. Rudolf Steiner, *The Work of the Angels in Man's Astral Body*, lecture of 10/9/18, Rudolf Steiner Press, London, 1988.

4. Rudolf Steiner, The Last Address, Rudolf Steiner Press, London, 1967.

5. See note 3.

6. Ibid.

7. See note 2.

8. Rudolf Steiner, *Awakening to Community*, lecture of 2/27/23, Anthroposophic Press, Spring Valley, 1974.

9. Rudolf Steiner, *The Challenge of the Times*, lecture of 12/7/18, Anthroposophic Press, Hudson, 1941.

10. Wooden group sculpture ("The Representative of Humanity"), sculpted by Rudolf Steiner and Edith Maryon, representing Christ between Lucifer and Ahriman. The sculpture may be seen in the Goetheanum in Dornach, Switzerland.

11. See note 1.

12. Ibid.

13. Rudolf Steiner, *The Archangel Michael: His Mission and Ours*, lecture of 11/23/19, Anthroposophic Press, Hudson, 1994.

14. Rudolf Steiner, *The Inner Aspect of the Social Question*, lecture of 2/11/19, Rudolf Steiner Press, London, 1974.

15. Rudolf Steiner, *Karmic Relationships*, vol. 2, lecture of 5/9/24, Rudolf Steiner Press, London, 1974.

16. Ita Wegman, *To the Friends: Transactions and Reports from 1925-27*. 2nd ed., Natura Verlag, Arlesheim, 1968. Not translated. This passage dates from 6/7/25.

17. See Rudolf Steiner, *The Christmas Conference for the Foundation of the General Anthroposophical Society 1923/1924*, Anthroposophic Press, Hudson, 1990.

18. See note 16.

19. *How to Know Higher Worlds*, Anthroposophic Press, Hudson, 1994.

20. See note 3.

21. Rudolf Steiner, *Occult History*, lecture of 12/30/10, Rudolf Steiner Press, London, 1982.

22. See note 2.

23. Ibid.

24. Rudolf Steiner, *The Easter Festival in the Evolution of the Mysteries*, lecture of 4/19/24, Anthroposophic Press, Hudson, 1988.

25. Ibid.

27. Ibid., lecture of 7/21/24.

28. C.f. Emil Funk, Calendar for 1913-14: An initiative of Rudolf Steiner, Dornach 1973 (not translated).

29. See note 27.

30. Rudolf Steiner, *Man and the World of Stars* (including "The Spiritual Communion of Hunanity"; see this volume, lecture of 12/24/22), Anthroposophic Press, Spring Valley, 1982.

31. Ibid.

32. Orally transmitted by Friedrich Rittelmeyer.

33. See note 17, lecture of 12/25/23.

34. The four stages in a human encounter can be seen as corresponding to stages of higher cognition. Cf. Rudolf Steiner, *Stages of Higher Knowledge*, Anthroposophic Press, Hudson, 1990.

35. See note 3.

36. Rudolf Steiner, *The Mission of Folk Souls*, Rudolf Steiner Press, London.

37. Ibid.

38. See note 1, lecture of 3/2/24.

39. See note 8.

40. Ibid.

41. *Wir Erlebten Rudolf Steiner*, edited by M. J. Krtick von Poturzyn, 6th ed., Stuttgart 1980 (not translated).

42. Ibid.

43. Rudolf Steiner, *Human and Cosmic Thought*, lecture of 1/23/14, Rudolf Steiner Press, London, 1991.